After the Interval

After the Interval

Michael Melford

The Crowood Press

First published in 1990 by
THE CROWOOD PRESS LTD
Gipsy Lane
Swindon
Wiltshire SN2 6DQ

Text copyright © 1990 by Michael Melford
Design by Karyn Claridge

Unless otherwise indicated the black and white photographs in the plate section
of this book are reproduced by permission of Ken Kelly *(KK)* and John
Woodcock *(JW)*.
The cover photograph of Don Bradman taken in 1948 is courtesy of Ken Kelly,
the 1989 picture of Robin Smith ducking a Merv Hughes bouncer is courtesy of
Patrick Eagar as is the portrait of the author.

British Library Cataloguing in Publication Data
Melford, Michael
    After the interval.
    1. Cricket, history
    I. Title
    796.35809

    ISBN 1-85223-266-8

Typeset in Sabon by Novatext Graphix, Edinburgh
Printed in Great Britain by Butler & Tanner Ltd, Frome

Contents

Preface

WHEN I was asked to write a book about cricket since the Second World War, I replied, with more truth than modesty, that I am not of the stuff of which historians are made. This seemed to surprise no one and we settled for a contemporary view of events in the last 45 years.

It is probably inevitable that some will think that certain cricket and certain cricketers receive more, or less, attention in this book than is merited. The first-class and Test cricket which keep the cricket correspondent of a national newspaper fully occupied give him little chance of seeing much of the game at other levels. He may see a little youth cricket but other flourishing parts of the game live in departments of their own. There are, for example, the leagues and the ladies who, if given any attention at all, have their own correspondents.

I can only claim that I did try to broaden my knowledge of both. One Saturday in the early 1950s I set off from east of the Pennines to watch a league match in Rochdale. Alas, though the weather was tolerable in Leeds, Rochdale was awash.

In 1951 I reported the second day of a women's Test match between England and Australia which was played on a turning pitch at Worcester. The lady spinners performed very creditably and a close final day was in prospect.

That night I was instructed to leave Worcester and go to Trent Bridge where Wilfred Wooller was having an amicable routine row with the opposition about the lifelessness of the Trent Bridge pitches. By way of protest he had employed all 11 bowlers.

In those pre-motorway days it took three hours to drive from Worcester to Nottingham and I arrived to find that all was quiet and both sides were united in going through the motions until three o'clock, at which hour Glamorgan had to depart for Swansea. Meanwhile Australia were winning an exciting contest at Worcester by two wickets.

I cannot believe that any other game has a better work of reference than *Wisden*, the great memory-jogger, and I am indebted to the last two editors, John Woodcock and Graeme Wright, for maintaining the lofty standards.

I have been fortunate in being able to draw from Ken Kelly's store of fine pictures and much appreciate his enthusiastic co-operation. For 40 years, too, I have admired John Woodcock from the target end as a no-nonsense photographer who takes aim and fires without keeping you hanging about. I now realise that the end product is of high calibre and I am grateful to him for allowing me to look after his 23 albums while he was in Australia.

And so to Jo and Chris Forster whose kindness and encouragement have been a great help, as has that of the ever considerate editor, Graham Hart.

Michael Melford
May 1990

Introduction

IT was 1945. The War was over and, in relation to the start of a new cricket season, in smarter time than its predecessor three decades before. This time there were eight months of peace – eleven in Europe – in which to pick up the pieces of cricket again, to reassemble them and to make preparations for the first post-war English season.

Inevitably these were going to be makeshift arrangements. Many grounds still had to be derequisitioned, the materials and labour needed to restore them properly were in short supply. Equipment was not easily available, some players were still overseas, some only recently returned from prisoner-of-war camps and some were not certain to be released from military service by April or May 1946.

Yet in some ways the first-class counties were better placed than 16 of them had been in 1919. (Glamorgan were not elevated to first-class status until 1921.) Certainly the Second World War had been two years longer than the First and six seasons had been lost – for many years afterwards one heard it said of this or that cricketer that "he had lost his best years in the War". But county clubs had been kept alive and throughout the hardest times there had been an official emphasis on the need for recreation and on playing and, within reason, watching sport.

Nowhere had this policy been more successfully followed than at Lord's which Sir Pelham Warner, then in his late 60s and early 70s, kept going with all the enthusiasm and devotion to the game which had marked his long career. It was soon realised that despite all the handicaps, discomforts and preoccupations of contemporary life, including bombs, there was a huge appetite for watching cricket. There were, after all, few outdoor counter-attractions. Few people had the petrol to drive out of London at weekends. The youthful television had been put aside until after the War. As early as 1942 a crowd of 22,000 watched a match at Lord's between a joint Middlesex and Essex side and one from Kent and Surrey.

The players for these war-time matches came largely from the Services. Many pre-war first-class players were still stationed in Britain either because they were above the age groups usually posted overseas or because they were training for the invasion of Europe. Some were in the home forces, such as anti-aircraft units and the fire services. Some younger players were at Universities awaiting call-up or, on rare occasions, unfit for military service. Some were still at school, the best known schoolboy cricketer of the era being Trevor Bailey. Many charities profited from the matches played at Lord's and on grounds elsewhere in the country.

In cricketing countries overseas the problems were different. In Australia and New Zealand the domestic difficulties were naturally not on the scale of Britain's though by the end of the War many of their best games-players were overseas. Evidence for this lay in the high quality of the Australian Services cricket team captained by Lindsay Hassett in England in 1945 and of the New Zealand Kiwis rugby team which toured Britain during the following winter. Though by the 1945–46 season Australia, New Zealand and South Africa had their cricket flowing again, even then they were not ready for a resumption of a full first-class programme.

However, in India, not yet partitioned, first-class cricket had even raised its standards with the presence on the sub-continent of English players in the Services. Denis Compton's 249 not out for Holkar in the Ranji Trophy final of 1944–45 attracted interest throughout the cricketing world and so, to a lesser extent, did occasional scores from Egypt where Walter Hammond and less well known English cricketers such as a Yorkshireman called J.C. Laker were to be found playing at Gezira.

In the West Indies huge scores were being made by players called Weekes, Worrell and Walcott, none of whom had been in the 1939 West Indian side whose tour of England had been curtailed by the outbreak of war.

No other country had quite as tough a post-war return to cricket as England. Those with smaller populations may have been relatively as hard hit by the loss or absence of players but they did not have still with them the burdens of rationing and shortages. They did not have as unhelpful a climate.

After the First World War English cricket had taken much longer to recover than Australia's. The memories lived on of two-day championship matches in 1919, of a defeat 5–0 in Australia in 1920–21 and an almost equally conclusive defeat by Warwick Armstrong's powerful Australian side in England in 1921. One Test was won in 1924–25 but seven years passed before the Ashes returned to England. History was to repeat itself with remarkable accuracy after the Second War.

However, in early 1946, English cricket was not without hope of doing better this time, as grounds were patched up, new county secretaries were appointed, old players were rediscovered, new ones found with qualifications. This was not without hazard in those times of limited information. One county was said to have found later that the captain they had appointed was not the one with the same name of whom they had been thinking.

Test selectors were appointed. There was a world-wide call for a swift resumption of international cricket and India, whose cricket had been relatively uninterrupted, were an obvious choice as the touring team for the first post-war English season. It was also a choice with some political significance, for there was much talk at the time of future independence and partition for India. A cricket tour putting aside religious differences and bringing back old friends remembered from the 1936 tour had much to commend it.

After the visit from the Indians there was to be a full-scale M.C.C. tour of Australia. It was clear to all concerned that English cricket would not be properly prepared for this but the pressure from Australia was irresistible, and it was a time when enthusiasm and goodwill were clearing many obstacles.

The hopes which the English cricket observer of those days nursed were based not only on the fact that in the recent War some cricket of good standard had been played but on the state of English cricket immediately pre-war.

The passing of six seasons without regular cricket was certain to be a big handicap. Many fine players would not return. The loss of the great Yorkshire left-arm spinner Hedley Verity, who died of wounds as an Italian prisoner of war in 1943, was much in everyone's mind.

But the events of the last two pre-war seasons had been greatly encouraging at the time. The arrival on the scene in the late 1930s

of two young players of the very highest class in Len Hutton and
Denis Compton had promised a new golden era of English batsmanship. Moreover the last two Test matches played against
Australia and South Africa respectively, one at home, one abroad,
had lingered in the memory not only for their prolific scoring but
for England's prominent part in them.

In August 1938 England had scored 903 for seven against
Australia at The Oval, the 22-year-old Hutton making 364.
Victory by an innings and 579 runs in this last Australian Test
between the Wars was something on which to look back fondly
during the dark days of war. So was the Durban Test of March
1939. Needing 696 to beat South Africa, a below full strength
England side scored 654 for five before they had to leave the
match drawn after ten days in order to catch the ship home.

Lessons had been learnt from these two matches and from the
rebirth of cricket in 1919. Cricketing discussions during the War
invariably decided that there should be no more "timeless" Tests.
And in 1946 there was to be no two-day programme but a full
county championship of three-day matches.

There was every reason to believe that big crowds would be
drawn to first-class cricket. An exciting new chapter in cricket
history was about to open. The game would undoubtedly change.
But how? How deeply would the changes penetrate? Would the
vital things like a desire to play cricket and the enjoyment of it
survive?

Nobody knew for certain in the first peace-time winter of
1945–46. For the moment, all that was wanted was one of those
fine cricketing summers of abundant sunshine with which the
years of war had perversely been blessed.

Cricket is used to 'intervals' – lunch intervals, tea intervals, rest
days, wet days and so on. But never before had competitive cricket
been suspended for nearly seven years. No one quite knew what
to expect after *this* interval.

1

Back to First-Class Cricket

IT is seldom wise to rely on co-operation from the British climate and in the summer of 1946 it was back at its least helpful, cold as well as wet. Yet between the interruptions the leading batsmen of seven years before were soon re-establishing themselves. So were the stronger county sides. Yorkshire and Middlesex, first and second in the 1939 Championship, were first and second again and the most eminent player in each side was carrying on much as before: Len Hutton, approaching his 30th birthday, averaged 50 for Yorkshire; Denis Compton, two years younger, averaged 61 for Middlesex.

Compton's form in Indian cricket had made his successful return to the game in England a near certainty, but Hutton's future was far from assured. During the War he had suffered a serious injury. His left arm was now noticeably shorter than his right. It had to be proved that the arm was strong enough to cope with the best bowling and that the exemplary technique of his batting would help him to rise above his disability.

The worst fears were soon set at rest. Hutton almost certainly profited from having several summers after the accident without first-class cricket. There was no need to rush his recovery. He had time to sort out what he could do as fluently as before and what required adjustment before Yorkshire and England needed him again.

When that day arrived he still felt the effects of his injury but the evidence was soon forthcoming that it was not going to reduce his timing and basic soundness. In Yorkshire's first Championship match, against Glamorgan on a turning pitch at Cardiff, he made 90 out of a total of 195. He followed this with 62 in another low-scoring match at Canterbury before making 111 in Yorkshire's first post-war home match against Leicestershire at

13

Headingley. Len Hutton was back and in form. Only if one sat down and tried to imagine how one's own activities would be affected by such an injury did the magnitude of his achievement begin to sink in.

Denis Compton's return to English first-class cricket was also eagerly awaited, though without the same doubts and concern. He had a more robust physique than Hutton's and within a few days of returning from India early in 1946 had played football for England against Scotland. There was as yet no public knowledge of the knee trouble which was to haunt the last decade of his career, though it originated from an injury incurred when playing for Arsenal in 1938. Seldom one to do things in half measure, he began with 0 for M.C.C. against Surrey but in Middlesex's first home match made 74 against Leicestershire on a wet pitch at Lord's. When in the next match he made 147 not out and 54 against Northants it was a fair assumption that the teenage genius of the 1930s had not lost much of his flair. By the end of May he was making a hundred in each innings against Lancashire at Old Trafford.

Then, however, he ran into a bad patch which, though lasting barely three weeks, became a matter of national interest and concern, such was his stature and his ability to capture the public's attention. There was a lot of rain in that period and wet pitches could take some of the blame, but Compton certainly did the job in style, beginning with 10 against Nottinghamshire and seven and one against Derbyshire, both matches at Lord's.

An ideal cure for a barren spell seemed to be an innings on an immaculate pitch at Fenner's and he duly made 202 at a run a minute against Cambridge University. But that proved to be just a fleeting sight of blue sky between the clouds as he followed it with some really spectacular failures – 0 in the Whitsun match against Sussex, 0 in the Test Trial at Lord's, eight and 0 against Yorkshire, one against Glamorgan at Swansea and then 0, bowled first ball by Amarnath, in the First Test against India at Lord's.

At this point he had made four noughts in six innings and had been bowled four times by bowlers of such different types as James Langridge (slow left-arm), Jack Martin (fast-medium), J.C. Clay (off-spinner) and Lala Amarnath (medium pace).

Forty years later Compton would not have it that he was genuinely out of form. "I never had enough time at the wicket to establish that I was out of form," he said. "I just got out. I have never understood it."

Certainly there was little time for post-mortems, for on the day after the Test match Middlesex were at home to Warwickshire at Lord's and Compton came to the wicket as bemused by it all as were the spectators.

"I was desperate as I went to the wicket that day. I had almost forgotten what it was to feel the impact of ball on bat." In the mind of many a spectator there was a nasty fear, encouraged by the number of times that he was being bowled, that with the resumption of first-class cricket, in a dimmer light than that in which he had been playing in India, some flaw in his eyesight had been exposed.

Thus it was in an atmosphere of some apprehension that he took guard that day against Eric Hollies' leg-spin. He pushed forward to the first ball and, from the inside edge, it ran on at more than just a trickle to hit the outside of the off-stump.

The bails stayed on. To the spectators it was the turning-point. To Compton, it was encouragement to try something more positive and almost at once he pulled Hollies for six, a long way over the midwicket boundary. With that, he was away and playing with all the old panache. He made 122 and by the end of a wet season, and despite this unproductive interlude, he was one of only three batsmen in the country averaging over 60.

The others were Walter Hammond and Cyril Washbrook. Hammond had been the outstanding English batsman of the 1930s, a majestic sight in full flow. In 1946 he was obviously in the evening of his Test career but at the age of 43 he made batting look absurdly easy. He averaged 108 for Gloucestershire and resumed the England captaincy which he had first held in 1938.

Cyril Washbrook was now 31. In the late 1930s he had been a consistent opening batsman for Lancashire for several seasons. In 1946 he left his pre-war form far behind. With his cap tipped to one side and his upright bearing, head held high, he would walk out to bat giving the impression of a certain amount of lofty contempt for the bowler. He soon made himself the obvious opening partner for Len Hutton.

Of the other batsmen resuming after a gap of six seasons, Joe Hardstaff had mixed fortunes. In the final Test of 1938 he had made 169 not out against Australia but he was now almost 35 and his early season form for Nottinghamshire suggested that his best playing days might have been left behind. However, he was picked on the England side for the Test Trial and, having survived a confident appeal first ball, made 115. On the strength of this he was picked for the First Test in which he made 205 not out. He was an elegant batsman whose stance at the wicket, upright and relaxed, was a model for young batsmen and bore little resemblance to the bat-brandishing styles favoured in the 1980s.

Another batsman making runs in 1946 was W.J. Edrich who had returned from the War with a D.F.C. and an outstanding record as a bomber pilot. Bill Edrich – small, tough and determined – had already had a career of unusual ups and downs. It seemed that when he was in favour with the selectors, he was not in favour with the Press – and vice versa. Coming from Norfolk, the first of five from his family to play first-class cricket, he had had to qualify for Middlesex and did not play a full season until 1937 when he was 21. He then made three hundreds and averaged nearly 50. In the next year he made 1000 runs before the end of May and was picked for England throughout the series against Australia. When Len Hutton made his 364 in the last Test at The Oval, his unsuccessful opening partner was Edrich who in six Test innings that summer mustered only 67 runs.

When he continued in the same vein on the winter tour of South Africa, 21 runs in his first five Test innings, there was much moaning about the selectors' indulgence. They and Edrich may be said to have had the last laugh when he made 219 in the second innings of the "Timeless" Test in Durban. Yet he was not picked against West Indies in 1939 and only for the last Test against India in 1946. This was washed out before he could bat. A week before, however, he had been selected to fill one of the last three places in the M.C.C. side about to sail for Australia.

One other batsman who made a big contribution to the first two post-war seasons in England and was almost certainly the best left-hander in the world at the time was a New Zealander at Oxford University, Martin Donnelly. Rugby footballers will remember him also as the brilliant attacking fly-half of the formidable Oxford XV of 1946–7 who played once that winter for England against Ireland in Dublin.

A trim figure of only medium build, he might have been played in a film by Sir John Mills. He had first come to England in the New Zealand side of 1937 when he was 19. He played in all three Tests then. Though he had only a short career in post-war cricket, he left behind memories of several superb innings at Lord's, all played with the charm and timing of a player of the highest class. After serving in an armoured regiment in the Middle East and Italy, he arrived in England in 1945 in time to make 133 for the Dominions with a sparkling innings to mark the last season of war-time cricket at Lord's.

His 142 in the 1946 University match at Lord's was an innings to grace any occasion and it was followed a year later by 162 not out for the Gentlemen against the Players at Lord's. He made the runs in only three hours and the ball seemed to go wherever the fielders were not. Two seasons later, he returned with the New Zealand touring team captained by Walter Hadlee and played a superb innings of 206 in the Lord's Test.

Hutton, Compton, Hammond, Hardstaff, Washbrook, Edrich, Donnelly – all batsmen adding to their reputation. But what of the bowlers in 1946?

Through the ages good bowlers have usually been harder to find than batsmen and have had a shorter span at their peak. Now, after a six-year gap, the shortage was more acute than ever, though there was one newcomer who was to prove of immense value to Surrey and England through the next decade.

Alec Bedser had been the most successful bowler in the Surrey Second XI in the last two seasons before the War. He had played in only two first-class matches, against Oxford and Cambridge. Both were reduced by rain and he had yet to take a first-class wicket. His twin brother Eric, marginally the older, played in the same matches. Rather than flood the market with fast-medium bowlers, Eric became an off-spinner. As he also became a sound opening batsman, he too was to play a big part in the Surrey successes of the 1950s.

The brothers were in France in 1940, leaving through Dunkirk. Later in the War they served in North Africa, Italy and Austria and had not long been demobilised when Alec took six for 14 in the second innings for Surrey against M.C.C. at Lord's. Within seven weeks he was playing in his first Test match, also at Lord's, and taking 11 wickets in it.

This was not a great surprise to those who had seen him bowling in one-day matches at Lord's in 1943 but since then he had played little or no cricket. He was six feet three and weighed over 15 stone. Strongly built and with a fine economical action and run-up, he moved the ball about with great accuracy. The leg-cutter which swung into the batsman and left him off the pitch was to account for many of the world's leading batsmen. He could bowl a large number of overs and had an exceptional record of fitness. He himself attributed his fitness and stamina largely to the fact that he was 28 when he played his first full season of first-class cricket and had by then come to his full strength. As chairman of selectors later in life, he had plenty of experience of fast and fast-medium bowlers who were full of promise in their early 20s but were still not fully developed physically and were subject to frequent breakdowns.

Alec Bedser's leap to fame in May 1946 coincided with a notable period in the history of the Surrey County Cricket Club. The year 1945 had been the centenary of Surrey and of cricket at The Oval. The ground had been badly damaged during the War and a centenary restoration fund was launched. After a lot of hard work during the winter of 1945–6 the ground was ready, not only for the resumption of first-class cricket but for a Centenary Celebration one-day match on 23 May attended by King George VI, the Patron of the Club. Surrey's opponents, Old England, included many of the most successful English cricketers between the Wars and the pictures of the King laughing with the players added a joyous note to the return of cricket.

Two weekends before, the first-class game had come back at The Oval with an historic piece of cricket when Surrey played the Indians. With some difficulty the Indians reached 205 for nine, five of them having succumbed to Alec Bedser. The last pair of Sarwate and Banerjee then batted together for three hours 10 minutes and added 249. This not only exceeded the previous highest last-wicket stand in England – the 235 of Frank Woolley and Arthur Fielder for Kent in 1909 – but was the first occasion when a number 10 and number 11 had made hundreds in the same innings. Sarwate made 124 not out, Banerjee 121. Though Sarwate made 200 in India several years later, he and his partner were not batting out of position in that side at The Oval. In his other 18 innings on the tour Banerjee mustered 174 runs. A fast bowler, he did not play in a Test match on either of his two tours of England. Sarwate, a leg-spinner, played in one Test in 1946 and was out for 0 and two – in each innings to Alec Bedser whom he had played with some comfort in early May at The Oval.

The Indians, who had toured England twice in the 1930s, included six players from their side of 1936. Three of these – Vijay Merchant, Mushtaq Ali and the all-rounder Lala Amarnath – were players of high quality. The captain, the Nawab of Pataudi, had yet to play in a Test match for India but had played three times for England in the early 1930s, all against Australia.

This probably sounds strange in the 1990s but in those days the English cricketing public took Indian princes in its stride.

There had been the great Ranji – K.S. Ranjitsinhji who played in 15 Test matches for England around the turn of the century. His nephew "Duleep" – K.S. Duleepsinhji of Cheltenham, Cambridge University, Sussex and England – had delighted crowds in the late 1920s and early 1930s with the wristy charm and nimble foot-work of his batting. He played in 12 Test matches for England in a career cut short by ill-health.

The Nawab of Pataudi senior – his son was to captain India in the 1960s – had an outstanding record for Oxford between 1929 and 1931. In his last year he made six hundreds and his 238 not out remains the highest ever made in the University match which dates back to 1827. After coming down from Oxford, he went on the "Bodyline" tour of Australia in 1932–3, making 102 in Sydney in his first Test match. He lacked the sparkle of Duleepsinhji but was correct and patient and hard to dislodge when well established at the crease. During his brief career for Worcestershire he made three double hundreds in 1933 and another in 1934 before he too had to yield to ill-health.

In theory, Pataudi's experience of English conditions and his class and soundness as a batsman should have stood him and his side in good stead in 1946 but his long retirement from the first-class game was no help. He made four hundreds on the tour but his highest score in the three Test matches was 22 and he was clearly not fully fit. He did, in fact, die five years later, at 41, suf-fering a heart attack while playing polo.

Even without major contributions from their captain, India had several batsmen good enough to make a lot of runs on true pitches and in fine weather. Vijay Merchant, now 34, had long been recognised as a batsman of the highest class. A complete player though only five feet eight in height, he made seven hundreds on the tour including one in the Third and last Test. His opening partner, the dashing Mushtaq Ali, needed more reliable pitches than many of those encountered in this wet summer. So did others, such as Gul Mahomed, Rusi Modi and Vijay Hazare who had been prolific scorers in their own country. On two good pitches at Sheffield and Lord's, Hazare, who was to captain India on their next tour of England, made 244 not out against Yorkshire and 193 not out against Middlesex.

The side had two fine all-rounders in Vinoo Mankad and Lala Amarnath. Mankad is probably remembered in England mostly for his batting and bowling in the Lord's Test of 1952 but he had a remarkable tour in 1946, scoring 1120 runs and taking 129 wickets with his left-arm spin. Only one English cricketer did the double that summer, Dick Howorth of Worcestershire, also a left-arm spinner.

In those days of uncovered pitches few visiting sides had the experience to cope with a wet English summer and in the First Test at Lord's Alec Bedser proved too much for the Indian batsmen, taking 11 wickets for 145. Joe Hardstaff's 205 not out greatly facilitated England's win by 10 wickets. Without it, they would have been hard pressed to win in the three days allotted.

At Old Trafford Bedser again took 11 wickets, but in a low-scoring match India, who had put England in, held out for a draw with their last pair at the wicket for the last 13 minutes.

There was much good cricket played in this match but the last Test at The Oval was hopelessly ruined by rain. At Lord's the gates had been shut on the first two days and 15,000 were present on the third day. On the second day at The Oval, the Monday, 26,000 turned up. Of these more than 20,000 paid three shillings and sixpence (17½p) at the gate. As expected, the grounds all over the country had been packed and though the whole season had been a struggle against the weather, the great thing was that Test cricket and the County Championship had been resumed and had not lost their attraction for the public.

The Indians had, as expected, improved on the record of their two previous tours, though there was no guarantee that the improvement would continue. Many of their best batsmen were near retirement and, when partition came to the sub-continent, they were likely to find it even harder to produce fast bowlers. The required physique was more common in the northern provinces which were to become Pakistan.

Of their 1946 side they were soon to lose Abdul Hafeez, a 21-year-old left-handed all-rounder. His next Test was against India as A.H. Kardar, Pakistan's first captain, and he was to be a leading administrator in the game in Pakistan for many years. After the 1946 tour he went up to Oxford and played three times against Cambridge as well as for Warwickshire.

Gul Mahomed, also a left-hander, was another who eventually took Pakistan citizenship, but he had played in eight Test matches for India before his solitary appearance for Pakistan when his days of prolific scoring were long past. Though he achieved little in England, on returning home he made 319 in the final of the Ranji Trophy of 1946–7.

In that first post-war season Yorkshire, the champions, and

Middlesex, runners-up, finished in the same order as in the last three pre-war seasons.

Captained and firmly disciplined, as before, by Brian Sellers, Yorkshire were the better equipped side, though some of their players were at an age when not many more seasons could be expected of them. For Maurice Leyland, the great left-hander, it was the last season. Though he was 46, he was still highly effective on the many awkward pitches of that season. Frank Smailes was 36 and still a useful enough all-rounder to be picked for England at Lord's. That was his only Test and he played for only two more seasons. Two batsmen, Cyril Turner (43) and Wilfred Barber (44), retired at the end of the 1946 season.

In the spring Yorkshire cannot have been quite sure of what to expect from two of their Test players of 1939 – Len Hutton because of his arm injury, and Bill Bowes who had been a prisoner of war. In the event both played big parts in winning the Championship. Hutton's skill on wet pitches put him well ahead of the other batsmen. Bowes, tall and fast-medium, gradually recovered his strength and by the end of the season had taken 56 wickets in the Championship at 13.89 apiece.

But Yorkshire's victory was based on spin bowling that year – on the remarkable season of Arthur Booth. They still had their off-spinner of 1939, Ellis Robinson, and he took 129 wickets at 14.03 each, but his partner before the War had been the much lamented Hedley Verity. Now Yorkshire looked around for a left-arm spinner and settled on Booth whom they had let go in 1931 when Verity was establishing himself as a left-arm bowler of rare talent. Booth had spent several seasons playing for Northumberland. On being recalled to Yorkshire at the age of 43 he took 84 wickets at 11.90 each. It was a one-season triumph, for he played only four matches in the dry summer of 1947 and then, beset by arthritis, dropped out.

Middlesex's strengths were in direct contrast. In the 1930s they had hit on a rich seam of young batsmen under the captaincy of R.W.V. Robins. By 1939 when Robins handed over to Ian Peebles, their batting order, starting with Jack Robertson aged 22, Sid Brown 21, Edrich 23 and Compton 21, was unusual both for its talent and its youth. The future looked promising indeed but six seasons, in which all sorts of batting records might have been broken, were lost.

In the cold and wet of 1946, with Walter Robins (now 40) in command again, the batsmen were no disappointment and the

bowling was strengthened through the left-arm spin of Jack
Young. He had been around a long time – he had played in a few
matches as far back as 1933 – and was 33 when a decision to
release him to Glamorgan was reversed abruptly. He took 95
wickets at 16 apiece and in just over a year was playing for
England. Jim Sims (42) was not quite the force of the 1930s but
took 88 wickets with his leg-spin and Laurie Gray (30) had
improved enough as a fast bowler to take 81 wickets.

Overall, Middlesex's policy could be interpreted as making as
many runs as possible as quickly as possible in order that the
bowlers could be given extra time in which to work.

It was generally accepted that Yorkshire were worthy champions. They had beaten Middlesex in the wet at Lord's in June
and had had the better of a draw in mid-August at Sheffield. This
last match, also reduced by rain, was played during the final Test
match to which Yorkshire lost Hutton and Middlesex Compton
and Edrich.

The composition of the Middlesex side for this important contest was a reminder that as yet there was still a place for the amateur in English first-class cricket. Yorkshire still had an amateur
captain, Brian Sellers, commanding 10 professionals. At Sheffield
Middlesex included four amateurs, one of whom, G.O. Allen
aged 44, was playing only his second first-class match of the season. The other had been at Whitsun. Gubby Allen made many
runs during the later stages of his playing career and, with his fine
action, still had his moments as a fast bowler. In the first innings
of this match he bowled 25 overs and took five for 26.

A great uncertainty existed about the future of the amateur in
English post-war cricket. It was not an immediate problem
because the best of the pre-war amateurs would usually be available still and the numbers of amateurs leaving the Services and
going up to Oxford and Cambridge would sustain the supply of
relatively mature amateurs for some years. National Service was
likely to continue for the foreseeable future and though it would
interrupt the careers of young professionals on county staffs, the
University sides would be older and stronger as a result of it.

Before the end of this wet summer the selectors had to pick an
M.C.C. team to tour Australia and New Zealand. It was still the
responsibility of M.C.C. and remained so until the formation of
the Test and County Cricket Board in 1968. Even then the custom of calling England representative touring teams "M.C.C."
lived on for nearly a decade, though the Marylebone Cricket Club

by then was merely an influential club which owned Lord's and had a special responsibility for the Laws of Cricket.

The selectors, not for the last time, were choosing a side for a major overseas tour on the evidence of a home season's cricket played in very different conditions. On this occasion, they had much less than a full season's cricket evidence before them, for the team was due to sail on the *Stirling Castle* on 31 August before the County Championship programme was completed.

For the England players it was going to be a tremendous experience after the privations of the war years. They were certain to receive a hero's welcome and the unrationed food and drink, the sunshine and the bathing were only a few of the attractions which lay ahead.

The last match in Auckland was not due to end until 29 March 1947. The real heroes, perhaps, were their families who had only just been reunited with them after war-time absences and now were surrendering them for nearly eight months.

2

The Don's Farewell

IT would be wrong to say that Australian cricket awaited Walter Hammond's M.C.C. team in September 1946 with any shortage of confidence but there were several issues to be determined, not least the health of Don Bradman.

The influence of Bradman on England–Australia series since he made a hundred in each of the two Melbourne Tests of 1928–9 aged 20 is hard to over-estimate. It was not only the huge scores which he made and his consistency but the rate at which he scored – 309 in a day at Headingley in 1930, 304 there in 1934 in under seven hours – and all this apparently without taking risks. Perfectly balanced and with lightning reflexes and footwork, he was always in position, always waiting for whatever the bowler produced. The ball seldom left the ground but was struck through the gaps in the field with extraordinary frequency.

How Bradman would have fared against modern field-setting, with an almost square cover-point on the boundary and defence in depth on the on-side, became a matter of speculation in later years. Certainly he would not have received as many balls in an hour as he did then but anyone who saw him in the 1930s would surely back him to find a way through somehow, especially as to add to his technical genius, he had the perfect temperament for all occasions and for making vast scores. By the outbreak of war he had already made 15 Test hundreds against England and of those two were of over 300 and five others over 200.

Even in 1932–3, when England under Douglas Jardine sadly but successfully brought down Australia with short, accurate fast bowling at the batsman's person, Bradman averaged 56. The last sight of him in a Test match had been a melancholy one as he was carried off at The Oval in 1938 with an ankle injury sustained while bowling in England's innings of 903 for seven. But he had made a hundred in each of the other three Tests in that series – one Test, at Old Trafford, was completely washed out.

Now, eight years later, he was only 38 but no one knew if his health, which had not always been of the stoutest, would stand up to a return to cricket at the highest level. He had played a bit for South Australia in the 1945–6 season and had made runs but without clearing away all doubts about his full fitness.

Bradman apart, Australia could take encouragement from a look at their post-war resources. The Australian Services team in England in 1945 had left no one in doubt that Keith Miller was a fast bowler and all-rounder of high quality and that Lindsay Hassett, the Services captain, had many more runs left in him. But while England were on their way with a side of whom seven had played against Australia pre-war, the restricted programme of 1945–6 had left Australians fairly confident that their Test team would be well stocked with good, young players.

Sidney Barnes, who had played in one Test in England in 1938, had made hundreds of runs for New South Wales. Arthur Morris, a left-handed opening batsman of great charm and consistency, had first come on the scene in 1940–1 when making a hundred in each innings for New South Wales against Queensland in his first first-class match. Don Tallon, taller than most of his craft, was regarded as a wicket-keeper of the highest ability.

The best news of all for Australians was probably that there was an obvious candidate to open the bowling with Miller. Ray Lindwall, a young fast bowler with a splendid action, had emerged from three years in the jungles of New Guinea and the Solomons to take a lot of wickets in high-class company.

A short Australian tour of New Zealand in March 1946 under the captaincy of Bill Brown, the opening batsman of the 1930s, had done nothing to dent confidence. It had also made a piece of history, for Australia had never played a Test match against New Zealand before. To New Zealanders this omission may have seemed no great hardship when the one played in Wellington in 1946 lasted only two days and they were bowled out for 42 and 54.

The clashing of their seasons must have been one reason for the previous failure of Australia and New Zealand to meet at Test level. The ideal time for a tour of New Zealand was January and February and that coincided with the climax of the Sheffield Shield programme in Australia. Moreover, Australia had until then undertaken few full-strength tours apart from the trip to England every four years. Air travel was still in its infancy for cricketers and official Australian teams had played only one series against West Indies, in Australia in 1930–1, and none against India. They had played more often against South Africa, first of all as far back as 1902–3 when Joe Darling's side stopped there on their way home from England. In the 1930s there had been one full series of five Tests in each country.

Lest it be thought that Australia were totally lacking in missionary fervour towards New Zealand cricket, it should be added that there had been private Australian visits to New Zealand since before the First World War. The great Victor Trumper had played there. But even if the opposition had seldom been strong enough to justify a Test series, it was still remarkable that after the Test match in Wellington in 1946 another 28 years passed before the next Test match between the two neighbouring countries. Then two three-match series were played in the same season of 1973–4, one in each country. By then England had had 16 Test series with New Zealand, South Africa had had five, West Indies four, India four and Pakistan five.

Australia, of course, had communication problems of their own before air travel developed. Western Australia, which was to produce many of their best players, was still so remote from the east that they did not compete in the Sheffield Shield until the 1947–8 season and then it was with a half-programme wherein they played the other states only once. It was 1956 before the first West Australian, John Rutherford, was picked for an overseas tour.

Walter Hammond's M.C.C. team can have had few illusions about the strength of their bowling when they arrived in Fremantle in September 1946. But the mere fact that a Test series between Australia and England was going to take place again overshadowed all other considerations, including that of how Australia were to be bowled out.

England had two main bowlers, Alec Bedser and Doug Wright. Bedser was a great asset but he was likely to have to bowl too much. Wright, who with his long, bounding run-up bowled his leg-spin at near medium pace, was an unusual type but it was a type born to be unlucky. When he produced the unplayable ball, it tended to miss everything, most importantly the edge of the bat and the stumps. When bowlers of his type bowl a loose one, it seems to sit up conveniently for the batsman.

Two other leg-spinners were in the side. Peter Smith of Essex had taken 107 wickets in the recent English season and had batted number three for Essex. John Ikin was a courageous left-handed batsman and a fine close fielder who had bowled 333 overs for Lancashire in 1946 and had taken 38 wickets at 19 apiece. He played in all five Tests in Australia but was only required to bowl seven overs in them. James Langridge, a left-arm slow bowler and middle-order batsman, might have played in the Third Test but for an injury which eventually put him out for the rest of the tour.

The faster bowlers, besides Bedser, were Dick Pollard and Bill Voce. Pollard had taken five for 24 against India in his first Test that July. He was 34 and had been successful for Lancashire for several seasons before the War. Both he and Voce had still been in the Forces during 1946 and had not played a full season. The selection of Voce, now 37, 14 years after his partnership with Harold Larwood had helped to win the 1932–3 series, pointed all too eloquently to the shortage of fast bowling. In subsequent selections of teams for a tour of Australia a useful guideline was to pick young fast bowlers on the way up rather than more experienced players who might have passed their best. The eight-ball over, in vogue in Australia then and for 30 years to come, called for greater resources of strength than did the six-ball, especially in a hot climate.

As things worked out, Bedser and Wright bowled the most overs and the most effective of the other bowlers were Norman Yardley and Bill Edrich. Yardley, the vice-captain, destined to become captain of England in 1947 and of Yorkshire a year later, was one of the outstanding Cambridge batsmen of the 1930s and had toured South Africa in 1938–9, playing in one Test match. He had been wounded in the Western Desert but had played a full season for Yorkshire in 1946. As a sound middle-order batsman, he had restored many an innings which had made a sticky start. What he was not required to do for Yorkshire was bowl. In 1946 he bowled only 31 overs and did not take a wicket. However, his gentle medium pace was deceptive and his ability to move the ball about on a nagging length was unexpectedly useful in Australia. In the limited-over cricket of modern times, in which the batsmen are forced to take risks on slow pitches and when the ball is not coming on to the bat, he would have been invaluable. But his bowling was a surprise in Australia in 1946, especially as in South Africa eight years before, under the same captain, he had bowled only three overs in first-class matches.

Yardley took 10 Test wickets and, rather less surprisingly, Bill Edrich took nine. Edrich, small and tough, had taken 68 wickets for Middlesex that year. In later years he became a serviceable off-spinner but in 1946 he hurtled up to the wicket with an abandon which made one fear that he might do himself an injury. For a few overs he could be genuinely fast but without the subtleties of movement in the air and off the pitch which take good wickets.

The welcome in Australia had all the warmth of reunions with old friends and the tour off the field began, as it was to continue, on the happiest note. On the field during the three and a half weeks in Perth the M.C.C. batsmen were soon making runs, Hammond himself starting with 131 retired in a country match and 208 against Western Australia. The bowlers in his side, however, were soon being made aware of their limitations. There was a brief moment of optimism in early November when M.C.C. beat Victoria, generally regarded as the strongest state side, in a match in which Hutton and Compton made hundreds on their first appearance on the Melbourne Cricket Ground, but that was to be the only first-class win in Australia.

And so, eventually, to Brisbane for the first post-war Test match between the old adversaries. England could not be said to have had insufficient practice, for three months had passed since they sailed from Southampton. In the past they had been lucky in Brisbane and had won all three of their previous Test matches in the city.

To the general delight Don Bradman had been fit enough to accept the Australian captaincy. The fact that the legendary figure of pre-war years had not left the stage of world cricket was a boost to the game. If he played in this series and the next in England two summers later, young cricket followers in England as well as Australia would have a chance to see the great man of whom they had heard from their fathers. For older spectators another sight of Bradman at the wicket was a dream which they had feared would never be realised. But there was a tentativeness about his return to first-class cricket which sounded a note of caution. The fear was that if he was unsuccessful, he might accept that his astonishing career was over.

So far his season had been a mixed one. He had played for South Australia against M.C.C. and had had to field throughout the first day's play while Hutton and Washbrook were making 237 without mishap. It was the third day before Bradman came to the wicket, looking far from robust, and made 76 in a some-what exploratory two and a half hours. He was soon out to Pollard in the second innings.

A fortnight later he played again against the touring side for an Australian XI in Melbourne. He made 106 before being out to the left-arm spin of Denis Compton, off whom he might have been stumped when 78. The offender behind the stumps was Godfrey Evans who at the age of 26 was shortly to settle into a Test career which lasted almost without interruption to the end of the 1950s. He had played in the largely washed-out final Test against India at The Oval but the expectation was that he would be second wicket-keeper to Paul Gibb on the tour. Gibb, neat and competent, had opened the innings throughout the 1938–9 series in South Africa, averaging nearly 60. A Cambridge Blue of the 1930s, he was the third amateur (with Hammond and Yardley) in the touring side of 1946–7.

Bradman played once more before the First Test – in the Sheffield Shield against Victoria in Melbourne. He made 43 and 119 but was troubled by a leg strain.

So the Don came to Brisbane with his future still unsettled in the public's mind and probably in his own. He made 187 and led Australia to victory by an innings and 332 runs. Surely this almost guaranteed that he would carry on playing and would take the side to England in 1948! Well, so it did but, without dramatising a single incident unduly, one was entitled to wonder what might have happened if he had been given out just before lunch on the first morning when he had made 28 and the Australian score was 74 for two. Then it was that he chopped at a ball from Voce and to many watchers seemed to be caught waist-high by John Ikin at second slip. The umpires took a differ-ent view and Bradman, who had so far been ill at ease against Bedser, went on to share in a third-wicket stand of 276 with Lindsay Hassett.

Australia batted on into the third day before they were out for 645. By then the weather had changed. England batted in each innings after a deluge. The ball lifted off a length, Miller and Toshack took nine wickets each and Lindwall, who was struck down by chicken pox during the first innings, was not greatly missed.

Keith Miller, with his powerful, athletic frame, was a formidable opponent at the best of times. He never allowed a batsman to settle in. No slave to a bowling mark, he would turn and bowl as the mood took him. His faster ball would often bounce more than expected and when the ball lifted, as in Brisbane, nobody would back the batsman with confidence.

Ernie Toshack was rising 32 and his Test career ended after the 1948 tour with a knee injury. But for two years he was an important member of the side. A tall, left-arm, unathletic-looking figure, he bowled medium pace, mostly around the leg-stump. His strength was his accuracy and once he had found the length required on a wicked lifting pitch, he was very awkward indeed.

Skilfully handled by Bradman, Toshack was to be especially useful to Australia on good pitches by keeping the batsmen quiet while the fast bowlers were recharging their batteries before taking the new ball. In England the new ball had been taken usually after 200 runs had been scored but in the early post-war years the availability of a new ball became governed by the number of overs bowled. Various numbers were tried, some as low as 55 six-ball overs.

Before Christmas Australia won again by an innings in Sydney, as in Brisbane on the sixth day. Test matches in this series were played over six days of five hours apiece. This time Australia, having bowled England out for 255 on a pitch which took spin, had to bat after rain on the second day but after the weekend the pitch had rolled out. Bradman, who had been limping on the first day and did not field on the second, held himself back until the fall of the fourth wicket at 169. He and Barnes then shared in a fifth-wicket stand of 405 which remains the highest ever made for the fifth wicket in all first-class cricket. Both made 234, the solid determined Sidney Barnes batting for 10 hours 40 minutes, his captain for four hours less. On the England side, Bill Edrich, one of the last choices for the tour, made 71 and 119.

It was a measure of Australia's all-round superiority that here they bowled out England with spin. Ian Johnson, an off-spinner who had played in Brisbane but had not been required to bowl, took eight wickets. So did Colin McCool, the leg-spinner, who had bowled only one over in the First Test. McCool, a compact batsman with a lot of strokes, had made 95 at Brisbane and was to become a successful all-rounder for Somerset in the late 1950s. In the New South Wales team against M.C.C. was another all-rounder destined for Somerset. Bill Alley never played for Australia but he became a familiar figure in English cricket as a left-handed batsman who made over 3000 runs in 1961 at the age of 45 and later became a Test umpire.

Bradman's emphatic return to Test cricket continued with 79 and 49 in the New Year Test in Melbourne where England escaped with a draw. McCool, who usually batted six or seven, and Lindwall at nine advertised the depth of the Australian batting by making a hundred apiece. The Fourth Test in Adelaide was also drawn after Denis Compton, who had done little in the previous Tests, made a hundred in each innings. So did Arthur Morris. On the second evening of this match, after England had made 460, Alec Bedser brought to reality what had only been a dream by bowling Bradman for nought.

Back in Sydney in the final Test, England led on first innings but Australia won by five wickets. Len Hutton was 122 not out after batting through the first day, but after a washed-out second day and a Sunday, he was stopped from resuming by tonsillitis and took no further part in the match. Don Bradman's 63 was mainly responsible for Australia's 214 for five which won the match.

Bradman played only the one Sheffield Shield match for South Australia that season and only the first (in which he made exactly 100) in the following season. But the Indians were playing a full five-Test series then and he warmed up in that for the coming tour of England. He averaged 178. The Indians were without two of their senior batsmen in Merchant and Modi and were outplayed by a side which had now acquired another high-class performer in Bill Johnston, a powerfully built left-arm fast-medium bowler, who added variety to their attack, as well as accuracy and stamina.

While Australia had been demolishing India 4–0, England had been considerably less successful in the West Indies. Captained and managed by G.O. Allen, they set off without Hutton, Washbrook, Compton, Edrich, Yardley, Bedser and Wright, who were either resting or unavailable. Within 72 hours of arriving by sea in Bridgetown, they were playing the first of two matches against Barbados. Their immediate form not surprisingly indicated that long sea voyages were a better preparation for batsmen than for bowlers but, before long, injuries were plaguing the side so much that an urgent request was made to Lord's for another player.

In the dire situation in which the M.C.C. team found itself, two valiant individual feats were performed. The assistant-manager and second wicket-keeper, S.C. Griffith, was required to open the innings in the Second Test in Trinidad. Billy Griffith, later to

become a much respected Secretary of M.C.C., had batted nine or
ten in his three previous innings on the tour. He had never made a
first-class hundred and for Cambridge University and Sussex was
a vigorous late-order batsman.

In Port of Spain he laid aside his aggressive instincts and batted
through the first day for 100 not out. Next day his first Test
innings ended for 140, a monumental piece of devotion, patience
and determination.

The batsman who came out as a reinforcement was Len
Hutton. He flew out, which, considering that up to the recent
War flying the Atlantic had been a pioneering job for intrepid
aviators, cannot have been a very restful journey for the less
adventurous. However, when Hutton went to the wicket three
days later against British Guiana in Georgetown, he too batted
throughout the first day, making 138 and 62 not out in the
match.

England lost the last two of the four Test matches and did not
win a match on the tour, though it did establish two things. One
was that in future the strongest possible side should be sent to the
West Indies and, coming from an English midwinter, should be
given a week at least for acclimatisation and practice. The other
was that English cricket had a pretty good off-spinner in the making in Jim Laker, a 25-year-old Yorkshireman who, after service
in the Middle East, had been found by Surrey playing for Catford
in London club cricket. He had taken 79 wickets in 1947 in barely half a season's matches. In the Caribbean, though not fully fit,
he took 18 Test wickets at 30 each.

As preparation for the summer's series with Australia, this tour
had not been a great help. More relevant, it was hoped, was the
tremendous batting of Denis Compton and Bill Edrich in the previous summer of 1947. However, the Australians' tour of 1948
already had a special significance as Don Bradman's last tour and
the British public could look at his figures against India and con-
clude that the old genius had far from faded. He had only once
been out for less than 132.

The passage of an Australian cricket team to Britain was widely
reported in those days. Some newspapers sent their representatives to join the ship as far away as Colombo. After 10 years,
Bradman was back – for the last time – and it was something not
to be missed, even with the counter-attractions of the London
Olympic Games.

The Australians' first match at Worcester was of special significance, for on his three previous visits there Don Bradman had made 236, 206 and 258. The weather was uninviting and there was something peculiarly spiteful in the way that after a long dry spell the first drops of rain fell as Lindwall ran up to bowl his first ball in England. However, 32,000 turned up in the three days and on the second day Bradman made 107 in just over two and a quarter hours. All was well with the Don – and not only with him.

Rarely can the batsmen of a touring side have mastered the conditions of an English spring more swiftly. At Worcester, Arthur Morris, playing his first innings in England, made 138. At Leicester, Keith Miller made 202 not out. At The Oval, Barnes, Bradman and Hassett all made a hundred in a total of 632. At Cambridge, Bill Brown, on his third tour of England, made 200. Then, as early as 15 May came the feat for which the Australians of 1948 are especially remembered.

On the first day at Southend against Essex they made 721, the greatest number ever scored in a six-hour day of first-class cricket. Bradman's contribution of 187 was made in two hours five minutes. Brown made 153, the all-rounder Sam Loxton 120 and the second wicket-keeper Ron Saggers 104. Keith Miller, as unconventional as ever, was bowled first ball by Trevor Bailey, who suffered an injury which prevented him from batting on the Monday when Essex were bowled out twice. Essex's attack, after Bailey's injury, was mostly confined to slow and medium-pace bowling and they bowled 129 overs in the day.

The Australians moved on, winning most of their matches by an innings, until they reached Trent Bridge for the First Test. There they met an England side which included four of the batsmen who had played in a high-scoring draw on the ground 10 years before – Hutton, Edrich, Compton and Barnett. Charles Barnett of Gloucestershire, who now batted number six, was a fine sight in full flow, a tall, forthright driver and cutter. In 1938 he had opened the innings with Hutton and at lunch on the first day had been 99 not out.

In 1948 Australia had Bradman, Brown and Hassett left from the Trent Bridge Test of a decade before. England never quite recovered from being bowled out for 165 on the first day – they had been 74 for eight before Laker and Bedser added 89 together – though the going was never easy for Australia. Bradman's 138 took him four and three-quarter hours, Hassett's 137 an hour longer. Lindwall suffered a groin strain and could not bowl in the second innings when England's resistance was led by Compton, between showers. Miller bowled 44 overs, Johnston 59 and the match was into its fifth and last day when one of Compton's finest innings ended, a shade unluckily, for 184. He had batted for nearly seven hours and was only out when he changed his mind about hooking a high bouncer from Miller, slipped on the wet surface and broke his wicket. Australia won by eight wickets on the last afternoon.

This First Test confirmed the all-round excellence of Bradman's side, not least by the high standard of fielding and the mighty efforts of Miller and Johnston who took four wickets each.

At Lord's in the Second Test Johnston again played an important part, this time in support of Lindwall, who took eight wickets in the match. In the second innings Ernie Toshack, also left-arm but of medium pace, took five for 40 and the absence from the attack of Miller, who played in the match but could not bowl, was not felt. Indeed Australia had 409 runs to spare.

Bradman made 38 and 89 in his last Lord's Test. As at Trent Bridge he was out in both innings to Alec Bedser whose success was founded on a late in-swinger which the "Master Batsman" would, just occasionally, glance to backward short-leg. If this relative failure by the Don was a disappointment to the public, he put it right in his last match of all at Lord's in late August by making 150 against the Gentlemen. His farewell appearances elsewhere were also marked in appropriate manner – at the Hastings Festival 143, at Scarborough 153 and at Aberdeen, where 10,000 turned up to see his last innings in Britain, 123 not out.

By then Australia had won the Test series 4–0. England led them on first innings at Old Trafford when Compton, having been felled by a ball from Lindwall early on, returned to make 145 not out. England also had their moments at Headingley when Norman Yardley's declaration early on the last day left his bowlers five and three-quarter hours in which to bowl Australia out on a pitch taking spin.

Australia, it seems, were themselves far from confident, especially after Hassett was out to Compton for 17. It was Compton, indeed, who came nearest to upsetting the Australian batting with his recently acquired chinaman and googly. Bradman was dropped at slip off him and Morris survived a stumping chance. If it was not a day for English cricket to remember, at least the world could marvel at the second-wicket stand of 301 between

Arthur Morris and Don Bradman which set up the famous 404 for three on this turning pitch. Morris made 182, Bradman 173 not out and Australia won by seven wickets with 15 minutes to spare. This certainly was the mark of a great side basking in the confidence of great players in form.

There was really just the one disappointment in the Don's last tour. After England had been bowled out for 52 in the Fifth and last Test on a drying pitch at The Oval – Lindwall six for 20 – Bradman came out for his last Test innings, a historic moment even with the Olympic Games in progress in other parts of London on that Saturday. The packed crowd had to wait while Morris and Barnes had an opening stand of 117. Then, near the end of the first day, Bradman came out to an ovation without parallel. The crowd stood, the England captain Norman Yardley shook the great man's hand as he arrived at the crease and called for three cheers from the England side.

Eventually the tumult died down and Bradman was able to take guard. But even for one as disciplined as Don Bradman it must have been a moving experience to find that you meant so much in the lives of people the other side of the world. Perhaps, just for once, that normally unshakeable concentration was dented. He played forward to his second ball from Eric Hollies, a googly, and was bowled. The ovation was resumed as he walked back and disappeared into the pavilion. In the Test matches of the previous 20 years he had averaged 99.96. If he had hit just one four in that last innings, he would have averaged 100.

On that last tour in 1948 Don Bradman made 11 hundreds in 31 first-class innings and averaged nearly 90. If there had been no pre-war Bradman, the post-war version would still have been a sensation. Yet those who had also seen him batting before the War were in no doubt that he had been even more brilliant then. That merely underlines the heights which his genius reached.

He also captained what is usually considered the strongest side ever seen in England. What lifts it over modern West Indian teams is that the 1948 Australians had the strength and desire to go all out to win every match of their tour. Out of 31 matches in a summer not always blessed by the weather they won 23 and drew eight. Moreover, in the victorious present they had not neglected the future. They had brought with them the 19-year-old Neil Harvey who had played in the last two Tests against India, making 153 in the last. On the tour an injury to Barnes brought Harvey into the Test team at Headingley and he made 112 in the first of his many Test innings in England.

When the last match was played in Aberdeen, the Australians were invited to Balmoral where some of the last pictures of the Don in England were taken of him walking in the grounds with King George VI and Queen Elizabeth. On returning home he was knighted, the first still active cricketer to be so honoured. Still to come were many years of service as an administrator.

For the moment, Raymond Robertson-Glasgow put the feelings of the British cricketing public fairly in the following year's *Wisden*:

"Don Bradman will bat no more against England, and two contrary feelings dispute within us: relief, that our bowlers will no longer be oppressed by this phenomenon; regret, that a miracle has been removed from among us. So must ancient Italy have felt when she heard of the death of Hannibal."

3

Compton, Edrich and their Heyday

NOTHING helped to re-establish English domestic cricket after the War more than the spectacular batting of Denis Compton and Bill Edrich in the almost unrelieved sunshine of 1947. The manner in which Middlesex won the County Championship gave a great fillip to the game and so did the way in which the same pair addressed themselves to the South African bowling in the Test series.

Certainly the bowling which they met was not of the very highest class. Certainly the shortage of fast bowlers with their long run-ups provided the batting side with more overs per day than would be received in modern times. In those pre-covering days many pitches took spin. Every county had several slow bowlers and no one had to worry about a slow over rate. Sometimes a day's play was of six and a half hours or even seven hours in order to allow an early finish on the third day when trains had to be caught.

Petrol, of course, was still rationed, a circumstance which contributed to the big crowds which watched some matches. Many people did not have the means to go away at weekends. Nobody owned villas in Spain and the beaches of Britain had been covered too recently with mines and barbed wire for the seaside to be instantly attractive. So, weather permitting, which it nearly always did in 1947, people went to the cricket.

Just as even great actors would struggle to succeed in a bad play with an ineffective supporting cast, so Edrich and Compton benefited from being preceded by one of the most consistent opening pairs in the country. Jack Robertson and Sid Brown made respectively 2760 and 2078 runs that season. To follow Edrich and Compton there was George Mann, who played almost

a full season, a fine driver of the ball who captained England in
South Africa two winters later; Alec Thompson, a hard-hitting
middle-order batsman who occasionally played a match-winning
innings; and Walter Robins. The lively and imaginative captaincy
of Robins was a great asset and, though 41, he remained remarkably nimble between the wickets and in the field.

Robins did not have an outstanding fielding side but its bowling did have variety and with huge scores behind them the
bowlers could usually operate to attacking fields.

One match, at The Oval against Surrey over the second weekend in August, provides a good example of Middlesex's cricket
that year and its popularity. The match was watched by 54,000
of whom 47,000 paid at the gate. The 30,000 present on the
Saturday when the gates were closed saw Middlesex make 537
for two, Robertson 127 and Brown 98. Compton joined Edrich at
250 for two, which is scarcely penury, and they added 287 in two
and three-quarter hours, Edrich making 157 not out and
Compton 137 not out. Surrey, who had bowled 118 overs in the
day, were by no means a weak side – they finished sixth in the
Championship – but when they batted after the weekend they
succumbed to a "new" bowler. Denis Compton took 12 wickets
for 174.

In what one would have thought was a fairly hectic season
Compton had found time to change from orthodox left-arm spin
to an assortment of chinaman and googly. As recently as March,
in the last match of M.C.C.'s tour of Australasia, he had taken 11
wickets for 49 on a drying pitch against Auckland as an orthodox
spinner. In the home season of 1947 he was persuaded that his
bowling future lay in the chinaman, the off-break to a right-handed
batsman bowled by a left-arm bowler, and the googly, which
would be a leg-break to a right-handed batsman.

Compton's mentor was a most entertaining cricketer, Jack
Walsh, an Australian who had begun to qualify for Leicestershire
before the War and played a few matches as an amateur then. In
1946 he was 33 and for several seasons Leicestershire's main
wicket-taker, bowling about a thousand overs and taking 150
wickets each season. He was a prodigious spinner of the ball and
though sometimes expensive, as are most of his method, he concealed one of his two googlies so well that the batsman would
sometimes miss by a quite remarkable margin. When the pitch
was taking a lot of spin, spectators could have the droll sight
of the batsman preparing to guard his stumps against a huge

off-break while the wicket-keeper Jack Firth, who had learnt to read Walsh well, set off to take the googly a yard outside the off-stump.

In July 1947 Compton had a week with Walsh, first while Middlesex were playing a highly eventful match with Leicestershire at Leicester and then when both were in action for the Players against the Gentlemen at Lord's.

"Why don't you try the chinaman?" Walsh asked him. "You'll get a lot of fun out of it."

Nothing appealed to Compton more than getting fun out of cricket and his flair for the game was such that he quickly taught himself the subtleties of a different form of bowling. He bowled off two or three strides, spun the ball a lot and soon had a well concealed googly under fair control. The speed with which he bowled an over on accurate days meant that a baffled batsman had little time to marshal his thoughts and organise his defences.

The new method was successfully unveiled at Northampton a week later after Edrich had made 267 not out and Compton 110. In the context of Middlesex's cricket in this era Compton could afford to give away runs and his 46 overs in the match cost 178 of them. But he took nine wickets and Middlesex bowled Northants out twice and won the match.

He was fortunate that, as a batsman, anything he did with the ball was a bonus. Here lies the major factor in the development of spin bowlers. They need time and, perhaps costly, experience to perfect their craft. A slow bowler with no other contribution to make will often not survive the formative years. If he has other parts to play, he can hold his place in the side while developing as a sideline an extra weapon such as the chinaman and its variations. A prime example of this in the 1950s was John Wardle.

In 1947 Middlesex were already well equipped with spin. Jack Young, an orthodox left-arm spinner without a lot of flight but with a high degree of accuracy, was bowling his way into the England Test team. Jim Sims, though well into his forties, was still taking wickets with his leg-spin. A 17-year-old schoolboy leg-spinner, Ian Bedford, took 25 Championship wickets in his holidays.

The match at Leicester provided another instance of Middlesex's batting powers. Leicestershire made over 300 in the first innings and nearly 400 in the second but lost by 10 wickets. On the second day 663 runs were scored of which Bill Edrich made 257 and Compton 151. Between lunch and tea 310 were made in two hours 20 minutes.

The conditions were so much in the batsmen's favour that by lunch on the last day Leicestershire, batting with spirit, seemed to have earned a draw, for they had lost only four wickets and were 17 runs ahead with only 80 minutes of the match left.

After lunch, however, the long resistance led by their captain Les Berry crumbled. After Compton had taken the last three wickets, Middlesex needed 66 to win in 25 minutes. Edrich, captaining Middlesex for the first time – he had turned amateur in the spring – took Compton in with him and they made the runs off seven overs with four minutes to spare.

In one period of 28 days, starting at the end of June, Bill Edrich made 1176 runs in six matches. Only two of these matches were at Lord's. The others were at Old Trafford, Headingley, Leicester and Northampton. One marvels nowadays at the excellence of pitches all over the country in those early post-war days – pitches which cannot have had a lot of attention during the years of war. Perhaps the rest did them good. The exception was Headingley where in a low-scoring match after rain Edrich made 70 and 102 out of totals of 124 and 234.

On the whole Middlesex negotiated fairly well the matches when Edrich and Compton were away playing in Test matches. One of their replacements, Alan Fairbairn, a left-hander from London club cricket, made a hundred in each of his first two first-class matches. But serious challengers had emerged in Gloucestershire. In their first Championship match of the season they had been brushed aside by Middlesex at Lord's but they had two formidable slow bowlers in Tom Goddard, the 46-year-old off-spinner, and Sam Cook, a left-arm spinner. In the Championship that year these two took 206 and 120 wickets respectively.

The second meeting between the two sides, which could well decide the Championship, was keenly awaited. It took place in mid-August on the College ground at Cheltenham which had the reputation for taking spin. It clashed with the Fifth Test at The Oval, so that Middlesex could expect to be without Edrich and Compton. In fact, Edrich, who was having trouble with a shoulder strain, could not bowl. He withdrew from the Test match, not considering himself fit enough for a four-day Test especially as in the previous matches of that series he had been required to open the bowling. He was replaced in the England team by Jack Robertson, which was scarcely a surprise as Robertson had made a hundred in each of Middlesex's last five matches.

England already had a 3–0 lead in the Test series and at least as much attention was paid to affairs at Cheltenham as to The Oval Test. The excitement in the West Country was tremendous, for Gloucestershire last won the Championship in 1877 and on the evidence of the previous match at the Festival were going to have a pitch on which Goddard and Cook would be in their element.

Middlesex had come from losing at Lord's to Kent. There had been a fascinating duel between Compton and Doug Wright, both at their best. Wright took 11 wickets in the match. Compton's 168 in the last innings when Middlesex needed 397 to win a stirring match is ranked very high amongst his achievements. Gloucestershire's previous opponents at Cheltenham had been the South Africans who had beaten them, the off-spinner Athol Rowan taking 11 wickets for 87.

The famous match began in front of a crowd of 14,500 who were somehow fitted into the College ground. Most of those present probably did not realise what an important toss it was to win and for a time were well satisfied with what they saw. Bill Edrich could not bowl but he opened the innings after Middlesex had won the toss and he made what was to be the only individual 50 in the match. There was then a major collapse before Tom Goddard, and Middlesex were reduced to 143 for nine.

By then, however, a new Middlesex hero had come on the scene in Harry Sharp who, considering that this was his first match of the season, was an inspired selection. He had stood firm while Jim Sims made 32 and he hung on for 14 not out while Jack Young laid about him in a last-wicket stand of 37 precious runs. Sims and Young then bowled Gloucestershire out for 153.

In their second innings Middlesex were soon in trouble again against Goddard and Cook but Sharp, elevated in the batting order, hit Goddard with the spin for eight fours in his 46. The last six wickets fell for only 16 runs and Gloucestershire needed 169 to win.

In the last innings Robins used only three bowlers. Young bowled throughout, taking five for 27 in 19 overs. When it seemed that Sims should be relieved, on came Sharp, who had not bowled in the first innings, and promptly took three good wickets with his off-spin. George Emmett, short of inches but not of skill, could play brilliantly on this sort of pitch but Harry Sharp had him caught at the wicket for nought. By the second evening Middlesex had won by 68 runs and went on to beat Derbyshire, Surrey and Northamptonshire and clinch the Championship.

England meanwhile had won the Test series against a South African team led by Alan Melville which was better than its 3–0 defeat suggested. Melville must have had a greater knowledge of English conditions than any other visiting captain at that time, for he had captained Oxford University for two seasons in the 1930s and Sussex for two seasons. He began the series with three hundreds in his first three Test innings. Dudley Nourse was another batsman of the highest class and English bowlers knew from experience that Bruce Mitchell was never easily dug out. He had made the first of his seven Test hundreds 16 years before and he made eight first-class hundreds on this tour in 1947 including one in each innings of the Fifth Test at The Oval. His 189 not out in the second innings earned South Africa a draw and put them within sight of what would have been a record-breaking win. Needing 450, they finished at 423 for five.

Among their bowlers, the South Africans had Athol Rowan who was just about the best off-spinner in the world at the time. He had a very able partner in "Tufty" Mann, an accurate left-arm slow bowler who played in glasses. He had commended himself at Trent Bridge by starting his Test career with eight maidens to Edrich and Compton. Before the War, Mann had won a golf Blue at Cambridge but, after taking eight wickets in the 1939 Freshmen's match, was not required on the cricket field. Since then he had been a prisoner of war in Italy before escaping to the mountains and being sheltered by peasants. He was a cricketer of character who was greatly mourned when, after his second tour of England in 1951, he died at the age of 31.

The main problem of the 1947 South Africans was that they could not contain Edrich and Compton. Bill Edrich in the first four Tests averaged 110. Compton made 758 runs in the five-match series. In fact, the South Africans scarcely laid eyes on Compton without his making a hundred against them – one each in four of the five Tests, one for Middlesex against the Springboks and one for the South of England against them at the Hastings Festival.

By now, however, the prolific pair were both showing signs of wear and tear after a long hot summer of hard grounds. A week before, while bowling in Middlesex's last Championship match against Lancashire at Lord's, Compton had a recurrence of the old knee injury acquired on the football field in 1938. He had to be helped off the field. The injury yielded to manipulative treatment and he was back after the weekend, making 139 in the second innings. This equalled Jack Hobbs's record of 16 centuries in a season.

Sixty thousand watched this match, though the Championship had already been won. The sporting public was watching with increasing excitement Compton's approach not only to Hobbs's 16 centuries but to the 3518 runs in a season made by Tom Hayward in 1906. Normally by the first week in September the Arsenal Football Club might have been becoming restless, wanting to have him at Highbury for training. It is sometimes forgotten that as late as 1950 he won an F.A. Cup-winners' medal. But in 1947 he had the utmost cooperation in his final assault on the two records.

The first of his two matches for the South of England at Hastings was against the South Africans. They gave him nothing and, having had the best of the pitch, they won by 10 wickets. However, Compton played superbly in the first innings to make 101 in 108 minutes. When he reached his 17th hundred of the season amid a rare hubbub, the proceedings were stopped for five minutes as the crowd stood and cheered, other players came out from the pavilion to shake his hand and one and all rejoiced. It was a weight off everybody's mind because, though no one knew the future of first-class cricket, it was a fair bet that no batsman would ever be in a position to make a 17th hundred in a season again, even if the weather was on his side.

Compton still needed 122 runs to pass Tom Hayward's record aggregate. He had two matches left, one at Hastings for the South of England against Sir Pelham Warner's XI, the other for the Champion County, Middlesex, against the Rest.

As in the first match of the Festival he had no easy passage. When he batted on the second day at Hastings there had been overnight rain and though he himself played immaculately, he ran out of partners when he had made 87. This left him needing 35 and he made them with some care on the last day in an innings of 86.

So the records were broken and all that was left of the golden season of 1947 was the match over four days at The Oval between the Champion County and the Rest of England. This had last been played in 1935 but before that had been played annually and had only twice been won by the champions – by Yorkshire in 1905 and 1935. For Middlesex in 1947 it might have smacked of anti-climax, though this was not an approach which one associated with a side captained by Walter Robins, especially in the last

match of his captaincy. Yet it seemed almost too much to hope
that their batting, and especially its two main exponents, would
do it one last time. The Rest had a strong bowling side on that
season's form – Alec Bedser, Doug Wright, Tom Goddard and two
of the bowlers destined for the winter's tour of West Indies,
Harold Butler, genuinely fast on his day, and Dick Howorth, the
Worcestershire left-arm spinner. Between them they took 815
wickets in 1947.

The toss which Robins won was obviously important in the
long term but autumn mornings at The Oval can hold special
problems for batsmen and Robertson and Brown were soon out
to Bedser. When George Mann was stumped off Wright,
Middlesex were 53 for three.

This brought Compton in to join Edrich and they added 138
together before Compton found himself in so much discomfort
from his knee that, for once, he had to retire. When he resumed
on Monday morning, Edrich was still there and they added
another 72 runs before Edrich was out for 180, having also
passed Hayward's long-standing record aggregate. By then
Compton was playing with much brilliance and went on to make
246. Once when his knee gave way as he was playing a stroke, he
swept the ball for four while lying on the ground.

It was one of the peculiarities of the chips of bone and other
foreign bodies lurking in his knee that there were still times when
he could bowl without discomfort and he bowled 35 overs in this
match, taking six of the wickets as Middlesex made the Rest of
England follow on and won by nine wickets.

One of the many attractions of watching Edrich and Compton
that summer was the contrast between them. They mostly batted
bare-headed but even if hidden by the helmets and bars of the
1980s, there would have been no mistaking them either physically
or technically. Edrich, small and belligerent, would day after day
come in and carry on as he had left off the day before. No reconnaissance seemed to be needed. He was the epitome of a batsman
in supreme form and utterly confident.

Compton, nearly a head taller, would take more care in settling
in – or appear to do so. One of his characteristics was the ability
to convey to the crowd his difficulties or lack of them. The spectator would be at his side as he negotiated the rough ground,
admittedly fairly swiftly, and as he emerged on to the plain
beyond. Then he would reel off the strokes to all quarters, the
ball seeming to accelerate, as with other masters of timing, when

it was halfway to the boundary. He had a reputation for unortho-
doxy but it was more an inventiveness based on a sound and
completely natural technique.

Of his 18 hundreds that summer, only two were extended to
200, the 246 at The Oval and 208 in the Lord's Test. He was not
one who, on reaching 100, took a fresh guard. Partly this was
because the need of his side by then was for runs made quickly;
partly because he was blessed with a temperament which created
the feeling that having done his duty to the side by making a hundred, he was now entitled to take the risks which he had denied
himself previously. Heaven knows how many more runs he might
have made if he had been of a more cautious and less adventurous disposition.

The year 1947 is rightly remembered as the one in which Bill
Edrich and Denis Compton broke records and probably reached
the pinnacle of their respective careers. Certainly things were
never quite the same again. Middlesex in the 1950s were not the
same force, though with Edrich and Compton given the responsibility of being joint-captains, their cricket was never dull. It was
said that the captain for the match was the one who turned up
first, usually Edrich. In time, as Compton's playing days were
interrupted by operations on the knee, Edrich took over and
proved to have a flair for manufacturing finishes.

If a side was not strong enough to mount a serious challenge
for the Championship – and not many were in that Surrey-domi-
nated era – it could still keep itself in the upper half of the
Championship table by winning half of its close finishes – and
provide entertainment in the process.

Edrich and Compton played on until the late 1950s. Inevitably
the weight of runs and the consistency of 1947 were no longer
there but there were numerous occasions when the old brilliance
surfaced again. Edrich was held in high regard by Len Hutton as
a batsman of boundless courage and determination and though
he did not go to Australia in 1950–1, he went in Hutton's side in
1954–5 and was the captain's opening partner. Later in his career
it was said, not entirely frivolously, that what he needed to bring
out his best was a bang on the head or a really difficult pitch. He
played two memorable innings against Northamptonshire in
1954. Hit in the face by Frank Tyson at Lord's, he spent the night
in hospital but as soon as a wicket fell next morning he emerged
from the pavilion looking as if relishing the chance to engage
again the redoubtable bowler on a rather fiery pitch. A week later

at Northampton, Tyson again bowled very fast. Edrich made 102.

The magic of 1947 did last for one match at Lord's early in the next season. A year before, Somerset had beaten the future champions there by one wicket. Now vengeance was nigh. Compton came in to join Edrich at 54 for two and they played circumspectly to lunch and into the afternoon. At tea both had reached 100.

In the next 70 minutes they made 209 runs of which Compton's share was 139. A number of Middlesex matches are played towards the extremities of the Lord's square. This one was near the top side. It was a siting of which Compton was wont to take full advantage by hitting everything possible to the shorter boundary. This had other virtues besides saving him and his partner a lot of running. The ball would bounce back off the railings and the fielding side had no option but to pick it up and bowl again. A Somerset survivor of the massacre spoke later of the art of doing this while avoiding the captain's eye as he looked round for his next bowler. Anyhow, 120 overs had been bowled when George Mann, the new captain, declared at half past five. The partnership was then worth 424 in four hours and was closing fast on the 445 which was the highest recorded for the third wicket. Edrich had made 168 and Compton 252 which included relatively few sixes (three) – and 37 fours.

In 1949 one of Denis Compton's finest innings, 97 not out, enabled Middlesex in their last match of the season to beat Derbyshire at Lord's and earn a share in the Championship with Yorkshire. The pitch was a fastish one of uneven bounce and with Cliff Gladwin, Bill Copson and Les Jackson, all Test bowlers, Derbyshire were well equipped to use it.

Earlier in the week Alec Bedser had caught Middlesex on a drying pitch and they had lost a match which they had for two days appeared to be winning. Against Derbyshire things continued to go wrong for them. George Mann had put Derbyshire in on a soft pitch which played better on the first day than it did later. Derbyshire led by 89 runs on first innings and though a Cambridge freshman, J.J. Warr, many years later to become President of M.C.C., took five for 35 in Derbyshire's second innings, Middlesex needed 193 to win. Against this bowling on a lifting pitch, it seemed far too many, especially when the score soon stood at 36 for five.

However, to this critical situation Denis Compton brought his many talents. For three hours 40 minutes he fought it out with the Derbyshire bowlers, supported first by Walter Robins, seldom found wanting when courage and improvisation were needed, then with Leslie Compton, his brother, and then for a few overs with Jim Sims. The runs were made and Middlesex had a share of the Championship which they were not to see again for 27 years.

In the 1950s Edrich and Compton were not often in partnership together for England, though they were at the wicket at The Oval in August 1953 at the moment when the Ashes were recovered after an interval of 19 years. Except under Len Hutton's three-year captaincy, Edrich was seldom picked for Test matches. Reg Simpson, a well-organised Nottinghamshire batsman highly effective off the back foot, had come on the scene, as had the youthful Peter May from 1951 and later Colin Cowdrey. Compton missed much of the 1950 and 1956 seasons but when he was fit enough, much of the old sparkle was still there. The highest score of his career was made in 1954 at Trent Bridge and in a strange context. Though Pakistan drew the series by winning at The Oval, nothing went right for them at Nottingham.

Having bowled out Pakistan for 157, England, captained by David Sheppard in the absence of Len Hutton, were well on the way to a big lead on the second day when Simpson was out for an elegant 101. Compton was approaching 50 but so brilliantly did Tom Graveney play while making 83 in 85 minutes that nothing excessive was required from Compton at that stage. He had reached 100 when Graveney was out and Trevor Bailey came in at 339 for four.

By this time the Pakistan bowling was in a sorry state. Their best bowler, Fazal Mahmood, was still bowling, though with a pulled muscle and off a short run. Their fast bowler Khan Mohammad kept going but became slower and slower. Their leg-spinner, Khalid Hassan, was playing in his first, and only, Test match at the age of 16.

Joined by Bailey, who was not likely to do anything violent himself but would be adept at giving his partner the strike, Compton was in an ideal position. The pitch was still playing well, the opposition's bowling was in disarray and England were so well placed that it was unlikely to matter much if he failed to add many more to his 100. The snag was that it looked almost too easy. The likelihood was that after a few minutes of spectacular strokes he would get out when playing one which took too great a liberty.

So he began to fire off strokes, doing just as he liked with the bowling. He did not get out after a few minutes. In fact, he was twice dropped before he reached 200. His stand with Bailey lasted an hour and three-quarters in which Compton made 165 out of 192 before missing a leg-break. He had batted only four hours 50 minutes for his 278. When Hanif Mohammad made his 337 against West Indies, he took 16 hours 10 minutes. Gary Sobers's 365 in the same series occupied over 10 hours.

Still to come from Compton were two superb innings of 158 and 71 in the Third Test against South Africa at Old Trafford in 1955. Earlier in that season, against Sussex in the Bank Holiday match at Lord's, he played an innings which might have come from his most prolific days. When Middlesex were bowled out for 206, Compton had made 150 of the total and the second highest score was 13.

After another operation, this time for the removal of his kneecap, he did not play until the end of June in 1956. He then played so well that he was picked for the last Test against Australia at The Oval. England had won the two previous Tests by an innings but began the final Test with a lead of only 2–1 which did not seem much when they were 66 for three just after lunch on the first day. Peter May had carried the England batting through much of the series and he was looking set to do so again when Compton came in and after a careful start played almost as well as ever in their stand of 156 to which he subscribed 94. He also shared a stand with his young captain in the second innings of a match spoilt by rain.

His form was such that he went on that winter's tour of South Africa. His last tour was followed by his last home season in 1957. He had always had a happy touch in marking special occasions with some of his best batting and it was no surprise when in the last match of the season, against Worcestershire at Lord's, he made 143 and 48 and again played as well as ever.

In an age when there was an increasing number of amateurs who played like professionals, Denis Compton was a professional who played like an amateur. Cricket was not a job to him. It was a game which he loved greatly and which he played without ever seeming to consider what material rewards he obtained from it.

He became a successful executive in the advertising world in which he was still engaged when in 1988 he, and many others, celebrated his 70th birthday. He had been told that his knee was unlikely to allow him to play games after he was 55 but he exceeded this by more than 10 years as an active and much revered member of Denham Golf Club. He remarried and became the father of two charming little girls.

Bill Edrich gave up the Middlesex captaincy after the season of Compton's retirement. He played in half the matches in 1958 under John Warr and then returned to his native Norfolk whom he captained throughout the 1960s. In his second year Norfolk finished top of the Minor Counties Championship, though they lost in the challenge match to Lancashire Second XI. Edrich averaged 53 with the bat and as an off-spinner took 43 wickets at 16 apiece. He played his last matches for Norfolk in 1971 aged 55, having played his first for them in 1932 aged 16.

In his later years, while working in the City as a financial adviser, he was a valued member of the Middlesex cricket committee and his death after a fall in his home came as a severe shock to the many cricketers with whom he was still in touch.

4

The Calm before a Hurricane of Spin

IT did not take long after the War for what is now a perennial problem to be exercising cricket administrators. Too much cricket was being played at international level.

As early as the winter of 1947–8 Alec Bedser and others were being rested from an M.C.C. team to the West Indies after 17 months of almost continuous cricket. The surfeit mainly concerned England as the only Test-playing country with a cricket season in the Northern summer. When the other countries played against each other it was in or close to what would anyhow be their season. Thus they had a winter's rest, except when they were going to England.

Australia's strength at that time was such that while in 1949–50 they were winning a five-match Test series in South Africa 4–0 under Lindsay Hassett, they sent a team under Bill Brown on a short non-Test-playing tour of New Zealand. Neither team lost a match. Nor was that the only Australian involvement. England had been invited to tour India that winter but had refused. Their place was taken by a Commonwealth team captained by an Australian, Jock Livingston, later to play for Northamptonshire for many years, and including eight other Australians.

In the first flush of enthusiasm after the War a programme of international tours had been drawn up aimed at making up for the lost years. England would receive touring teams in every summer up to and including 1952. M.C.C. teams would be sent abroad every winter until 1950–1 inclusive.

By 1948, however, there had been a sharp change of thinking, especially in England, for several reasons. The strain on the leading English professionals had become evident. National Service was to continue indefinitely. There was an economic crisis which had led to something called the Control of Engagement Order making the recruitment of young players difficult. It was a period of full employment with high wages which undoubtedly put off some young players who might have made a career in cricket.

By the autumn of 1948 two other considerations weighed heavily on M.C.C. The high injury rate of their players in West Indies could be partly attributed to the strain put on some of them who had lost the suppleness of youth and during the years of rationing had not had an ideal diet. A look at the ages of the two teams picked for the Test Trial played at Edgbaston in June 1948 also produced a worrying statistic for M.C.C. – not one player was under 27.

At their meeting that autumn the Advisory Committee – the forerunner of the Test and County Cricket Board – agreed to an M.C.C. proposal to set up a committee to explore ways and means by which better facilities could be given to the youth of the country in obtaining cricket experience. A start was already being made with the formation of the English Schools Cricket Association (ESCA). The M.C.C. Youth Cricket Association was set up under the chairmanship of H.S. Altham.

Meanwhile, M.C.C. set about pruning international tours as they affected England. Ten years before, a commission recommending a reduction in such tours had found that the counties still wanted an overseas team in England each summer. Mindful of this no doubt, M.C.C. accepted the policy of having a Test series in England each summer but recommended that if a blank year did occur it should be in the season after the visit of an Australian team. In fact, the last peace-time season without a touring team was that of 1927.

Tours overseas by M.C.C. teams presented a much more urgent problem. It was agreed that priority should be given to England's oldest opponents, Australia and South Africa. The visit to India in 1949–50 was therefore postponed for two years and England players had that winter off.

In the previous winter M.C.C. had had a happy tour of South Africa and what was then Rhodesia. Captained by George Mann, they won the series 2–0. South Africa, like England, were still relying largely on pre-war players. So were New Zealand, whose troops had fought with such distinction in the Middle East and Italy, but that did not stop them from emerging with much credit from a Test series in England in 1949.

This series comprised four three-day matches and that was
nothing like enough for two sides which batted better than they
bowled. Though the result was four draws, the way that New
Zealand batted and fielded made them a popular and attractive
side. They were well led by Walter Hadlee and had a manager,
Jack Phillipps, who earned such a reputation that he not only
managed the next New Zealand side in England nine years later
but also the M.C.C. team under Dennis Silk which went on a
non-Test-playing tour of New Zealand in 1960–1. By then New
Zealand–England cricket links had become stronger than ever
with the appointment as Governor-General of Lord Cobham
who, as the Hon. Charles Lyttelton, had captained Worcestershire
before the War. His Excellency, then 51, captained the Governor-
General's XI in a three-day match against M.C.C. at Eden Park,
Auckland and, ever a robust striker of the ball, made 44 in 20
minutes to the immense satisfaction of 23,000 spectators.

In England in 1949, batsmen such as Martin Donnelly, Hadlee
himself, Mervyn Wallace, the youthful John Reid and a left-hander
of the highest class, Bert Sutcliffe, were not to be disposed of easily on the good pitches of a dry summer. Rumours that New
Zealand had one of the best opening batsmen in the world had
preceded Walter Hammond's M.C.C. team's arrival in 1946–7
and Sutcliffe had hammered the point home. In Dunedin, for
Otago against M.C.C. he made 197 and 128 with a wide range of
attractive strokes and in his first Test match a week later he had
made 58. He was then aged 23.

Two years later he had a successful first tour of England, but
was eclipsed in the first month by Wallace who, like Hadlee,
Donnelly and the fast bowler Jack Cowie, was a survivor of the
previous New Zealand tour of England 12 years before. Wallace
had an unusual tour this time. Having started with 82 and 126
against Yorkshire at Bradford, he followed up with hundreds at
Worcester, Leicester and Cambridge, so that, with 11 days of the
month left, it was conceivable that he might join the distinguished
band who had made 1000 runs before the end of May. He needed
273 runs in three matches. At this point, alas, the runs dried up.
It was July before he reached 1000 runs and August before he
was in full working order again. Then he made two fifties in The
Oval Test.

Though it was soon clear that a series of four draws was a
near-certainty, the quality of the batting on both sides made up
for a lot. At Headingley in the First Test Hutton and Compton

and in the second innings Cyril Washbrook all made hundreds. At Lord's, the injured Washbrook was replaced by Jack Robertson who in the second innings of what was to be his second and last Test in England made 121. He was a batsman of undoubted quality who was unlucky in being the contemporary of several other high-class opening batsmen. Denis Compton found that he could take few liberties with the slow left-arm accuracy of Tom Burtt, but made 116. He and an unusually fluent Trevor Bailey made more than two-thirds of the 313 for nine at which George Mann declared.

This was an unusual declaration because it was strictly illegal. In English first-class cricket players sometimes find themselves operating under different playing conditions or under modifications of the Laws of Cricket according to whether they are engaged in a County Championship match or a Test match. Mann had declared around six o'clock in order to give his bowlers a few overs at batsmen tired after a day in the field. This would be standard practice normally but at that time was not allowed on the first day, by Law 15.

Luckily New Zealand did not lose a wicket on the Saturday evening, a point touched on by George Mann when he took the unusual course of issuing a statement next day:

"When I declared the England innings closed on Saturday evening I thought that the experimental rule which allows a declaration to be made on the first day of a three-day match applied to the present Test series. I regret very much that I was wrong in this respect, but I am very glad indeed that we did not in fact gain any advantage from the declaration."

The New Zealanders, of course, took this in their stride. The time had not yet come when it is almost impossible to make a genuine error without someone attributing a sinister reason for it. The most remarkable thing about the incident was that the umpires – one of them the doyen Frank Chester – allowed the declaration when it was made.

After this, Martin Donnelly played his superb innings of 206 to give New Zealand a big lead but a draw was always the likeliest result. Faced with the probability of a series of four draws, M.C.C. now asked the New Zealanders if they would agree to adding a fourth day to the remaining two Tests at Old Trafford and The Oval. The New Zealand team were prepared to do this but after consultation with their Board at home, they decided that it would be wrong not to fulfil the original programme. Adding a day to the Old Trafford Test would have meant cancelling a three-day match against Yorkshire at Sheffield. The fact that more than 47,000 watched this match was testimony to the disappointment which might have been caused by a cancellation.

On their tour of 35 matches Walter Hadlee's team lost just one match – towards the end of May. It was an historic defeat, for their conquerors were Oxford University, but it did not come as a complete surprise. In the previous week Oxford had beaten Yorkshire for the first time since 1896.

On a pitch drying out after flooding, Oxford probably had the best of the conditions on the first day when their South African opening batsman Murray Hofmeyr carried his bat through the innings for 95. Thereafter the ball lifted awkwardly and the University's fast-medium bowlers Philip Whitcombe and Michael Wrigley bowled a length which gave the New Zealanders little chance. The bowlers were supported by brilliant fielding and catching which also was not surprising, for Oxford's first four batsmen, Hofmeyr, Brian Boobbyer, Christopher Winn and Clive van Ryneveld, were already, or shortly to become, rugby internationals.

Whitcombe and Wrigley took 16 wickets in the match and their captain, van Ryneveld, scarcely needed his main wicket-takers of that season. George Chesterton, who as a Malvern schoolmaster was to spend many hours in the summer holidays bowling for Worcestershire in the 1950s, was required to bowl only 12 overs; Abdul Hafeez Kardar, the future captain of Pakistan, bowled his left-arm spin for only 11 overs.

Halfway through the Test series of that summer the England selectors made a change of captain, not because of any failing on the part of the recent incumbent but with an eye to the future. Since the War five different captains had led England on the field in a Test match. The first, Walter Hammond, had retired after the 1946–7 tour of Australia. Norman Yardley, who had been vice-captain there, took over for 1947 but was not available for the tour of West Indies in the following winter. G.O. Allen took the side to the Caribbean. When he was injured and unable to play in the Barbados Test, Ken Cranston led the side. Cranston, a dentist, was 30 and had only come into first-class cricket in 1947 on being appointed captain of Lancashire. It is a tribute to his all-round ability – he was a fast-medium bowler and a middle-order batsman with plenty of strokes – that by the time he had to resign the captaincy of Lancashire after the 1948 season in order to

apply himself to teeth rather than Tests, he had played eight times
for England.

Norman Yardley was back for the 1948 series against Australia
but was again unavailable for the winter's tour of South Africa.
However, George Mann, another pre-war Cambridge Blue, had
played a full season for Middlesex in 1947 and had taken over
the captaincy of that county in 1948. He was a batsman reliable
in an emergency and a handsome driver of the ball. His selection
to captain the side in South Africa was particularly apt. His
father, F.T. Mann, had led the M.C.C. team of 1922–3 in South
Africa.

The series in South Africa was won 2–0 and the tour was a
happy one, Mann himself playing an innings of 136 not out in the
last Test. He captained England in the first two Tests of 1949
against New Zealand but his captaincy of Middlesex was only
going to be a brief one before he had to attend to affairs in the
family brewing business.

By now, however, a very considerable candidate had come on
the scene in F.R. Brown, who had just embarked on a second
career in first-class cricket. As a young amateur playing for
Cambridge and Surrey he had gone on the "Bodyline" tour of
1932–3 and had played in two Tests in New Zealand. Massively
built, he had played in four other Test matches in the 1930s as a
leg-spinner and powerful middle-order batsman. His last Test had
been at Old Trafford in 1937. He had played only twice for
Surrey that season but he took four wickets in the Test match and
was top scorer in the second innings when he hauled England out
of an awkward position with his 57.

Freddie Brown was captured at Tobruk and spent several years
as a prisoner of war. He did not return to first-class cricket in
1946 but in the odd match in 1948 showed that he was by no
reckoning a light of other days. Called on to open the innings at
Scarborough against the M.C.C. team about to tour South Africa,
he made 123. He took five wickets in the match, bowling Len
Hutton for one of them.

That winter he was offered a job which allowed him to captain
Northamptonshire who had resumed their pre-war position at the
bottom of the County Championship table. Under Freddie Brown
they staged an immediate revival, winning 10 matches and moving up from seventeenth place to sixth. In all matches in 1949 he
did the double, making 1077 runs and taking 111 wickets. For
the Gentlemen at Lord's during July he took eight wickets and in

the following week he led England out of the pavilion at Old Trafford against New Zealand.

He was 38. By chance this was the first Test match played by Brian Close who also performed the double that year but at the age of 18. In England, where cricketers mature later than else-where, Close had the same unusually well developed physique which Brown had had in his youth – and which the teenage Ian Botham was to have in the 1970s.

Brown led England with gusto in the last two Tests but even with eight bowlers in his side at The Oval and with Len Hutton's 206 and Bill Edrich's 100 there was no beating this New Zealand side in three days on good pitches.

The selectors who needed a captain for the 1950–1 tour of Australia and New Zealand did not commit themselves at this stage. Presumably they wanted confirmation that Brown's 1949 season was not just a flash in an ageing pan. There were certainly few of his contemporaries of 1932–3 still playing, though one of them, Leslie Ames, made five hundreds in 1950, including his 100th.

At this stage Brown was still bowling swiftish leg-breaks and googlies but he broadened his repertoire to include medium-paced cutters. He could bowl long spells of these. There was no sugges-tion that he would fail in Australia on the point of fitness but he was not quite in the form of 1949 and the selectors turned back to Norman Yardley at the start of the 1950 series against West Indies. Few of the leading amateurs could make themselves avail-able for the long tour of 1950–1 and Brown was obviously the main contender. But no decision had been made when he came in to bat at Lord's in July for the Gentlemen, who were having a dif-ficult time against the Players' bowlers, the best in the country except for Trevor Bailey who was in the Gentlemen's side.

In the next 110 minutes he solved the whole matter with an astonishing exhibition, making 122 out of 131. On the second day he took three good wickets and at the end of play was invited to captain M.C.C. in Australia and New Zealand.

First he had to preside over the fourth and last of the five-day Tests played with the West Indies in 1950. This was a strange series for its extremes of failure and success. In May, as John Dewes and the freshman David Sheppard made 343 for the first wicket on a flawless pitch at Cambridge against the tourists and Cambridge rattled up 594 for four before declaring, it was hard to foresee the England batsmen suffering much hardship in the

Test matches. West Indies had replied at Fenner's with 720 for three, Everton Weekes 304 not out, Frank Worrell 180 but this was no more than was expected of the prolific West Indian batsmen.

Also in May, at Bradford, England staged a Test Trial which was a classic in its unhelpfulness. On a drying pitch The Rest were bowled out for 27. Jim Laker took eight wickets for two, one of the runs, it is said, being allowed his Surrey colleague, Eric Bedser, to get him off the mark. In the second innings, Eric Hollies, who two years before had bowled Bradman in the Don's final Test, took six for 28. In between, Len Hutton batted brilliantly to make 85 out of England's total of 229.

The performances of Laker, Hollies and Hutton merely confirmed what was already known. The young batsmen, who by now included another Cambridge freshman Peter May, were submerged in the trial and the selectors can scarcely have been any wiser about how to fill the place left vacant by Denis Compton. After his knee operation Compton needed a long rehabilitation and was likely to miss most of the season.

The First Test was at Old Trafford where some strange pitches were being produced that summer, partly through limited watering. When Sussex played Lancashire there in July, they were beaten in a day by an innings, the off-spinner Peter Greenwood taking nine for 67 and the left-arm spinner Malcolm Hilton 11 for 50. They bowled all but three of the 56.1 overs needed to dismiss Sussex twice.

The pitch on which the First Test was played a month earlier was not dissimilar. In view of the dominance of Ramadhin and Valentine for the rest of the series and the fact that Valentine, the left-arm spinner, had taken eight for 26 against Lancashire on an adjacent pitch earlier in the week, it takes some working out how England won by 202 runs.

The answer is that England had some advantage from batting first and their bowlers knew better how to bowl on the pitch than the young West Indian pair. The England batsmen, with greater knowledge of such pitches, also improvised the better. The vital partnership was that on the first day between the dogged Trevor Bailey, who made 82 not out, and Godfrey Evans, who made 104 out of their sixth-wicket stand of 161. Evans was in his element when something unconventional was required and Bill Edrich, the top scorer in the second innings, had a history of playing imperturbably on pitches which others found impossible. Valentine did take 11 wickets in the match but was struck for 204 runs in the process.

One last incongruity of this Test was that England's most successful bowler in the match – with nine for 116 – was Bob Berry for whom there was not always a place in the Lancashire side on the rough pitches. Hilton, who was quicker through the air, was preferred to him and in the one-day rout of Sussex in July Berry bowled only the three overs which Greenwood and Hilton did not bowl. The England selectors, however, had to think about the type of slow left-arm bowler most likely to be effective on good pitches. Berry, with his flight, was much more the type for whom they were looking and he did, in fact, go on the tour of Australia and New Zealand that winter.

For the rest of the series West Indies, and especially Sonny Ramadhin and Alf Valentine, were in complete control. The West Indies' fast bowlers caused little trouble but this previously untried pair, aged 21 and 20 respectively, took 258 first-class wickets on the tour and seemed to tighten their grip on the batsmen with each encounter.

John Goddard, their captain, knew little about them at the start of the tour. He was not the worst off-spinner himself but as the tour progressed, he was able to put the young bowlers on, stand back and marvel at the effect on even the best batsmen of two youths whose previous first-class cricket amounted to just two trial matches in Port of Spain.

Alf Valentine, from Jamaica, was an orthodox left-arm spinner who spun the ball a lot. Sonny Ramadhin, a Trinidadian, was far from orthodox. Only five feet four inches and with a slight boyish figure, he bowled with his cap on and sleeves rolled down. He was mainly an off-spinner with a quick arm who pushed the ball through without a lot of flight. But he had variations to that and also, with a trick of the fingers not apparent to the batsman, would produce a leg-break which often turned quite sharply. There was a theory that the leg-break was the one which was given slightly more air, though not too much reliance could be put on that. One heard of many batsmen who decided to play him as an off-spinner, relying on the leg-break turning enough to miss everything. But his command of length was such that mesmerised batsmen found ways to get out to whatever he bowled.

Both the young bowlers undoubtedly improved as they gathered experience and as the batsmen lost confidence. In the Second Test at Lord's Ramadhin bowled 115 overs for 11 wickets conceding only 152 runs. Valentine bowled 116 overs for seven wickets and 127 runs. They bowled 145 maidens, though they could have afforded to have given the runs away.

The bowlers, of course, never had to worry about how many runs their side had in the bank. Alan Rae, a consistent left-handed opening batsman who had played a lot of club cricket in London while reading law, made hundreds at Trent Bridge and The Oval. After Clyde Walcott's 168 not out in the second innings at Lord's, the other two members of the "Three Ws" put on 283 for the fourth wicket at Trent Bridge, Frank Worrell making 261 and Everton Weekes 129. Worrell followed this with 138 at The Oval without reaching the pinnacles of batsmanship attained at Trent Bridge. Part of the attraction of the "Three Ws" was that they were so dissimilar. The crowds would see the slim and elegant Frank Worrell playing cultured strokes to all parts. Everton Weekes, shorter, sturdier and more obviously aggressive, would be remembered for the quick-footedness with which he moved into position. Clyde Walcott, taller than the others and powerfully built, would doubtless leave memories of his driving, especially if it was one of the days when he went on the back foot and hit a perfectly respectable ball straight for six. It could be a joy for the spectator but probably not a lot of fun for the bowler.

West Indies won the last three Tests by huge margins. Cyril Washbrook made a hundred in the second innings at both Lord's and Trent Bridge. He was not fit to play at The Oval where Len Hutton carried his bat through the innings for 202 out of a total of only 344. At Trent Bridge, Reg Simpson and Washbrook led an honourable fight-back with a stand of 212 in the second innings. But the match ended with the other opening pair, Rae and Stollmeyer, making the 102 runs needed for a 10-wicket victory with the utmost ease.

Jeff Stollmeyer, like his partner to become the leading administrator in West Indies cricket in later years, had been in the last West Indies team to tour England in 1939 when he played in all three Tests at the age of 18. He and the all-rounder Gerry Gomez were the only two in the 1950 side whose first tour of England had been curtailed by the outbreak of war.

This time the West Indies went home, not unnoticed, as in 1939, in the confusion of impending war but to the acclaim of the sporting public. West Indies cricket teams had long been a force in the Caribbean against M.C.C. teams not representative of England's full strength but now they had followed up a win in

India 18 months before with a victory in England against the strongest side which England could muster.

It was true that Denis Compton had not played against them until the last Test when he made 44 and seemed to be unravelling the problems set by Ramadhin and Valentine to his satisfaction when he was run out. But the margin of victory had been so great that West Indies had clearly established themselves as major rivals to Australia and England. In another 18 months they were due to tour Australia, an event keenly awaited even in neutral corners.

As for their next visit to England which, with the need to fit Pakistan into the fixture list, would not be until 1957, it was already evident from the scenes which greeted the West Indian wins at Lord's and The Oval and from the rate at which their compatriots were leaving their lovely islands in order to brave the harsher climate of Britain, that they were never going to be short of support and encouragement there.

While John Goddard and his side went back to various parts of the Caribbean, the M.C.C. team under Freddie Brown sailed for Australia. As after the First World War, the revival of English cricket in relation to the prevailing strength of Australia was slow and this M.C.C. side had proved a hard one to pick. Not for the last time, performances in English conditions against one type of opponents were no guide at all in choosing players who would do well against opponents of different strengths in Australia.

Winning Test matches is not everything but usually success at the top level can stimulate enthusiasm for the game at what it was becoming fashionable to call "the grass roots". This was important at a time when English cricket was bracing itself to withstand the end of the post-war boom and the end of full grounds for first-class cricket.

As the counter-attractions increased, people were not going to flock to often uncomfortable grounds. The administrators of the 17 first-class counties could scarcely look out of their pavilion windows without being reminded of what needed to be done to their grounds after a decade of war and shortages. Most county grounds, too, dated back to the turn of the century and beyond and would have been due for renovation even without a war.

The age of sponsorship had not yet dawned and cricket was badly in need of good publicity. A winning England team would help, not only by maintaining the number of county members and those who paid at the gate but by encouraging the young to play the game. It did not need a professor of sociology to predict that an expanding community would need new schools and that in urban areas there would not be the space to provide these schools with playing fields. Of all games, cricket would be the worst sufferer because it requires more space, takes up more time and needs more expert coaching than almost any other.

After five post-war seasons the problems, on and off the field, were many but, in the immediate future, signs that England could once again have Australia at full stretch would be a help.

5

The Second Career of F.R. Brown

FREDDIE BROWN, having already been named as captain in Australia and New Zealand that winter, had taken over from Norman Yardley for the last Test of 1950 against West Indies. The selection of his team for Australia was a difficult and prolonged exercise. Compton was pronounced fit for the tour but Washbrook, originally not available, only became a starter when allowed to follow later by air. Bill Edrich was not picked, which was predictable on his recent record against Ramadhin and Valentine but very surprising indeed after his resolute batting against fast bowling on the previous tour of Australia.

One of the main problems was finding bowlers to support Alec Bedser, Trevor Bailey and Doug Wright. The great irony was that four years later the larder of English bowlers was so richly stocked that Fred Trueman and Jim Laker, at the height of their powers, were not picked for the next tour of Australia. In 1950, however, the selectors agonised over their choice so painstakingly that a month elapsed between the announcements of the first names and the last. If this suggests that the selectors of 1950 were doddering old things unable to make up their minds, it should be added in haste that three of them, including that summer's chairman, Bob Wyatt, were still playing first-class cricket. Leslie Ames, the first professional to be appointed to the committee, made his 100th first-class hundred that August during the Canterbury Week.

Twelve names were announced at the end of July. A few days later, that of Brian Close could be added as he had required leave from National Service. In mid-August three more were added in David Sheppard (Sussex), Arthur McIntyre (Surrey) and Bob Berry (Lancashire). On 27 August J.J. Warr (Middlesex) became the 17th and for the moment last member of the side. In January, Brian Statham and Roy Tattersall, both of Lancashire, flew out as replacements.

The selectors could be said to have settled eventually on youth, an admirable decision in many ways, though the choice of seven players under 25 was considered by some to be rather overdoing it.

Three of the young men, Dewes, Sheppard and Warr, had been in that year's Cambridge side. Close had played only one championship match for Yorkshire that season because of his National Service but had had the extraordinary record for an 18-year-old in 1949 of 1098 runs and 113 wickets. Gilbert Parkhouse had had a successful season opening the innings for Glamorgan. The left-arm slow bowler Bob Berry had a method based on flight which was considered more likely to succeed on Australian pitches than those of the other Lancashire spinners, Tattersall and Malcolm Hilton, who had each taken roughly three times as many wickets as Berry had that season. Brian Statham was only 20 and had played barely half a season for Lancashire.

Of these, the unluckiest were John Dewes and John Warr in that they never really had another chance. By the end of the tour Dewes, aged 24, had played in five Test matches spread over three years but only against the very best – Australia and West Indies.

Warr, 22, was chosen partly on the strength of the unusual number of wickets which he had taken on the immaculate and, to a fast bowler, unhelpful pitches of Fenner's. In each of his first two years at Cambridge he had bowled well for Middlesex in the vacation. It was his misfortune that he was not as good a bowler then as he became later in his career when he was an outswinger who troubled the best batsmen and a shrewd analyst of a batsman's weak points. But by then, the England selectors had so many good bowlers from whom to choose that Warr, with his modest record on the 1950–1 tour for ever in the reference books, was never seriously considered again.

Freddie Brown's side proved a popular one and did at least crack the ice on the lake of Australian success by winning the last Test. They had the outstanding batsman of the Test series in Len Hutton who played superbly on all sorts of pitch to average 88. This was double that of any Australian batsman and 50 more than the next England batsman, Reg Simpson. Denis Compton, probably never entirely confident of his knee's soundness, made runs in the minor matches but had easily his least productive Test series.

Brown, with his image of rugged determination in the face of adversity, was the sort of Englishman of whom Australians approve. Much publicity was earned by a Sydney greengrocer who was reported as extolling his produce with the words: "Fine lettuces, fine lettuces – hearts like Freddie Brown's".

Whereas in the 20 years since he first played first-class cricket Brown had been known as a leg-spinner, here he realised that he was needed as a medium-pacer who could cut the ball. He bowled for long hours with remarkable control and not without reward. Alec Bedser took 30 wickets at 16 each in the Test series but the next most effective bowler was Brown with 18.

Of the five Tests, only the Third and Fourth were played on good batting pitches. These two coincided with an epidemic of injuries to the England bowlers and were John Warr's only Tests. At Sydney, in great heat, all but six overs in an Australian innings of 426 runs and 129 eight-ball overs were bowled by Bedser, Warr and Brown.

Things had started to go wrong for Brown in Brisbane during the First Test. Alec Bedser bowled magnificently and was mainly responsible for having Australia out for 228. But by the time that England batted, a tropical downpour had flooded the ground and left The Gabba square living up to its most sinister reputation. The ball kicked off a length when it was not scudding along the ground and Johnston and Miller soon reduced England to 68 for seven.

At this point Brown declared in the hope of bowling Australia out before the pitch dried out. In fact, Australia had made 32 for seven against Bailey and Bedser and the innings was only in its 14th over when Lindsay Hassett also declared. England thus needed 193 to win. Next day this might be a reachable target – if only they could survive the 70 minutes' play left that evening. If only. . . ! Lindwall's first ball of the innings bowled Simpson and that evening England finished at 30 for six.

Next day the going was certainly a little easier but though Len Hutton played the turning, lifting ball brilliantly to make 62 not out, England lost by 70 runs. In this match, Hutton batted lower down the order in an attempt to bolster the middle batting.

England's last four wickets fell to Jack Iverson whose unusual skill had received a lot of publicity. Tall and heavily built, he was 35 and a former fast bowler who while serving in the Army in

New Guinea had taught himself a grip which involved bending back the index finger and holding the ball between the ball of the thumb and the middle finger. There were said to be ways of detecting from his grip which way the ball would turn but while the England batsmen were trying to work it out he took 21 wickets in the series at 15 apiece. Then, after injuring an ankle, he disappeared from the Test scene as suddenly as he had arrived.

England's selection for this First Test had been difficult. Warr had bowled well in the previous match against Queensland and, as the pitch played, might have done well in the Test match. But the worries about the middle batting led to the inclusion of the second wicket-keeper, Arthur McIntyre, as a batsman. He had not made many runs on the tour but he was nimble in the field while Warr had recently been caught by almost every photographer in Australia while in the process of dropping a catch.

The Brisbane Test had suggested that Australia were not quite the force they had been while the now Sir Donald Bradman had been playing, especially as Arthur Morris, the scourge of English bowlers in the previous two series, was out of touch. He made 206 in the Fourth Test in Adelaide but mustered only 115 runs in his other eight Test innings. As the series advanced, it became clear that not only was Len Hutton the outstanding batsman on either side but that Alec Bedser was the outstanding bowler. As a wicket-keeper, Godfrey Evans was at least in the same lofty class at Don Tallon.

With a little luck and composure at critical stages England might also have won the Second Test in Melbourne where they led on first innings and lost by only 28 runs. Bedser, Bailey and Brown did a great job by bowling Australia out twice, but England's batting let them down. The hopes that Denis Compton might be coming into form had been kindled by his 115 in the previous match against an Australian XI but his knee became swollen during that match and he could not play in the Test.

On better pitches in Sydney and Adelaide England lost by large margins. By then they were weakened by injuries. It was in the final Test in Melbourne that an England revival became something more than wishful thinking. It was Australia's 26th Test since the War and the first they had lost.

Alec Bedser was at his best, while Freddie Brown's victims in his five for 49 included Morris, Hassett, Harvey and Miller. When England were 171 for one, with Hutton and Simpson engaged in a stand already worth 131, they seemed to have at last worked their way into a winning position. But the middle batting failed again and at 246 for nine their advantage had disappeared.

Yet Reg Simpson, who had come in at number three, was still there and had made 92 when he was joined by Roy Tattersall who, soon after his arrival by air with Statham, had played in his first Test in Adelaide. Tall and lean, he was 28, an off-spinner of near medium pace, no great spinner of the ball but accurate and well equipped with variations of flight and pace. Remarkably he had not been needed to bowl a single ball in Lancashire's one-day demolition of Sussex in the previous July, but he had taken 193 wickets that season. As a batsman, he was a left-hander of modest achievement, though far from the worst tail-end batsman.

Here it was that he had his finest hour with the bat. In that hour he made 10 against the might of Lindwall, Miller and Johnston with Iverson and the off-spinner Ian Johnson in support; while Simpson, emerging from his dour resistance of previous hours, made 64 with a scintillating range of strokes. When Tattersall eventually succumbed to Miller, Simpson (156 not out) had played one of the decisive Test innings of the post-war years. After Bedser, who had taken five wickets in the first innings, took another five in the second, England needed only 95 to win and were steered home to an eight-wicket win by Hutton.

Thus England could look back on the series with genuine satisfaction. For the first time since 1938 they had beaten Australia in a Test match and they were entitled to think that, with a little luck, they might have won the first two Tests of the series.

They added a win in the second of the two Tests in New Zealand. The captain suitably made the winning hit in Wellington five and a half months after the first match in Australia and could return home in the knowledge that his difficult job had been well done and the tour had had a happy ending. Australia, under Lindsay Hassett, had been competitive but friendly opponents. The two captains were old friends who had led sides against each other before in very different circumstances. They were the captains of British and Australian Army sides at Gezira in Egypt in 1942, a few weeks before Freddie Brown was taken prisoner at Tobruk.

Ahead of him in 1951 lay a home series against South Africa, after which a new captain would be needed. M.C.C. had a long tour of India – with an interlude in Pakistan – to undertake in the following winter but it was accepted that few of the leading players would be available for that. Of wider interest would be the progress of West Indies in Australia.

By the end of the English summer South Africa had been beaten again, though this was probably a better performance by England than was fully appreciated at the time. The South Africans came with a number of little known young players captained by Dudley Nourse. They still had the experience of Eric and Athol Rowan and somewhat improbably had brought a medium-paced bowler aged 40 who bowled in glasses and had yet to play in a Test match. In fact, Geoff Chubb was already an able cricket administrator – within five years he was President of the South African Cricket Association – and he was a great success as a player in England, bowling more overs on the tour than anyone else and taking more Test wickets, 21.

However, it was the younger players in the side who were to take South African cricket into more prosperous times. Cheetham, McGlew, McLean, Waite, Endean and van Ryneveld were to become familiar names in the Springbok sides of the 1950s. To these should be added that of Hugh Tayfield who was soon flown in as an understudy to Athol Rowan whose fitness was in some doubt. Tayfield did not have a great tour but within a few years was probably the best off-spinner in the world on hard pitches.

Having survived a particularly nasty English spring, which included sleet in Bradford where in a drawn match Yorkshire nearly bowled them out in each innings for under 100, the South Africans put an ugly dent in the recovery of English cricket by winning the First Test at Trent Bridge by 71 runs.

Their first innings was built on a sterling 208 by Nourse who was batting in much discomfort from his left thumb which had been broken three weeks earlier. England also made over 400 through hundreds by Simpson and Compton. Nourse could not bat in the second innings and by early on the fifth and last day Bedser (six for 37) and Tattersall had bowled South Africa, now led by Eric Rowan, out for 121.

This left England needing 186 to win but the ball was now turning a lot and they made only 114 against the spin of Athol Rowan and Tufty Mann.

If the Springboks had had the better of the conditions at Trent Bridge, they were out of luck at Lord's where a thunderstorm soaked the pitch after England had batted. Brown had won what proved to be a vital toss and England had batted with spirit to make 311. Their batting now included Willie Watson, a Yorkshireman who hitherto had been better known as a footballer and had been in England's side in the previous year's World Cup in South America. A graceful left-hander, he had made 57 in his first Test innings at Trent Bridge and now was joint top scorer with Denis Compton, each making 79.

On the second day, after the early morning thunderstorm, Tattersall took seven for 52 with the left-arm spinner John Wardle taking the other three. The follow-on in a five-day match was enforceable then with a lead of 150 – not the 200 of later years – and South Africa, 196 behind, had to bat again before the pitch had had time to recover. By early on the third afternoon the Second Test was over with England winning by 10 wickets.

They won again, by nine wickets, at Old Trafford where Cuan McCarthy, South Africa's tall young fast bowler, had his chance but bowled too short on a lifting pitch. Len Hutton batted with great skill and courage, with John Ikin in stout support, and England led 2–1. This was the position when, after a draw at Headingley, they came to the last Test at The Oval.

This, the last Test of Freddie Brown's captaincy, was an eventful contest with an appropriate ending when it was reaching its climax on the third afternoon. The pitch had rewarded both good batting and good bowling but only Eric Rowan and Denis Compton had passed 50. After Jim Laker had taken six wickets in the second innings, there was no certainty that England would find it easy to make the 163 needed against the spin of Athol Rowan and the medium-paced accuracy of Chubb. However, Len Hutton was at the peak of his form and with his young Yorkshire opening partner, Frank Lowson, he had taken the score to 53 when he was out in a rare way. A ball from Rowan turned and lifted to hit him on the glove and run up his arm. Thinking that it might be going to drop on or near the wicket, Hutton automatically made to knock it away. In so doing he inadvertently prevented the wicket-keeper Russell Endean from making a catch. It was a clear case of "obstructing the field" and he was given out by the umpire Dai Davies while his colleague, the redoubtable Frank Chester, nodded his approval from square-leg.

After this mishap England declined to 90 for four and were beginning to labour when Brown arrived, clearly bent on recovering the initiative. Before scoring, he was nearly caught by Jack Cheetham running in from deep square-leg but, having survived that, he struck Rowan far and wide and made 40 in quick time. Though he was out before the end, the last innings of his captaincy was ideal in its context and the perfect finale to his vigorous period in command. It won the match by four wickets and the series 3–1.

After the setback at Trent Bridge it had been a good series for England who had not only won it but had brought in some young players of undoubted ability. Brian Statham had bowled well in his first home Test matches. Tom Graveney had played the first of what were to be 79 Test matches. Willie Watson, though 31, had looked good enough, both technically and temperamentally, to establish himself in Test class now that he had finished his football career with Sunderland and England. Most significant of all, Peter May, a 21-year-old undergraduate, had played a first Test innings of 138 at Headingley which left little doubt about his quality.

It was 18 years since the last M.C.C. tour of India. Cricket on the sub-continent was known to be very different from that elsewhere but, until the 1960s, tours there were so widely separated that the lessons of one were not acted on in the next. Fast bowlers who were too lively for Indian batsmen in England were played with panache on slow mud pitches in India. Spin bowlers who were thought to be sure to prosper in India were sometimes made innocuous by the slow low bounce, though they still bowled the bulk of the overs.

The senior players in England were not available and the captaincy fell to the young Lancashire captain Nigel Howard, with Donald Carr, later to become Secretary of the Test and County Cricket Board, as his vice-captain. As a batsman, Howard needed the ball to be coming on to the bat more readily than it usually does in India and he was ill with pleurisy later in the tour but he kept the side going through the five-month tour. This included a three and a half week visit to Pakistan after the First Test and nearly three weeks in Ceylon at the end.

The Test series was halved 1–1. England won the Fourth Test in Kanpur where the ball turned and Tattersall and Hilton took 17 wickets between them on a pitch too slow for India's two leg-spinners. India won the last Test in Madras by an innings. Carr, England's acting captain, won the toss but England never recovered fully from the damage done to them on the first day by the left-arm spin of Vinoo Mankad who took eight for 55. Four months later, Mankad gave further evidence of his all-round ability with a momentous performance at Lord's.

During that first day news arrived of the death of King George VI and the rest day was brought forward to what should have been the second day. After that, India made over 400 and by the time England batted again, the pitch was wearing.

M.C.C.'s visit to Pakistan earlier in the tour had been of much significance in that country which was due to be granted Test status by the Imperial Cricket Conference, as it then was, in the following July. In two minor matches on matting against very strong sides, M.C.C. were led on first innings and in one of them forced to follow on. Nothing was left to doubt.

In the first of the two matches against the representative Pakistan side, this on grass, though not much of it, in Lahore, M.C.C. easily earned a draw but had been led by 174 runs on first innings. The second, on coir matting in Karachi, was won by Pakistan by four wickets. In their early days as a cricketing nation Pakistan had a great bowler in Fazal Mahmood. On matting, and indeed on many other types of pitch, he was a wizard, medium-fast in pace and very accurate with his leg-cutter and other variations. His contribution in the first innings was six for 40 in 26 overs. The M.C.C. party returned to India having been given food for thought.

Meanwhile West Indies were in Australia on a tour which must have been a big disappointment to them. A year and a half before, they had beaten England, not only with the spin of Ramadhin and Valentine but with batting of high quality. It was not expected that Ramadhin and Valentine would have the same success in Australia but a batting order starting Rae, Stollmeyer, Worrell, Weekes and Walcott was surely going to be worth a wealth of runs.

In the event, West Indies won the Third Test in Adelaide on Christmas Day. They won by six wickets after 22 wickets had fallen on the first day. Rain had seeped under the covers and Worrell, Goddard and Gomez bowled out Australia for 82. But Australia won the other four Tests.

West Indies lacked the fast bowlers needed on Australian pitches and their batsmen had no answer to Keith Miller, Bill Johnston and Ray Lindwall who, with more than usual recourse to the bouncer, each took more than 20 wickets in the series. In the 1980s, when West Indies could often have fielded several sets of menacing and effective fast bowlers, it was strange to think that in 1951-2 in Australia they lost through a lack of them.

By the 1980s, of course, there had long been a market for West Indian fast bowlers in England. Almost every English county had one – some had two – and were prepared to give them vital experience of English conditions. This helped them to develop into formidable opponents for England Test teams, a state of affairs often sternly criticised by the same counties who had contributed to it.

Since 1947 when Middlesex had won the County Championship with their batting, the honours had moved around. In 1948 there was a distinct touch of romance about the result. The champions, Glamorgan, were the county most recently admitted to the Championship, in 1921, and they had never before finished higher than their sixth place of 1946. Moreover, when they beat Hampshire at Bournemouth to clinch the Championship, their side included J.C. Clay, who had been in the original Glamorgan side of 1921.

John Clay was an amateur, a Wykehamist, and for most of his career a slow right-arm bowler. He had long been closely associated with Glamorgan's cricket as captain or secretary with another revered figure, Maurice Turnbull. Turnbull had been killed in action in Normandy as a major in the Welsh Guards.

In 1948 Clay was 50 and a Test selector, a commitment which limited his matches in the Championship to five. But when he came into the side in August at a crucial stage and played at Cardiff against Surrey, who were to finish second in the table, he took five wickets in each innings. In the following match at Bournemouth he took nine wickets, including six for 48 in the second innings, and he was the bowler who had the last Hampshire batsman lbw and set Wales rejoicing.

Clay had played in one Test match, against South Africa in 1935. Wilfred Wooller, the Glamorgan captain in 1948, never played in one, though he had to refuse an invitation to go on the M.C.C. tour of South Africa in 1948–9. He too became a Test selector. The giant long-striding Welsh centre three-quarter who had played a big part in the famous victory over the 1935–6 All Blacks, Wooller was a great figure in Welsh sport. A middle-order batsman and a medium-paced bowler, he was a brilliant close catcher and required standards which made Glamorgan the outstanding fielding side of the day. His players were still mostly Welsh, though two of their most successful bowlers – Len Muncer and Norman Hever – had been released by Middlesex. Muncer, aged 34, an off-spinner who had been at Lord's for many years, took 139 wickets at 16 apiece; the fast-medium Hever took 77 at 17 apiece.

In August 1948 Allan Watkins, a left-handed all-rounder,

became the first Glamorgan player chosen for England against Australia. He was unlucky to strike that melancholy match which began with England's being bowled out for 52, but he survived to play in all five Tests in South Africa that winter, making 111 in the Fourth in Johannesburg. Three years later, on the M.C.C. tour of India, he averaged 64, the highest on either side.

In 1949 Glamorgan resumed their position in the middle of the Championship table and the joint champions were Middlesex and Yorkshire. Middlesex at various times had five players absent through Test selection. Yorkshire lost Hutton, who was in tremendous form, and, for one Test, Brian Close.

Close was the powerfully built 18-year-old phenomenon whose all-round talents did not stop at becoming the youngest player ever to do the double of 1000 runs and 100 wickets in a season. He would also bowl in two styles, opening the bowling and swinging the ball at a lively medium pace and later in the innings reappearing as an off-spinner.

Yorkshire had to win their last six matches to draw level with Middlesex but they finished in tremendous form. The runs were seldom a problem. In a season of three-day Test matches, Len Hutton only had to miss one of the six matches. Willie Watson seldom failed and Ted Lester, for many years in later life the Yorkshire scorer, made 140 not out and 186 in successive matches at a good pace. Norman Yardley, the captain, was a good class batsman to find around number six.

The bowling had its most severe test at Bradford when Derbyshire, having been bowled out for 94 in the first innings, batted for 213 overs in the second and made 491. To this, John Eggar, a pre-war Oxford Blue who was now a master at Repton, contributed 219. They were eventually worn down by Close and the two other Yorkshire bowlers who took over 100 wickets that season. Alec Coxon was an enthusiastic fast-medium bowler who had played in one Test match in 1948, but he was 32 and by 1951 had withdrawn to League and Minor County cricket for Durham. John Wardle was 26 and a slow-left-arm bowler with an eventful future.

Scoring in the County Championship in those years was relatively simple – 12 points for a win and four points for a first-innings lead in a match lost or drawn. But it was still remarkable that the next year's Championship also ended in a tie, this time between Lancashire and Surrey. No provision was made to separate the sides in a tie or the winners might well have been Surrey who had won 17 of their 28 matches against Lancashire's 16.

The two sides met at The Oval at the end of August. It was Lancashire's last match and Surrey's last but one. The Oval pitches were not yet as rewarding for good bowling as they soon became and the match was a dour struggle for first-innings points. The four points would have made Lancashire champions outright. This sort of situation is not a recipe for an exhilarating cricket match but there were some worthy individual performances, not least from Jack Parker, one of Surrey's senior players and one of the best all-rounders never to play for England. A tall fast-medium bowler, he took five for 30 in 24 overs and made an invaluable 50 when Surrey's reply to Lancashire's 221 was only 39 for three.

However, the main innings for Surrey, against a strong Lancashire attack led by Statham and Tattersall, was played by Peter May, who batted five hours for 92. It was only his 10th Championship match for Surrey but he had made such an impact that he was given his county cap after this innings. He played against Leicestershire in Surrey's final match, which they won with ease to earn their half-share in the Championship. When he was next free to play for Surrey, in the following July, the match against Middlesex at Lord's, in which he made a hundred, coincided with his selection to play in his first Test match.

Surrey's share in the Championship was seen at the time as of historical interest because they had last become champions in the fateful month of August 1914. Their captain then had been C.T.A. Wilkinson, who later became one of the most famous and indefatigable of club cricketers. Every year he played throughout August on the delightful ground beside the sea at Sidmouth, where a high standard of club cricket was maintained against touring sides, and as late as 1953, when he was 69, he took all 10 wickets against the Nondescripts.

However, Surrey's success in 1950 was to prove rather more than just an addition to successes of the past. It was the shape of things to come, as from 1952 when Stuart Surridge began his great years of captaincy.

Lancashire's future was equally unpredictable, but in the opposite sense. Their previous wins had not been in the distant past. They had been champions five times between the two world wars. The Lancashire League was still seen as a source of good players and they seemed to have the bowlers who would soon be bringing the Championship back to Old Trafford. Yet nothing happened –

and when they finished second in 1987 it was the first time for 12 years that they had been out of the bottom six. That half-share of 1950 remained their only taste of success in the Championship in more than half a century.

Unlike Yorkshire, Lancashire have had many overseas cricketers. Indeed they were one of the first in the field when the formidable Australian fast bowler, Ted McDonald, was signed up in 1924. From the mid-1960s they have probably been the victims of their own success in limited-over cricket.

Before Surrey's golden era began, Warwickshire were the unexpected champions of 1951. It was 40 years since their only previous Championship under the legendary all-rounder F.R. Foster, but since the Second World War they had become a hard side to beat. Now that Eric Hollies, with his accuracy and rather flatter trajectory than most leg-spinners, was no longer required by England, he played in every match for Warwickshire and took 145 wickets at 17 apiece. Charles Grove, a burly medium-paced bowler, took 103 and gave little away in the process. Since 1947 Tom Pritchard, a New Zealander in his early 30s, had been as awkward and penetrative as any fast-medium bowler in the country but, oddly, he was not at his best in 1951. He still took 93 wickets but was out of the side through injury during much of August. In fact, by then Warwickshire were running away with the Championship and had been almost out of reach when on 31 July they won their 15th victory out of 21 matches played so far.

Professional captains were still a rarity but Warwickshire were admirably led by one. Tom Dollery was for years one of the soundest and most consistent batsmen in the country and would have played in many more than four Test matches if his career had not clashed with that of Compton, Edrich and Simpson. He made the most of the talent at his command, not least by producing a fine fielding side from what did not look to be a particularly athletic lot of players.

Warwickshire were the first county to win the Championship under a professional captain and with an all-professional side. One amateur, the reserve wicket-keeper Esmond Lewis, did play in the last match of the season. For the rest of the season Dick Spooner not only kept wicket efficiently but opened the innings and finished top of Warwickshire's batting averages.

The end of the 1951 season was to some extent the end of an era, though this was only partly evident at the time. Surrey were about to embark on their seven years as champions. England were about to appoint their first professional captain of modern times and a period of prosperity was about to dawn for England at Test level. In 1953, the eighth post-war season, the Ashes might be recovered, just as they had been in 1926, the eighth season after the First World War.

6

Ashes Regained

IN March 1952 the England selectors, Norman Yardley, Bob Wyatt, Freddie Brown and Leslie Ames, were re-elected. In May they had to choose a captain for the series of four five-day Test matches against India. There was not a lot of doubt that this would prove to be Len Hutton.

His lack of experience as an elected captain of Yorkshire was no argument against him. Nor the fact that he would be the first professional thus honoured in modern times. Times were changing and though an amateur who did not have to carry a major responsibility as a batsman or bowler would have had an advantage, obviously a senior professional would have to tackle the job if no suitable amateur was available.

Denis Compton had been the vice-captain to Brown in Australia but he was not a candidate, even if he had nursed ambitions in that direction. The condition of his knee, one of the nation's best-known battlefields, made his future uncertain and indeed after two Test matches in 1952 he was so out of form that he asked the selectors not to consider him for the rest of the series against India. Perhaps he was out of luck too. He played, not in the Third Test but for Middlesex against Surrey at Lord's and was out in a freakish way. His full-blooded downward hook hit the top of Eric Bedser's foot as its owner took evasive action as a deepish backward short-leg. It lobbed up to be caught by the wicket-keeper fully 10 yards away.

The only other possible candidate for the captaincy was David Sheppard who had begun his season as captain of Cambridge with three hundreds in the first four matches. But he also had a dubious future, if such an adjective can be applied to a future bishop.

Len Hutton's experience as a player and his shrewd cricket brain easily outweighed worries that the captaincy might put too heavy a burden on one whose batting was of major importance and whose health and general fitness might be impaired. His was not a robust physique.

There was something in this last reservation, for in 1952 it was hoped that Hutton, then 36, would have more than three years left in him. In the event that was all he had, though they had been three very successful years for England under his captaincy. It began with an overwhelming victory over India who, under Vijay Hazare, were beaten 3–0. This Indian tour is usually remembered for the all-round performance of Vinoo Mankad at Lord's and for the score of nought for four with which India began their second innings in the First Test at Headingley.

The team selected for India's first tour of England since 1946 was short of experience of English conditions. Several of their senior players left behind were still not in their dotage but there was no guarantee that they were at one with the Board. Lala Amarnath, with his record of differences with the Board – he had been sent home from the 1936 tour of England – was fit enough later in 1952 to be appointed captain for the first series against Pakistan, but he did not come to England. Mankad, who had had so much to do with India's first Test win in Madras a few weeks before, was also not in the touring party. He was due to play for Haslingden in the Lancashire League.

It was only after India had lost the First Test that the Indian management asked Haslingden for Mankad's release for the three remaining Tests. This was granted and he came to Lord's and gave his astonishing performance with bat and ball.

India's resounding defeat at Headingley had been no surprise to those members of the M.C.C. side which had toured the sub-continent during the previous winter. The pitches there were so lifeless that fast bowlers were innocuous. Thus India not only had few fast bowlers of their own but had few batsmen who could play fast bowling on the livelier pitches in England.

Fred Trueman had first played for Yorkshire in 1949. It was clear that when fully developed he should have the pace and control to make him a fast bowler of the highest quality. With his National Service completed he had played a full season for Yorkshire in 1951 and, now 21, was being let loose in a Test match for the first time.

The Indians had been beaten by Surrey in their second match

and had not often been blessed with fine weather and good pitches
since then. However, the Headingley pitch was a good one and
after a start of 42 for three some excellent batting by the captain
Hazare and the 20-year-old Vijay Manjrekar added 222 for the
fourth wicket. That evening their 272 for six looked a fair score –
and even better when there was heavy rain in the night.

When Laker came on next morning he took the last four wickets in nine balls, but 296 seemed a healthy total as England toiled
for the rest of the day, mostly against the tall off-spinner Ghulam
Ahmed. That England eventually earned a lead of 41 was due to
Tom Graveney and the middle batsmen of whom Godfrey Evans
made 66 in quick time. With his quick-footed inventiveness Evans
could make life very difficult for spin bowlers.

As England came out to field they can scarcely have been confident about their position, faced as they were with batting last on
an uncertain pitch. Their 334 had taken them nearly 10 hours
and 165 overs.

A few minutes later, after the first 14 balls of the innings, they
were entitled to think in terms of an early victory. Trueman had
disposed of Roy, Manjrekar and Mantri, Bedser had accounted
for Gaekwad. The scoreboard showed nought for four.

Hazare changed his batting order and salvaged something from
the wreck himself during his sixth-wicket stand of 105 with
Phadkar, but on the fourth day England needed only 125 to win.
They batted with the prudence which was to mark much of
England's cricket in the 1950s to win by seven wickets.

Between the first two Tests the Indians went to Ireland to play
two two-day matches. When they returned they had achieved the
release of Vinoo Mankad from Haslingden. The effect was immediate and astonishing. Mankad opened the innings at Lord's in
the Second Test with Pankaj Roy, a sturdily built batsman aged
24. Mankad, 35, was also strongly built and rather taller. Neither
had much resemblance to the slight, elegant Indian batsman of
popular image. Indeed the match was barely half an hour old
when the leg-spinner Roly Jenkins was brought on and Mankad
hit his fourth ball over the sightscreen for six. The opening pair
made 106 together before Mankad, soon after lunch, was well
caught at short-leg by Watkins off Trueman for 72. With
Mankad's departure the Indians once again showed their capacity
for spectacular collapses. Seven of them were out by tea and
despite Hazare's 69 not out they mustered only 235.

Over the next two days England built up a lead of 302. A

brilliant 150 by Len Hutton and his partnerships with Simpson and May took England into the lead with only one wicket down. There was still 73 to come from Graveney who batted comfortably on the third morning when Godfrey Evans only just failed to make a hundred before lunch.

The most unusual statistics concerned Mankad and his slow left-arm spin delivered with the arm slightly lower than is recommended by the coaching manual. When the England innings ended halfway through the third afternoon, he had bowled 73 overs, 24 of them maidens, and had taken five wickets for 196. He had already bowled 31 overs on that third day when he opened the second innings and batted even better than on the first day, showing no signs of fatigue. By that evening he was 86 not out.

India finished with 137 for two, having graced that great day, the Saturday of a Lord's Test, with much entertaining cricket. In 20 minutes under six hours, 382 runs had been scored for the loss of seven wickets.

England's bowling – Bedser, Trueman, Laker, Jenkins and Watkins – was far from negligible but on the Monday morning Mankad carried on in the same mood, making another 93 out of 127 before lunch. When he was eventually out for 184, out of 270, he had batted only four and a half hours.

There had been periods during the match when batting had been seen at its best – while Len Hutton was passing from 100 to 150, towards the end of Graveney's innings and in the effervescent later stages of Evans' 104 – but none of the others had kept up their attack on the bowling as long as Mankad had and none of the other batsmen also bowled 97 overs in the match!

The match unfortunately ended in anti-climax. India collapsed once again and from 270 for two were all out for 377, so that England needed 77 in the 80 minutes left for play on the fourth day. They made only 40 as Hutton, safe in the knowledge that there was not a drop of rain forecast within 1000 miles of Lord's, made no attempt to finish the match that evening. Another 45 minutes were needed next day before England won by eight wickets. The ultra caution seemed unnecessary at the time and was in marked contrast with the lack of it two years later when a little of it might have turned a defeat by Pakistan at The Oval into a victory.

But it was Mankad's match and even in that last innings he played a big part. After one over he rubbed the ball in the dust and bowled another 24 overs, half of them maidens.

India's performance in defeat at Lord's was the high spot of their tour. On a damp pitch at Old Trafford they were bowled out for 58 and 82, being in considerable disarray against the fast lifting ball. In the first innings Trueman took eight for 31. The last Test, at The Oval, was ruined by the weather; though after an opening stand of 143 between Len Hutton (86), and his new partner, David Sheppard (119), there was time for India to be bowled out for 98 by Bedser and Trueman.

These were the first two Tests of Tony Lock who, since acquiring a new action in the winter, had found new powers of spin and an often devastating faster ball. He was a marvellously athletic close catcher and the first time that he touched the ball in a Test match was when he took a magnificent catch from Mankad at Old Trafford. At The Oval at the end of July Lock was no-balled three times for throwing by umpire Fred Price from square-leg. A month before, Cuan McCarthy, the South African fast bowler who was doing a year at Cambridge, had been called at Worcester. These were the first rumblings of a storm which was to bedevil the game for the rest of the 1950s.

The Indians had scarcely had an encouraging tour in preparation for the first series against Pakistan a few weeks later. However, their selectors recalled Lala Amarnath, aged 41, and they won the first of five Tests by an innings in New Delhi, Mankad taking 13 wickets. Neither he nor Hazare was playing in Lucknow a week later when Pakistan won by an innings. On jute matting Fazal Mahmood took 12 for 94. Nazar Mohammad, the opening partner of the prolific Hanif Mohammad, batted through the Pakistan innings of over eight and a half hours for 124 not out. Nazar passed on his technical soundness and his patience to his son Mudassar Nazar who in 1976, in the early days of his successful career opening the innings for Pakistan, made the slowest recorded hundred against England in Lahore, taking nine hours 17 minutes over it.

In the 1952 series India bounced back in Bombay when the Pakistan captain Abdul Hafeez Kardar, with an unenviable choice to make after winning the toss, decided to bat on a pitch drying after heavy dew. The Fourth Test, like many matches staged in Madras in late November, was washed out, after two days of the scheduled four. The Fifth, in Calcutta, was also drawn.

Two years later, Mankad led an Indian team which played five drawn Test matches in Pakistan. In 1960–1, with Nari Contractor and Fazal Mahmood the two captains, they added another series of five draws in India. At this point they stopped playing each other, which seemed sensible, especially in those periods when their two countries were at war. They resumed 18 years later.

In the same season of 1952–3 there were unexpected events in Australia. Since South Africa's defeat in England in 1951, pessimism over their coming tour of Australia and New Zealand had been widespread. In South Africa there were some faint hearts who maintained that the Test series in Australia would be so one-sided that the tour should be cancelled or postponed. In Australia there was concern at the higher administrative levels on financial grounds. A year before, the Australian Board had lost money on the disappointing visit of the West Indians. It was not going to be easy to interest their public now in the visit of a South African side which was not thought to be in the same class as Australia.

To their great credit, the South African Board, on learning of the Australians' fears, said that they were prepared to lose £10,000 on the tour which they hoped would be educational for their young players. They rejected the theory that heavy defeats would cause long-term damage to their cricket and stood firm in their view that it would provide valuable experience for their cricket's future.

Their players did them proud. They not only played some entertaining cricket but, to the general amazement, halved the series 2–2, which was the best result achieved by any touring side in Australia for 20 years. They even took home a profit of £3000.

Much the same was to happen again 11 years later but then it was brought about by some brilliant individual efforts. Now, in 1952–3, the basis of the success of the side led by Jack Cheetham was its enthusiasm which manifested itself in fielding of the highest possible calibre. Crowds even came to see them field.

Only one Test hundred was scored by a South African – Endean's 162 not out in the Second Test in Melbourne. By contrast, six were made by Australians, four of these by Neil Harvey. The Springbok bowlers lacked the penetration of Lindwall and Miller but the main wicket-taker in the series was Hugh Tayfield, an off-spinner whose accuracy and variations were made the more effective by the excellence of the catching. He took 30 wickets at 28 apiece.

In the First Test in Brisbane, Neil Harvey's 109 gave Australia an advantage which they never lost in a match of four innings under 300. Over Christmas South Africa levelled the series with their first victory over Australia for 42 years. Endean made his 162 not out and Tayfield took 13 wickets, a surprise, certainly in England, where the chances of an off-spinner in Australia were not rated highly. In Sydney, South Africa fell foul of Harvey, who made 190, and of Lindwall and Miller who took 13 of the wickets. Australia won by an innings and led 2–1 as they embarked on what was to be an extraordinary final Test played over six days in Melbourne.

Australia began it by making 520 (Harvey 205). That should have been enough to make any side safe but South Africa replied with 435 against Australian bowling lacking Miller and Lindwall who were injured. In the second innings Australia batted moderately against the fast bowling of Eddie Fuller who took five wickets. Tayfield and the leg-spinner Percy Mansell took the rest and on the afternoon of the fifth day South Africa needed 295 to win the match and halve the series. They played carefully that evening, reaching 84 for the loss of John Waite.

On the sixth day, however, they sailed into the attack, showing no fear of winning. It was a lot to have to score in the last innings of a Test match but the Springboks made light of their task and won by six wickets in cavalier fashion, Roy McLean, that dashing stroke-player, making 76 of the last 106 in 80 minutes.

This tour by a young South African side did much for cricket in South Africa. It also encouraged a quiet elation in England where it was seen as further evidence of Australian vulnerability and of England's excellent chance of winning back the Ashes at last in the summer of 1953. However, a certain wariness was prompted by the tremendous form of Neil Harvey, who had made 843 runs in the series, averaging 92, and by the selection of 17-year-old Ian Craig. After making 213 not out for New South Wales against the South Africans, Craig had been picked for the final Test and had made 53 and 47. His selection for the tour was a disquieting reminder of the habitual resilience of Australian cricket.

It was Coronation Year and the 1953 Australians, still under the amiable Lindsay Hassett, had many of their compatriots accompanying them to Britain. Television's presentation of cricket was developing all the time and the Test series was awaited with more than usual excitement.

England's best players had had a winter's rest to rekindle their zest for the battle but the first rounds undoubtedly went to the Australians. When the weather allowed, they beat Leicestershire, Yorkshire, Surrey and the two Universities, all by an innings. One

worrying feature of this for the English observer was that
Lindwall and Miller played relatively little part in it. It was a
sobering thought that the tourists could win their minor matches
with the leg-spin of Doug Ring and the youthful Richie Benaud
plus the lively fast-medium of Ron Archer, aged 19. The pitches
of early May were no doubt a help, especially at The Oval where
Archer took 11 for 61, but the Australians could scarcely have
started better.

After the loss of the first day's play at Lord's they bowled a
strong M.C.C. side out for 80. One of their victims there was
Peter May who had been the subject of a characteristically competitive piece of cricket when playing for Surrey against the
Australians. Here was a young man with a great future who had
come on the Test scene since England's last series with Australia.
He must be given the utmost discouragement. Thus Lindwall
wound himself up and bowled May a superb over in which the
young man was sorely exercised to make any contact at all. When
he did, he was caught at the wicket. Archer bowled him in the
second innings for one run, which was one more than in the first,
and when he was picked for the First Test, he had been out four
times to the Australian bowlers for 28 runs.

The Australians were rewarded when after he had been out at
Trent Bridge to Jack Hill who bowled brisk top-spinners which
would sometimes turn, May was dropped, or perhaps set aside,
from the Second Test. He did not reappear until the final Test in
which he played a valuable part.

The First Test, in which Alec Bedser bowled superbly to take
seven wickets in each innings, was drawn in the most frustrating
way for both sides and for an excited public. By the evening of
the third day, a magnificent cricket match was beginning to tilt
towards England. In Australia's first innings Hassett, who made
115, Morris and Miller contributed all but 12 of the total of 249.
England succumbed, mostly to Lindwall, and Australia led on
first innings by 105 runs. But when Bedser had finished with
them in their second innings, England required only 229 to win.
In the context of the scoring so far, this would have been a severe
task but there was evidence that the pitch might have less to offer
the bowlers after the weekend. On the Saturday evening Len
Hutton and Reg Simpson played with fair comfort after Don
Kenyon had been out to a full toss.

Everything was in place for an enthralling finish but over the
weekend it rained. It rained again on the Monday and play did

not restart until 4.30 on Tuesday by when it was too late for either side to win.

The England selectors that year were F.R. Brown (Northants) (chairman), N.W.D. Yardley (Yorkshire), R.E.S. Wyatt (Worcestershire) and Leslie Ames (Kent). During the weekend they made a piece of history. They brought their chairman into the side for the Second Test at Lord's.

Freddie Brown was still captaining Northants and recently had made runs and taken wickets at Lord's. There was a well-founded theory that a leg-spinner was needed at Lord's. Tattersall, the off-spinner, was dropped along with May and Simpson. Into the side came Brown, Willie Watson and Brian Statham. The 42-year-old chairman was known to be reluctant to resume a Test career begun 22 years before but it was seen as a necessary move for this match. It made sense.

The Lord's Test was a fine match with excellent batting on both sides but when Hutton and Kenyon began the last innings an hour before the end of the fourth day, there was not much doubt in anybody's mind that the 343 would be beyond them. The last hour that day was bound to be difficult against Lindwall, Miller and Johnston and the ball was turning enough for the Australians to believe that the tall leg-spinner Doug Ring would be too much for England on a fifth-day pitch.

The hour on Monday evening exceeded England's worst fears. Lindwall had Kenyon caught at mid-on and Hutton at slip. When Graveney was caught at the wicket off Johnston, England were 12 for three and though Compton and Watson held out until the end of the day, it was hard to see any future for England next day. The prospect would have been bleaker still if the left-handed Watson had not survived a sharp chance to short-leg off Ring.

Sometimes Test pitches at Lord's have lost pace by the last day and have made it very hard for bowlers to prise out determined batsmen. This was not entirely true of this one and the most widely accepted explanation of what followed was that the Australian slow bowlers did not bowl very well.

Compton played steadily for the first 95 minutes before he was lbw to a ball from Johnston which kept low. Trevor Bailey, a master of obdurate defence, then settled in with Watson and the hours passed without further mishap. By the time that Watson was out, having batted for five and three-quarter hours for 109, and Bailey was sixth out after four and a quarter hours for 71, only 35 minutes remained and England were almost safe.

Freddie Brown, who took four wickets and made 50 runs in the match, played a few robust strokes and at the end England were only 61 runs short, but the loss of early wickets and the struggle for survival had prevented victory from ever becoming a consideration.

The British public loves a successful rearguard action and there were, of course, a host of references to Dunkirk, but the Ashes still had to be won. The Old Trafford Test brought them no nearer, though it had an extraordinary finish.

Rain was seldom far away and by the last afternoon England had saved the follow-on and completed their first innings 42 runs behind Australia's 318. Only an hour remained and no drawn match was ever more certain. But at the end of the hour, after 18 overs, Australia's score stood at 35 for eight.

They themselves had no finger-spinners of the class of Laker and Wardle and were no doubt as surprised as everyone else at how much the ball turned. Wardle took four wickets, Laker and Bedser two each.

At the time, this piece of cricket was not taken too seriously and was attributed, at least partially, to carelessness and a lack of application at the end of a moribund match. Yet three years later, after Jim Laker's incredible match at Old Trafford, one could think back to 1953 and realise that the vulnerability of the Australian batsmen to the turning ball that evening had been of greater significance than was appreciated at the time.

The 1953 collapse was a source of amusement at the expense of those spectators who, assuming that nothing worth watching remained, had departed before the start of Australia's second innings. In those days the last train to London left Manchester at 5.25 and those members of the Press with commitments in the South next day received a nasty shock some hours later on arriving at Euston.

At Headingley in the Fourth Test England were put in by Hassett and for most of the match looked likely to lose it. Eventually after a long delaying action by Bailey and Laker, Australia needed 177 in an hour and 55 minutes. So far, England had performed with laudable courage and determination. Not everyone applauded their subsequent performance in the field.

Australia made a spirited effort and, at 117 for three, needed another 60 in 45 minutes. Hutton must have hoped that more of them would have got themselves out in assaulting Bedser, and Lock and Laker. Now they were going too well and he brought

on Bailey whom he had kept in reserve, partly no doubt because
Bailey had been batting nearly all day.

With Bailey bowling off his long run, the batsmen were not
going to face as many overs as they had been receiving from the
other bowlers; and with Bailey bowling, without a slip, outside
the leg-stump to a leg-side field, the rate of progress declined
sharply. At once Graeme Hole was well caught by Graveney
above his head on the square-leg boundary when the ball would
have gone for six. Thereafter, de Courcy and Davidson, both well
equipped with attacking strokes, could find no answer to this sort
of cricket. Australia still needed 30 at the end of the match.

In the passing years the Laws have been adjusted and the on-
side restrictions on fielders – only two allowed behind square –
and the admirable requirement of 20 overs to be bowled in the
final hour have eliminated extreme defensive methods.

After four draws, the final Test was to be played over six days
which allowed for interruptions through rain but otherwise was
more than enough as The Oval pitches had been playing. In
Surrey's home matches the ball had certainly turned at some stage
for Laker and Lock. This must have given the Australians to
think furiously. They had several leg-spinners but no specialist
off-spinner or left-arm spinner. They settled for bringing back
Johnston who was fit again, leaving out Richie Benaud who in his
previous three Tests on the tour had taken only two wickets and
made only 15 runs, and playing no specialist spinner at all. This
left Australia vulnerable if the ball turned, as seemed highly likely
at The Oval, especially in a six-day match.

England, for their part, made two significant changes. Simpson
and Watson were left out for May and Trueman. Peter May had
been in fine form recently. Trueman, restricted by National
Service to 10 matches for Yorkshire that summer, had been taking
wickets recently and had the asset in an English August of being
fresh.

The match began on a Saturday which meant that some
England players did not arrive in London until late on Friday
evening. Len Hutton had to come 250 miles from Scarborough –
and this was in pre-motorway days. The Australians had Friday
off, having beaten Essex in two days.

The Oval could accommodate 30,000 then and it was packed
every day. The tension was unparalleled in the experience of most
players and spectators. This was the chance to win back the
Ashes after 19 years. This was the ground on which Hobbs and

Sutcliffe had enabled England under Percy Chapman to win them back after the First World War. This was where the present captain Len Hutton had made his famous 364 against Australia in 1938.

The match began with a well-balanced first day as England bowled Australia out for 275. Trueman and Bedser bowled very well to take four and three wickets respectively. This was only moderately satisfactory for England, as they had dropped catches and, before Lindwall made a vigorous 62, had reduced Australia to 160 for seven. However, they had finished the day with a bit of luck – in fact, two bits – when Hutton was surprised by a fast shortish ball from Lindwall. It lobbed up just short of the slips at the same moment that his cap almost dropped on the wicket.

England's innings on the Monday was a determined one founded on a fine innings of 82 by the captain. Peter May played with great composure in a second-wicket stand of 100 but by evening the middle batting had subsided against the Australian fast bowlers to 235 for seven. Early on the third morning, however, Trevor Bailey conjured 69 priceless runs from the last two wickets with Trueman and Bedser and England led by 31.

It was during the third afternoon that England played the cricket which won back the Ashes. There had been nothing during their own innings to suggest that the ball would turn a lot, for Australia had no class spinners. Len Hutton was in little doubt and after five overs from his faster bowlers, he brought on Laker and Lock. By half past five they had Australia out for 162.

This left England needing 132 to win, a number which seemed somewhat more remote when Hutton went for a second run after a piece of misfielding in the square-leg area and was run out. But Edrich and May batted safely through to the end of the day by which time the number needed had been reduced by 38.

Next morning the excitement was even more intense as every run was grudged by the Australians and every run brought a roar from the dense crowd. Lindwall and Miller bowled scarcely a loose ball and Johnston, trying to fill a gap in the Australian attack, was used as a left-arm spinner. He could make the going hard for the batsman even if he lacked the expertise of Laker and Lock. Miller did remove May at 88 but it was too late to cause much concern and just before three o'clock Compton made the winning hit. The Ashes were back. One had to be at least 25 years of age to remember the last time that England had held them.

7

Hutton –
The Later Years

ENGLAND'S hand of Test-class bowlers was now growing stronger all the time and the side which Len Hutton took to the West Indies in 1953–54 was a formidable one. It was the first time that a truly representative team had been sent to the Caribbean. It was not a completely happy tour. The game in West Indies was now marred by bottle-throwing, disputes in the crowd about umpiring, threats to players' families and a general sensitiveness for which some players were not prepared. The strain that such a tour put on a reserved, gentle captain of dry humour must have been considerable but Hutton did not let it affect his batting. This was as important to the side as ever, even though Denis Compton was still capable of playing a great innings and young players such as Peter May and Tom Graveney had established themselves. Hutton averaged 96 in the Test series and seemed to enjoy captaincy on the field but the wear and tear of tours such as this may well have led to a shortening of his career.

The confidence built up by the recovery of the Ashes was soon shaken when England were well beaten in the first two Tests in Jamaica and Barbados. Like many sides, before and since, coming from an English midwinter, they were always struggling. There was a moment in the First Test when, needing more than 450 to win, they reached 277 for two, but West Indies soon regained control. In each match Jeff Stollmeyer could have enforced the follow-on but did not. England lost each match on the sixth day and in Barbados did the fair name of English batsmanship no favour by making only 128 runs in 114 overs on the third day. They were pinned down once again by Ramadhin and Valentine who bowled more than 50 overs each.

West Indies so far had not been at full strength. Worrell had missed the First Test through injury, Weekes the Second. But in British Guiana, as it was then, everyone was fit on the West Indies side – and England won by nine wickets.

This notable about-turn was achieved first by Len Hutton's fine 169, the product of seven and three-quarter hours of mastery, and the soundness with which Compton and the later batsmen helped the score up to 435. Statham then removed Worrell, Stollmeyer and Walcott, who mustered only six runs between them, and despite an eighth-wicket stand of 99 and a riot, West Indies had to follow on. The second-innings wickets were shared between all five bowlers – Statham, Bailey, Laker, Lock and Wardle – and England, needing only 73, won handsomely.

The jute-matting pitch in Trinidad had not allowed a Test match to be finished for 20 years and West Indies' 681 for eight declared (Weekes 206, Worrell 167, Walcott 124) was answered fairly painlessly by England's 537 (May 135, Compton 133). This left England needing to win in Jamaica to square the series.

How West Indies came to be bowled out for 139 on the first day in Sabina Park, Kingston, has never been satisfactorily explained, other than that it was the result of brilliant bowling by Trevor Bailey who took seven for 34. The pitch was a good one, West Indies had chosen to bat and England were without their most successful bowler, Brian Statham. It proved to be one of those days when the catches went to hand and when the odd ball which did the unexpected took a wicket.

Bailey's feat was achieved on a day when he had the distinction of opening both the bowling and the batting for England. He helped Len Hutton to negotiate the last half-hour safely.

The captain then devoted himself to building up the lead. He batted all through the second day and for nearly nine hours in all to make 205. The next highest score, until Wardle came in at number eight and made a vigorous 66, was 31. It was the first double hundred ever made by an England captain overseas. West Indies, 275 behind, were not easily bowled out in the second innings but when it finished on the fifth day, England needed only 72 to win. They won by nine wickets again.

West Indies did have one consolation. This was the first Test match of a 17-year-old all-rounder called Garfield Sobers who had taken four wickets with his orthodox left-arm spin and had batted promisingly in both innings. It was thought that more would be heard of him.

Pakistan's first tour of England, which followed in the summer of 1954, was a weird mixture of success and disappointment. Since the turbulent days of partition, cricket had had to be reorganised in those four north-western provinces of the sub-continent which, with East Pakistan, now Bangladesh, then constituted the new state of Pakistan.

They had advanced their claims to be a Test-playing country by winning a match against Nigel Howard's touring side of 1951–2. They had a few senior players with experience of top-class cricket in India. They had two players of outstanding talent in the medium-fast bowler Fazal Mahmood, who could be unplayable in certain conditions, especially on the mat, and in the schoolboy opening batsman, Hanif Mohammad. They had a captain, Abdul Hafeez Kardar, a left-handed all-rounder, with a broad knowledge of English cricket gleaned not only on India's tour of England in 1946 but subsequently from playing for Oxford University and Warwickshire. After being elected to full membership of the Imperial Cricket Conference in 1953, they had prepared carefully for this tour of England by sending senior players and a team of young players, the Pakistan Eaglets, to play in England where they were supervised by the eminent coach Alfred Gover at his school in Wandsworth.

Pakistan were thus not starting wholly from scratch, though they were not expected to trouble an England side which had swamped India in 1952, had won back the Ashes in 1953 and recently had won two Test matches in West Indies. This was borne out by the first three of the four Test matches. The weather for the First Test at Lord's broke records even by English standards. Play was not possible until 3.45 on the fourth day and then Pakistan were bowled out, mostly by Statham and Wardle, for 87. England did only a little better against Khan Mohammad and Fazal Mahmood. Khan Mohammad was more powerfully built than most bowlers from the sub-continent and had played in the Lancashire League.

The draw at Lord's was followed by a one-sided affair at Trent Bridge which contained several items of historical interest. This was the occasion of Denis Compton's 278 and of the brief appearance in Test cricket of a 16-year-old leg-spinner, Khalid Hassan. He took two wickets, bowling Reg Simpson for 101 and Compton for 278, and never played in another Test match.

This match was also notable as the first Test of one whom many regard, with some justification, as the best slow bowler of his day – and most other days too. Bob Appleyard was 30. In his first season for Yorkshire in 1951 he had taken over 200 wickets but had been struck down by a serious illness at the start of the 1952 season and did not play again until 1954. He could not be categorised as an off-spinner because at almost medium pace he had a variety of talents. He often took the new ball for Yorkshire. His flight frequently upset the batsman as did the unexpected bounce which he achieved from his height of about six feet two and his fine action. He was very accurate to the extent that he took many wickets when batsmen thought they could detect a loose ball at last and tried to drive or hook it. They found that it was faster or bounced more than they expected.

His arrival in Test cricket was spectacular. With his second ball he had Hanif lbw and in five overs he took four wickets for six runs. He took seven in the match and was then reserved by the selectors for Australia in the winter. Almost inevitably the series against Pakistan was by now being looked on as providing guidance for the winter tour and the glut of good bowlers was exercising the selectors in a way to which they and their immediate predecessors had not been accustomed.

Appleyard was to play in only nine Test matches. His health was seldom of the best and he retired in 1958. It was a sad story, for he was a great bowler prevented by fate from making the most of his rare ability. But the good news for the reader is that 30 years later he was still recognised as one of the most formidable opponents to be found on Yorkshire golf courses.

In this and the Third Test at Old Trafford England were captained by David Sheppard who from early June had been able to play for Sussex in the vacation of his theological college. At Trent Bridge he had the agreeable duty of declaring the England innings closed at 558 for six.

Sheppard declared again at Old Trafford where it rained and Pakistan had much the worse of the pitch. Bowled out for 90 by Bedser, Wardle and the Glamorgan off-spinner Jim McConnon, they were 25 for four in the second innings when they were saved by more rain.

From the events in the series so far, it was not surprising that the final Test at The Oval was regarded more as preparation for the tour of Australia and New Zealand than as one which would clinch the series. In fact, the story went that the selectors were concentrating so hard on picking the right touring team that the meeting was almost breaking up before they remembered that they also had to pick a Test team for The Oval. They then chose a

side which included several of those going on the tour who were
short of previous Test experience. Len Hutton was fit again and
back as captain, having played in only one and a half days of the
series so far. Inevitably his mind was on the tour rather than on
The Oval Test against opponents who had been largely outplayed
hitherto.

The main five batsmen were played – Hutton, Simpson, May,
Compton and Graveney. Sheppard was not available for the tour.
The 21-year-old Colin Cowdrey, that year's Oxford captain, was
given a first scent of Test cricket as twelfth man. But it was in the
bowling required for The Oval that the team was so eccentrically
picked. Laker and Lock, who 12 months earlier had bowled out
Australia here, were left out. So was Alec Bedser who had had
more experience of The Oval pitches than anyone. Even Trevor
Bailey, whom one would have expected to bowl well here and
who as a batsman was expert at repairing an innings which had
started badly, was omitted. Peter Loader was the only Surrey
bowler included. He and Frank Tyson were playing in their first
Test. Trueman, who had been so successful at The Oval against
Australia a year before, was not included because he, like Laker
and Lock, was not in the touring party.

The attack of Statham, Tyson, Loader, McConnon and Wardle
might well have been Trueman, Bedser, Bailey, Laker and Lock, if
the main consideration had been to win a Test match at The
Oval. But it was hard for anyone to get out of his mind the ease
with which Pakistan had been bowled out so far and to ignore the
belief that only the weather had prevented England from leading
3–0 instead of 1–0.

One factor overlooked, by the cricketing public in general and
not just the selectors, was that a pitch which rewarded good
bowling, as did most pitches at The Oval at the time, would bring
the best out of Pakistan's great bowler, Fazal Mahmood, who in
the series so far had taken only eight wickets at 38 apiece.

Yet when the match began on 12 August 1954, after a start
delayed by rain, it looked a repetition of previous suffering by
Pakistan. They were soon 10 for three and later 51 for seven to
Statham, Tyson and Loader. Though Kardar led a revival and the
last three wickets made 82, the relative ease with which the later
batsmen played suggested that England would make a lot of runs
when they batted on the second day.

In fact, a storm next morning flooded The Oval and on the
third day, the Saturday, May and Compton were the only batsmen

to pass 20. The ball lifted awkwardly and Fazal and the medium-fast Mahmood Hussain bowled the right length. Compton batted with great skill for two hours 20 minutes but England were out for 130. Fazal bowled throughout the innings, swinging the ball and cutting it either way, and took six for 53 in 30 overs despite having several catches dropped.

The pitch began to dry out during Saturday's play and, with the ball now turning, Pakistan finished at 63 for four. After the weekend this soon became 82 for eight as Wardle passed through the middle batting, but the last two wickets doubled the score, mainly through Wazir Mohammad, Hanif's eldest brother, and Zulfiqar Ahmed. Wardle, who had not bowled in the first innings, took seven for 56 in 35 overs.

England needed 168 and had more than two and a half hours of the fourth day's play left. Even then, they did not seem to appreciate the dangers, partly perhaps because Peter May played so handsomely for his 53 that others were entitled to think that victory was assured, especially at 109 for two. Even when May was out, England still seemed to be hoping to finish the match in the final half-hour, for Evans was promoted seemingly with this in mind. It did not work and both he and Graveney were soon out. When Compton, who had played well in a third-wicket stand with May, was caught at the wicket off Fazal just before the end, England's parlous position was at last exposed.

On the Tuesday they still needed 43 from four wickets with all the main batsmen gone. They lasted less than an hour against Fazal, who again bowled 30 overs and this time took six for 46.

The delight in Pakistan was easy to understand. They had halved the series and they were the first country ever to win a Test match on their first tour of England. The cricket of the new nation could not have had a better boost. England, as they prepared to set off for Australia, had to look on it as an unfortunate hiccup. It was to be 28 years before they lost another Test match to Pakistan.

However critical one might be of the choice for The Oval Test against Pakistan, the selectors had picked a team for Australia which was both imaginative and successful. Under the wise and kindly Harry Altham, the selection committee for Test matches at home, augmented for picking touring teams, included Walter Robins, Leslie Ames and Norman Yardley, all of whom had toured Australia. They took some brave decisions based on their estimates of how effective the bowlers available might be on

Australian pitches. In those days the difference between Australian and English pitches was greater than it became when pitches in England were partly or completely covered.

In the wet summer of 1954 the difference was greater than ever. Len Hutton headed the Yorkshire batting averages with an average of only 39. In the first-class bowling averages the top 31 bowlers took their wickets for under 20 apiece. By the late 1980s the number of bowlers with similar figures had fallen to nine.

The selectors steeled themselves and left out Trueman, Laker and Lock. Instead they picked Tyson, McConnon and Wardle. In his season and a half with Northamptonshire Frank Tyson, who had not been wanted by his native Lancashire, had looked as if he could become a genuinely fast bowler. At 24, of medium height and with hair already receding, he was not an obvious choice as a future scourge of Australia but he had unusually powerful shoulders and an intelligent head on top of them. McConnon had been taking wickets for Glamorgan for several seasons and had figured prominently in a rare win over Surrey at The Oval earlier in the summer of 1954, taking seven for 23 in the second innings against Jim Laker's five for 51. In the first innings of the same match Tony Lock had taken eight for 36. McConnon had a good action and was considered likely to be more effective in Australia than Laker and Lock who pushed the ball through more quickly. In the event he suffered a string of injuries and played in only five matches before coming home with a broken finger. Wardle was to become a vital bowler for overseas tours because he was developing, in addition to his orthodox left-arm spin, the chinaman and googly which were big assets on hard bouncy pitches in a warm climate.

The aforementioned imagination extended to the choice of batsmen. The old adage about there being no substitute for class led to the selection of the 21-year-old Colin Cowdrey who by now was an experienced infant prodigy. It was eight years since, at 13, he had made 75 and 44 for Tonbridge against Clifton at Lord's and had taken eight wickets in the match as a leg-spinner. Though rather heavily built for his years he had the lightning reflexes of a rackets player – one of his youthful achievements had been to reach the final of the amateur championship – and was a superb timer of the ball, a stroker of it rather than a hitter. Though he had not yet played in a Test match, he had an impressive record against the stronger bowling sides of the day. When he was only 18 he had made 106 for the Gentlemen at Scarborough against a Players attack including Alec Bedser and Roy Tattersall. At 20 he had made a fifty in each innings for the Gentlemen against the 1953 Australians. He was to be one of the great successes of the 1954–5 tour, though it started tragically for him when on arrival in Perth he learnt of the sudden death of his father who had inspired his cricket.

On his first appearance on the Sydney Cricket Ground Cowdrey made 110. Peter May, the team's vice-captain, was also making runs and so, after some unusual preliminaries, was Denis Compton who had stayed behind in England for more treatment on his knee. His flight out included an emergency landing in Karachi but characteristically he insisted on playing immediately after arriving in Adelaide and made 113. Against Queensland he made 116 and 69 and clearly had an important part to play in England's batting.

However, not everything was going right for Len Hutton's team. Alec Bedser had suffered an attack of shingles from which there was no quick recovery, though from early November he was bowling away in the sun and trying as hard as ever. Godfrey Evans was taken ill and could not play in the First Test in Brisbane. Jim McConnon was injured while fielding against Queensland. The misfortunes with illness and injury continued into the First Test when on the first morning Compton put his left hand in the boundary rails and broke a bone.

That morning Hutton had won the toss and put Australia in. In previous weeks M.C.C. had more than once put their opponents in and done well. They themselves had been put in by Ron Archer captaining Queensland the week before and it had taken a hundred apiece from Simpson and Compton and their fourth-wicket stand of 234 to repair the early damage. Moreover, Hutton and the tour selectors had gone into the match with four fast bowlers and, as his only spinner, the ill-fated Compton who had anyhow bowled only a few overs on the tour so far.

Thus it was not unreasonable to choose to field first and Hutton duly did so. Australia then made 601 for eight. From an early hour England were dropping catches, the left-handers Morris and Harvey made 153 and 162 respectively and at one time Australia were 456 for two. Their new captain Ian Johnson declared on the third morning and on the fifth of the six days England were beaten by an innings and 154 runs. As an additional irritation, eight of their wickets had fallen to the spin of Johnson and Benaud.

It was hard to imagine a more disastrous match for England, but salvation was at hand. In Brisbane Frank Tyson had started experimenting with a shorter run, which seemed particularly desirable in a hot climate. Having settled into this in Melbourne where he took six wickets against Victoria, he bowled with accuracy at a great pace and found the next two Test pitches in Sydney and Melbourne not unrewarding.

The turning-point in the series was reached on the third afternoon of the Second Test in Sydney. This time England had been put in and were bowled out for 154. Tyson, Statham and Bailey then kept Australia to 228 but when in the second innings Hutton, Bailey and Graveney were out for 55, England, still 19 runs behind, were perilously placed.

At this point May was joined by Cowdrey and the two young men added 116 for the fourth wicket (May 104, Cowdrey 54). Bill Edrich carried on and there was a priceless last-wicket stand of 46 between Appleyard and Statham. Australia now needed 223 and though Neil Harvey made 92 not out, Tyson and Statham were too much for his partners and England won by 38 runs on the fifth day. Tyson, one for 160 in Brisbane, had taken 10 for 130 here.

The Third Test in Melbourne over the New Year followed a similar pattern, though this time England chose to bat first. Against Lindwall and Miller they were soon 41 for four but a remarkable innings of 102 by Colin Cowdrey with support from Bailey and Evans helped them up to 191. This time Australia led by only 40 runs. Peter May sustained England's second innings, making 91, and Australia needed 240.

The end came swiftly on the fifth day when they were out for 111 (Tyson seven for 27).

When they came to the Fourth Test in Adelaide after a hefty win over South Australia with hundreds by May and Compton, England could take the field with morale high, in the comforting belief that they were the better side. Batting second they led by only 18 runs on first innings but by then the ball would turn a bit. Appleyard was soon bowling and disposed of Jim Burke and the left-handers Morris and Harvey.

It was widely assumed that Appleyard would finish off the Australians next day. But on another pitch of slightly uneven bounce Hutton began with Statham and Tyson. They bowled for the first hour and a half taking three wickets each and Appleyard was not required until the last pair were batting. England only

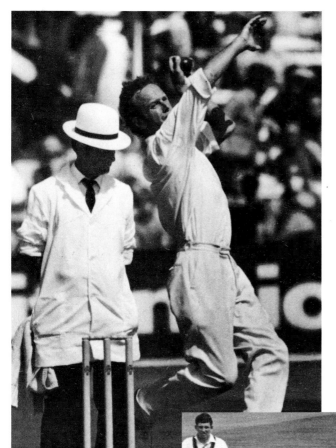

Derek Underwood was an important part of England's bowling for 10 years before the Packer interruption. He gave little away, could be next to unplayable on wet turning pitches and at 32 had already played in 77 Tests and taken 272 Test wickets. *KK*

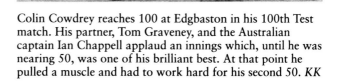

Colin Cowdrey reaches 100 at Edgbaston in his 100th Test match. His partner, Tom Graveney, and the Australian captain Ian Chappell applaud an innings which, until he was nearing 50, was one of his brilliant best. At that point he pulled a muscle and had to work hard for his second 50. *KK*

Clem Jones, the Lord Mayor of Brisbane, was also the curator of the Gabba, no sinecure in a city subject to violent tropical storms. *JW*

Vic Pollard, of New Zealand, who was seldom dislodged easily, stumped by Alan Knott at the Oval in 1969 off Ray Illingworth with something to spare. John Edrich at short-leg. The ball turned throughout the three-match series and Underwood took 24 wickets at 9.16, Illingworth took 10. *KK*

Headingley 1972. John Inverarity is caught by Illingworth off Underwood who took 10 wickets in the match. England's victory at Headingley in a low-scoring match put them 2–1 ahead but Australia squared the series by winning at The Oval. *KK*

Sixteen years earlier, when he played rugby once for England, Mike Smith in full stride had been a stirring sight. Here, in the Gillette Cup Final of 1972, he runs in vain, for umpire Charles Elliott is breaking the bad news to him that he is lbw to Jack Simmons to the evident satisfaction of Farokh Engineer and the bowler. Lancashire beat Warwickshire by five wickets. *KK*

The left-handed Roy Fredericks recovers quickly, after being beaten by Illingworth outside the off-stump, and just foils Knott. He survived to make 150. *KK*

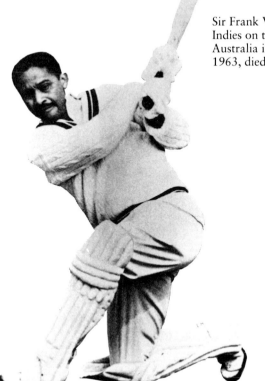

Sir Frank Worrell, captain of West Indies on the momentous tour of Australia in 1960–1 and in England in 1963, died much lamented in 1967. *KK*

Gary Sobers in one of his numerous roles, as a fast-medium bowler. *KK*

The last of the Test-playing amateurs. Alan Smith (*left*), the future chief executive of the TCCB, David Sheppard, later Bishop of Liverpool, and Ted Dexter who in 1989 became chairman of the England Committee. While they were away in 1962–3, amateurs and professionals in England became just 'cricketers'. *JW*
▼

Tom Graveney brought a touch of elegance to English cricket in a first-class career which lasted from 1948 to 1971, during which he made 122 hundreds and played in 79 Test matches. *KK*

Denis Compton and Walter Hammond flanked by David Allen and John Murray in South Africa in 1964–5. The match in Natal was Hammond's last. He died a few ▼ months later on 1 July 1965 aged 62. *JW*

▲
Bob Barber opened the innings for England in South Africa, and especially Australia, as if the whole thing was a great joke. His 185 in four hours 55 minutes on the first day of the Sydney Test in 1965–6 was the highlight of an all too short career. *JW*

Two distinguished men of ▶ letters, Jack Fingleton, before the Second World War a resolute opening batsman for Australia, and Ben Travers, author of the Aldwych farces and a passionate follower of cricket. *JW*

In 1966–7 South Africa's strength was such that they kept the 21-year-old Barry Richards in reserve during their series against Australia and did not bring in the year-younger Mike Procter until the Third Test. *JW*

During his years of captaincy M.J.K. Smith fielded for many hours in India, South Africa and Australia at short leg, a position which in modern times is usually reserved for the youngest, nimblest and presumably most expendable member of a side. Here he is catching David Sincock off David Allen, watched from behind the stumps by Jim Parks and Bob Barber. *KK*

Three great Indian spinners of the ▶ 60s and 70s, Prasanna *(left)*, Bedi and Chandrasekhar. *JW*

▲
Basil d'Oliveira batting at Edgbaston in 1970 against the Rest of the World. He made 110 and 81. Deryck Murray (West Indies) and, at slip, Eddie Barlow (South Africa) are in attendance. *KK*

Colin Cowdrey played in his first Test matches in 1954–5, the first just before his 22nd birthday. Here he is hitting the ball almost apologetically over the on-side field with effortless timing and a minimum of violence. *KK*

Canberra, December 1954. The Governor-General of Australia, Sir William (later Lord) Slim, under Len Hutton's guidance, reaches Frank Tyson near the end of the line while the Prime Minister, Mr Robert Menzies, lingers talking to the vice-captain, Peter May, and Tom Graveney. *JW*

Bob Appleyard, who played in
only nine Tests, bowling against
South Africa at Trent Bridge in
1955. Poor health shortened the
career of one of the very best
post-War English bowlers. *The
Hulton Picture Library*

Griffith, New South Wales, one of the many small
Australian towns where M.C.C. used to play country
teams – with the Griffith Oval a prominent feature. *JW*

Some of the M.C.C. team and accompanying press party on the golf course on a Sunday in Adelaide, with Sir Donald Bradman who played off scratch and nearly always won. From the left: Crawford White (*Daily Express*), Ken Barrington, Billy Griffith (acting manager), John Woodcock (*The Times*), Tom Graveney, Sir Donald Bradman, Alec Bedser (assistant-manager), Ted Dexter and Colin Cowdrey. *JW*

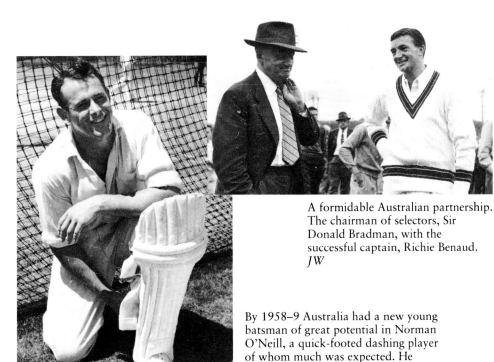

A formidable Australian partnership. The chairman of selectors, Sir Donald Bradman, with the successful captain, Richie Benaud. *JW*

By 1958–9 Australia had a new young batsman of great potential in Norman O'Neill, a quick-footed dashing player of whom much was expected. He averaged 56 in the series. *JW*

In 1962–3 M.C.C. set off for Australia on the *Canberra* with Ted Dexter as captain and the Duke of Norfolk, here seen with Fred Trueman, as manager. *JW*

Ted Dexter was flown out to Australia as a replacement in 1958–9 and by 1961 was making 180 at Edgbaston against Australia watched by Wally Grout, the wicket-keeper, and Alan Davidson at slip. *KK*

Alec Bedser in action during the Test Trial at Canterbury, July 1946. *The Hulton Picture Library*

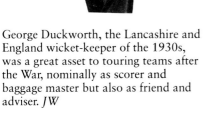

George Duckworth, the Lancashire and England wicket-keeper of the 1930s, was a great asset to touring teams after the War, nominally as scorer and baggage master but also as friend and adviser. *JW*

Norman Yardley and Hedley Verity while serving in the Green Howards in Northern Ireland in 1941. In July 1943 Captain Verity died of wounds received in Sicily. Yardley survived to captain England in fourteen Test matches and Yorkshire for eight seasons. *KK*

Don Bradman, in his 40th year, comes out to bat in 1948 at Headingley where, in three pre-war Tests, he had made 334, 304 and 103. Now he added 173 not out while Australia were making their 404 for three to win – in five and a half hours, but off 114 overs. *KK*

Neil Harvey, at 19 the youngest member of Bradman's all-conquering 1948 touring team, after making 112 at Headingley in his first Test against England. *KK*

Len Hutton batting against New Zealand in 1949, a marvel of technical perfection despite his shortened left arm. *KK*

England *v* Australia at The Oval, August 1953. Denis Compton, the master of footwork and timing, finds the gap with no obvious effort. *The Hulton Picture Library*

Brian Statham arrived abruptly on the first-class scene in 1950 and in a career lasting 19 years was probably the most reliable of the relative glut of excellent fast and fast-medium bowlers in England at the time. *KK* ▼

▲
Frank Tyson in 1954, his only full season before he and Statham between them took 46 wickets in the 1954–5 series against Australia, Tyson's share 28 at 20.82 apiece. *KK*

Peter May's 104 in the second innings of the Second Test in Sydney just before Christmas 1954 was the turning-point in the series. Of the other batsmen in a low-scoring match, only two, Neil Harvey for Australia and the youthful Colin Cowdrey for England, passed 50. *KK*

Two eminent net bowlers recruited from the press box in Perth in 1954, Freddie Brown, captain of the previous M.C.C. team in Australia, and Ian Peebles, who played 13 Test matches as a leg-spinner in the late 20s and early 30s. *JW* needed 94 and though they were 18 for three, Compton and May soon allayed fears in the dressing-room. England won by five wickets and retained the Ashes.

By the time the final Test in Sydney was due to start, much of New South Wales was flooded and operations did not begin until after lunch on the fourth day. England had the satisfaction of making Australia follow on and had taken six second-innings wickets when time ran out.

It had been the most gratifying tour made by M.C.C. for many years. Even the main news story of the series scarcely touched them. Over the weekend of the Melbourne Test a strange transformation had taken place in the pitch. On the Saturday the pitch had had cracks in it and in the prevailing weather, with a hot north wind blowing, it was conceivable that it would break up. Yet on Monday morning it was damp and the cracks had largely closed. The official inquiry "emphatically denied" that the pitch had been watered, so one was left to believe that it was a natural phenomenon, an act of God. In that case, powers beyond man's control had been on England's side, for the pitch was easier when they continued their second innings and had dried into its former awkwardness by the time that Australia batted.

After Sydney there were still four matches to be played in New Zealand. Len Hutton's team won them all, including two Tests. In the Second Test in Auckland they led by only 46 runs on first innings but did not have to bat again as New Zealand were out for only 26, a Test record unlikely ever to be beaten. Appleyard took four for seven in six overs.

Meanwhile the Australians had gone to the Caribbean which in later years would not have been the ideal place to restore shattered confidence. But in 1955 West Indies were still short of good fast bowlers and lost three of the five Test matches. The other two were drawn.

8

A Glut of Bowlers –
and Peter May

THERE was no hint of any change in the England captaincy as the M.C.C. team returned home in triumph in early April 1955 and began to prepare for the new season. Len Hutton did not appear until Yorkshire's third Championship match when he played at Headingley against Somerset and made 11 and 66. But Yorkshire began the last season of Norman Yardley's captaincy impressively by winning their first six matches. They managed well enough without Hutton and it was understandable that after a tiring tour he should be slow to come into action in the bleak weather of May.

He did not play again until the Roses match at the end of the month when he made two and 17 at Old Trafford. That night the Yorkshire team travelled down to Hove to play Sussex and next morning, Yardley being unfit, it was Hutton who went out to toss with Robin Marlar. He won and put Sussex in which, in the prevailing conditions and with Trueman, Close, Appleyard and Wardle in his side, seemed the sensible thing to do. But it rained at the wrong time for Yorkshire and Sussex won a low-scoring match by 21 runs. Hutton made 54 and 0.

From Hove, Yorkshire went to The Oval. Surrey had won all seven of their previous Championship matches and this one, Arthur McIntyre's benefit, was between two sets of bowlers exceptional in county cricket in any era. Norman Yardley had recovered and on winning the toss put Surrey in. They were bowled out for 85 (Appleyard seven for 29). After the weekend the pitch dried out and Surrey eventually won by 41 runs but on the first afternoon Yorkshire did only slightly better than Surrey. Len Hutton was caught at the wicket off Loader for 0.

The next day the England team for the First Test against South

Africa was announced. Peter May was the captain. During Saturday's play at The Oval even May had no inkling that Hutton would withdraw. It came as a complete surprise when G.O. Allen, the chairman of selectors, rang him to ask him to lead England in the First Test, as Hutton had dropped out with lumbago. May assumed that it would be only for the First Test. Trevor Bailey, far more experienced, had been vice-captain in West Indies two winters before but on the recent tour May had done the job. The selectors were thought to have preferred a batsman and to have agreed that May at 25 was more likely to provide continuity at the top than Bailey at 31.

Thus began a period of six and a half years during which May led England, first with conspicuous success, then with more difficulty as an improved Australia under Richie Benaud recovered the Ashes and May himself was plagued by a serious illness for nearly two years. As a batsman until then, he was probably the best in the world.

He was fortunate in the unusual number of high-class bowlers now available. It was a very strong England side but not invincible. It had two weak points. The best players of the day were not very mobile and though they had their moments when the catches stuck, there were other times when the bowlers' efforts were not fully supported.

The other vulnerable point was the lack of a consistent opening pair. A few years before, Hutton and Washbrook had been so dominant that as fine a batsman as Jack Robertson played in only two home Test matches. The prolific John Langridge of Sussex never played in a Test match at all.

Now there was seldom a settled England opening pair. Several batsmen came and played the odd valuable innings but without establishing themselves. Colin Cowdrey was asked to open, which technically was the obvious solution. He was a reluctant opener and though he made many runs when opening the innings, there was always the feeling that he would have made even more at number four. He was certainly adaptable and there was no greater compliment to his technical ability than that nearly 20 years later, when England were in trouble with the fiery and at times frightening fast bowling of Lillee and Thomson, it was Colin Cowdrey, aged 42, for whom the management sent.

There was also a problem in the middle of the order which was exposed when Cowdrey or Bailey was moved up to open. The

England sides of that era usually needed one more top-class batsman at six or seven. The best bowlers of the day and indeed the wicket-keeper Godfrey Evans saved many an awkward situation but Bailey was the only one who could be called a genuine all-rounder and he was not fluent enough to take charge of the second half of the innings. Time after time he would be left, perhaps 30 or 40 not out.

Thus though Peter May usually batted three or four he carried a much greater responsibility than was desirable in a captain. More often than not he went in with everything, so it seemed, depending on him. The figures for the 1956 series against Australia are illuminating in this respect. England won 2–1 and May averaged 90. The next batsman, English or Australian, who played throughout the low-scoring series averaged 45.

His importance to the side was clearly illustrated in his first series as captain against a fine South African side under Jack Cheetham in 1955. Many consider this to have been the best post-war series in England. England won it 3–2, the winning and losing of the rubber almost certainly resting on one umpiring decision in the last Test.

Before a damp and cold spring gave way to a fine summer the South Africans had a rough time. Worcestershire beat them and they had not found their form by the First Test at Trent Bridge which they lost by an innings. May began his captaincy with an innings of 83 and Frank Tyson, in the second of only four Test matches which he played in England, took six for 28.

The Second Test at Lord's was both unusual and spectacular. The Springboks now had two excellent fast bowlers in Adcock and Heine and in support the left-handed all-rounder Trevor Goddard. Goddard, who also opened the innings, was a medium-pace bowler who was to become a great swing bowler in the 1960s, though in the 1950s, before the restrictions on on-side fielders, he was considered largely negative.

On the first day at Lord's Heine and Adcock bowled England out for 133. The pitch, typical of Lord's in those days, was fast and lively. The stroke-player could enjoy himself if good enough and Roy McLean's 142 out of 196 in three and a half hours was rich entertainment for the packed crowd.

South Africa led by 171 runs but Peter May then played a brilliant innings of 112 with aid from Graveney and Compton. Though Tayfield, now established as one of the world's best off-spinners, was too much for the later batsmen, South Africa needed

183 to win when they began the last innings with half an hour of the third day's play left.

By now, however, the luck was running against them. They were unfortunate at the end of a tiring day in the field to have to face Statham at his fastest and in that half-hour they not only lost McGlew and Goddard to Statham but had their captain, Jack Cheetham, put out of action when Trueman's last ball of the day hit him an agonising blow on the elbow and chipped a bone.

The South Africans were unlucky again in Monday's weather which was dry but dark and play was interrupted by bad light. May was thus able to keep Statham fresh which was of high importance because for a long time Statham was the only bowler who looked likely to take wickets. With a two-hour break for bad light he was able to keep going throughout the innings, taking the first seven wickets for 22 before Wardle took the last two. England won by 71 runs.

Cheetham had not been able to continue his innings and he was out of the next two Tests too. Jackie McGlew, who took over the captaincy, had had the melancholy distinction of making a "pair" at Lord's – out twice to Statham – but the England bowlers were soon being reminded of what a rare coup this was. In each of the next two Tests, McGlew made a hundred and the sight of his stocky figure, patient and watchful, became all too familiar for them.

England were now able to bring in Colin Cowdrey for his first home Test match. Since his successes in Australia his life had been complicated, first by his joining the R.A.F. to do his National Service and then by the R.A.F.'s turning him down on medical grounds. He had a rare condition of the feet for which the R.A.F. did not wish to take responsibility.

To some members of the public it was incomprehensible that his feet could stand up to hard Australian cricket grounds but not to National Service. They wrote to the newspapers about it and they wrote abusive letters to Cowdrey. It all helped to make this an unsettled season for him. He played in only nine matches for Kent and though he was picked for the Third Test at Old Trafford, he missed much of the second half of the season through injury.

The Third and Fourth Test matches of 1955 at Old Trafford and Headingley were blessed by weather which did the North of England much credit. The snag was that on the hard pitches the ball often lifted to the gloves, as it had at Lord's, and broken fingers abounded. In the first innings at Old Trafford, Godfrey Evans broke a finger in two places while keeping wicket. He missed the rest of the series. McGlew had reached 77 in the first innings there when he had to retire with a hand injury but he returned when the seventh wicket fell and reached the third hundred of his side's innings.

These two matches were marked by exhilarating batting from the moment that Denis Compton set about repairing a start of 42 for two at Old Trafford. Playing with all his old flair, he made 158 out of England's total of 284. South Africa then made their 521 for eight, to which John Waite contributed 113, Paul Winslow 108 and McGlew his 104 not out. The tall Winslow was a powerful straight driver, great value on his day. On this occasion he reached his hundred by hitting Lock far over the sightscreen for six.

In their second innings England, though losing both opening batsmen, Don Kenyon and Tom Graveney, with only two runs on the board, made 381. This time May played the main innings, making his second hundred in successive Tests, though Compton's 71 in their stand of 124 in 105 minutes was of even higher quality than his first innings. In later years he would say that he did not often play better than in this innings.

At one time on the last day it looked as if South Africa would have little to do in the last innings, but Evans found that his broken little finger, now in plaster, was no great handicap to hitting the ball and he made 36 of a last-wicket stand of 48 with Bailey who as usual had survived earlier mishaps.

This left South Africa needing 145 in two and a quarter hours. There was a sad note in that the two wickets which Alec Bedser took were the last of his 236 Test wickets but nobody knew that at the time and South Africa went about their task in the same boisterous spirit which had marked their cricket throughout the match. The loss of two early wickets was brushed aside by McGlew and McLean who made 72 in 50 minutes and though both were out before the job was finished, South Africa won by three wickets with an over and a half to spare.

At Headingley South Africa won again, this time by 224 runs with two hours to spare. This was a remarkable win, not only because they were 98 for seven at one time on the first day and subsequently were led by 20 runs on first innings but because on the last day they were reduced in effect to two wicket-taking bowlers.

The Springboks had begun their second innings with an opening stand of 176 by McGlew and Goddard. McGlew made 133 and later Russell Endean advertised the South African's depth of batting by making 116 not out and taking the score up to 500.

This left them with eight hours 20 minutes in which to bowl England out. However, Adcock had retired with a broken bone in the foot early in the first innings and the powerfully built Heine, not one to skim lightly over the ground, found the foothold so dangerous that he did not bowl at all on the last day when eight wickets were still to be taken. South Africa were left with only Tayfield and Goddard to take wickets, with Mansell and his tidy but somewhat less than deadly leg-spin to rest them. In fact, Goddard bowled unchanged over the wicket for four hours.

As in the first innings there was a fascinating duel between May and Tayfield which Tayfield ended by having May lbw when he was 97. His great assets were his control and his subtle variations of flight and pace. He was not a prodigious spinner of the ball but every so often one would turn more – and more quickly – than expected and would surprise the best of batsmen. Tayfield and Goddard shared the wickets equally, having bowled 47.1 and 62 overs respectively.

So they came to The Oval for the last Test level at 2–2. Adcock was out of the South African side but Cheetham was back. England in their search for opening batsmen had moved on from Kenyon and Graveney, who had opened in the first three Tests, to Bailey and Lowson at Headingley and now to John Ikin and Brian Close. Both were left-handers, as was Willie Watson, who was picked for the first time in this series, and Dick Spooner, the wicket-keeper, who sometimes opened for Warwickshire. It was hoped that Goddard and Tayfield would find left-handers less easy to pin down.

The match started on a Saturday and the toss, which England won, was more than usually important because rain was forecast. It arrived soon after lunch when Compton and Watson were struggling to repair a start of 69 for three and it continued far into the night. On the Monday 17 wickets fell, mostly to the slower bowlers, and South Africa, having bowled out England for 151, succumbed for 112 themselves.

It was early in England's second innings, when they had already lost two wickets, that Tayfield turned a ball sharply to May and hit him on the back leg. May had then made four. He was given not out by umpire Tom Barclay. The likeliest explanation was that the ball was deemed to have done too much and would have missed the leg-stump. May went on to make 89 not out, a match-winning innings without doubt, for South Africa now needed 244. No side had made 200 in the fourth innings at The Oval that year.

Though John Waite, coming in at 33 for four, made 60 against Laker and Lock very well, it would have needed a miracle for South Africa to win. They took their disappointment extremely well, even though they were entitled to feel aggrieved at two more umpiring decisions early in their innings. In quick succession Endean and McLean were given out lbw by umpire Barclay when sweeping at Laker. There is a theory amongst players that umpires sometimes give batsmen out on the quality of the shot which finishes with them sprawled inelegantly across the line of the stumps, even though they believe they were outside the leg-stump and well forward at the moment of impact.

In the end South Africa lost by 92 runs and lost a marvellous series too. They would have been worthy winners, not least because of their lofty standards of fielding.

During the winter of 1955–6 M.C.C. sent an "A" team to Pakistan under Donald Carr on a three-month tour which eventually received more publicity than many a Test series. The team was mainly a young one and its members, by way of amusing themselves in a country short of other entertainment, had turned to practical joking. They would give each other the so-called "water treatment" wherein an unsuspecting victim would upset a bucket of water over himself as he opened a door.

No offence was caused until one day the trap was set for one of the leading Pakistan umpires, Idris Begh, with whom the M.C.C. party were on friendly terms. Idris Begh seemed to take the soaking in good heart and to accept it for the practical joke which it was intended to be, but when Pakistan players appeared on the scene, he took umbrage. His dignity had been outraged and it was soon being suggested in quarters unfriendly to Britain at the time that this incident was linked to umpiring decisions in the match being played which some of the M.C.C. players had clearly not liked. This was totally untrue. It was merely an ill-considered joke.

Within a few hours, the matter was elevated to the highest diplomatic levels. As it happened, that year's President of M.C.C. was Field Marshal Lord Alexander of Tunis who sent two cables of apology: one to the President of the Pakistan Board of Control and the other to the Governor-General, General Iskander Mirza, who was an old friend of Lord Alexander. The cable also offered to withdraw the M.C.C. team and cancel the rest of the tour. General Mirza replied in friendly terms refusing the offer of cancellation and the tour continued though under some strain. Donald Carr, the captain, took full responsibility when Lord Alexander conducted a subsequent inquiry.

It was a classic example of how dangerous it is to assume that others from different backgrounds have the same sense of humour as oneself. It was not the last time that Indians and Pakistanis saw an affront to their honour where none was intended. However forewarned by their Board at home, cricketers are not trained diplomats.

England's defence of the Ashes against Ian Johnson and the 1956 Australians was less colourful than the previous year's series with South Africa. For this the weather could take much of the blame. A new opening pair, Colin Cowdrey and the left-handed Peter Richardson, were just about the only players on either side to derive satisfaction from the First Test at Trent Bridge which was hopelessly reduced by rain. Their partnerships were worth 53 and 151.

Only once since 1896 have England beaten Australia in a Lord's Test and, though without Lindwall and Davidson, Australia won in 1956 by 185 runs. There were several brilliant catches, the most spectacular by Richie Benaud in the gully after Cowdrey had hit the ball in the middle of the bat. McDonald and Burke made 137 in their opening stand on the first day and Australia were always the likely winners thereafter, though it took a vigorous innings of 97 by Benaud on the fourth day to give them a decisive lead.

Peter May had been short of support in both innings at Lord's and the selectors made the bold but widely criticised decision of picking one of their own number, Cyril Washbrook, for Headingley. Washbrook was 41 and had not played in a Test match for five years. Now captaining Lancashire and batting number four, he had been making runs consistently. He was still a fine player of fast bowling and it was that which had been giving England most trouble.

The series really turned from the moment that Washbrook came out of the old Headingley pavilion on the first morning to join Peter May with the score 17 for three. It was not until 6.25 that evening that they were separated when May pulled a high full-pitch from Johnson downwards and was superbly caught by Lindwall at square-leg for 101. They had put on 187. Next day Washbrook was lbw to Benaud for 98 and the England innings subsided to 325. But the ball was now turning and Australia were 81 for six by the end of the second day.

Then the light faded and rain set in. There was no play on the Saturday and after a wet Sunday operations were not resumed until just before lunch on Monday. Keith Miller, who had not been fit to bowl in the match, fought hard for more than two hours but Australia followed on 182 behind and were bowled out a second time for 140. The series was level at 1–1 with two Tests to come.

The weather was much the same for the Fourth Test at Old Trafford which was to produce one of the most extraordinary bowling feats of all time. No one in the history of first-class cricket had ever taken 18 wickets in a match. Jim Laker took 19, his nine for 37 in the first innings (in 16.4 overs) being followed by 10 for 53 in the second in 51.2 overs.

In this match England's first five batsmen were all amateurs and they made the bulk of the 459 scored at a brisk pace in the first day and a half. Ian Johnson and Benaud bowled 47 overs each on a pitch already showing signs of taking spin. Richardson (104) and Cowdrey (80) launched the innings with a stand of 174. The Rev. David Sheppard followed with 113, though he had played only four innings for Sussex that season. May's 43 was his lowest score of the series. Bailey at number five made 20.

Australia began batting soon after lunch on the Friday and, despite a steady opening stand of 48 between McDonald and Burke, were bowled out for 84. Jim Burke had the distinction of being the only Australian batsman in the match not out twice to Laker.

Whereas Australia's first innings had lasted only 40.4 overs, beginning and ending on Friday afternoon, the second innings began on Friday evening and did not end until just before half past five on Tuesday. There was only 45 minutes' play on the Saturday and only an hour amid wind and rain on Monday when Australia did not lose a wicket. On the last day, Tuesday, play began only 10 minutes late and Colin McDonald, who had retired hurt on the Friday with a knee injury, played safely through to lunch with Ian Craig.

After lunch the sun came out and batting became fraught with difficulty as Laker, from the Stretford end, began to work swiftly through the middle order. One of the many weird facts about this amazing innings is that when McDonald was out after tea for 89, it was more than four days since he began his innings. Another is that Tony Lock bowled more overs in the second innings and in the match than Laker.

Tony Lock in that part of his career always bowled as if expecting to take a wicket with every ball. Laker, a prodigious spinner of the ball, nagged away at the batsman with his well-controlled variety of off-breaks. Earlier in that month of July 1956 Lock had himself taken all 10 wickets for Surrey against Kent at Blackheath. Laker had already taken all 10 Australian wickets that season, 10 for 88 in 46 overs for Surrey at The Oval. That was in the first innings of the Australians' first defeat by a county for 44 years. Lock took seven for 49 in the second innings.

It might be thought that Ian Johnson and his team did not look forward with much enthusiasm to a final meeting with Laker and Lock on their own ground, though victory at The Oval would have enabled Australia to halve the series.

In fact, Miller and Archer had the England batsmen in some difficulty on the first day and it took a fourth-wicket stand of 156 between Peter May and Denis Compton to restore a start of 66 for three. When it ended, 222 for three quickly became 247 all out. May was left 83 not out.

Compton's latest operation, for the removal of his right kneecap, had delayed the start of his season until July but he made 94 with most of the old charm and freedom. Rain in the second half of the match made a draw almost inevitable, especially as England, only 45 ahead on first innings, took precautions to ensure that their hard-won 2–1 lead in the series was not lost. Even so, Australia, needing to bat for only two hours after May's declaration, lost five wickets for 27 – Laker finishing with another set of bizarre figures, 18–14–8–3.

After five strenuous months in England and Scotland, the Australians of 1956 had not finished yet. After a short holiday in Europe, they gathered in Rome and flew to Karachi for their first Test match with Pakistan.

On the matting, of which they had scant experience, they were bowled out for 80 on the first day by the only two bowlers used in an innings occupying 53.1 overs, Fazal Mahmood and Khan Mohammad. It was the slowest full day's cricket ever recorded – only 95 runs were scored – but to many of the Australian players it was one of the most absorbing, such were the problems posed by the bowlers on the matting. Needing 69 to win, Pakistan spent two and three-quarter hours and 49 overs making the runs and winning by nine wickets. In the match Fazal bowled 75 overs and took 13 wickets for 114.

The Australians then played three Test matches in India, winning two of them, before slipping back into Australia in mid-November as athletes, games players and others from the rest of the world arrived for the Olympic Games in Melbourne.

Any cricket-lover in Australia at that time would have been depressed by the standing of the game in the eyes of the public there. They had some of the world's best athletes, swimmers and lawn tennis players. They seemed to be prepared to write off a game in which they had just lost to England and Pakistan.

Yet Australian cricket was as resilient as ever. In the following southern summer, with Ian Craig as captain, they went to South Africa and won 3–0. In 1958–9, under Richie Benaud, they easily beat England 4–0 and by 1960–1 when they beat West Indies 2–1 in a historic Test series which began with the tied Test in Brisbane and captured the public attention to an unprecedented degree, cricket was re-established as a game of colour and excitement.

Peter May's years of captaincy continued with a halved series in South Africa and wins at home against West Indies in 1957 and New Zealand in 1958. The batting was never quite right, for it relied too much for comfort on the captain. Colin Cowdrey had not been at his best for some time and was probably not helped by being required to open the innings. However, Denis Compton's 94 and 35 not out at The Oval had won him a place on what was to be his final tour and Douglas Insole, the Essex captain, who had not always been available for previous tours, went to South Africa as May's vice-captain. His homely bottom-handed method may not have been a thing of beauty but it was consistently effective and served him well in South Africa.

After the South Africans' buoyant performance in England 18 months before, the M.C.C. team can have been under no illusions about the severity of their task. Had they known of what the fates had in store for their captain, they would have been shocked.

From the first match against Western Province, May operated on a different plane from the other batsmen. In his first four first-class innings he made 162, 118, 124 not out and 206, and he made a fifth hundred in Durban before the First Test. But in the Test series he averaged 15. Certainly the Test pitches were such that no batsman on either side averaged as much as 40, yet May had just averaged 90 against Australia on pitches which were far from plumb.

It was inexplicable. The South Africans fielded superbly and in the early Tests May was out to some spectacular catches. Confidence can certainly be undermined by the feeling that if the ball is lifted even an inch off the ground, someone will catch it. But he went on making runs in the provincial matches, including a hundred against Western Province between the last two Tests.

The captain's shortage of runs meant that England batted stickily. The pitches did not encourage adventure; nor did the South African bowlers, Heine, Adcock, Goddard and Tayfield. Yet England won the first two Tests by large margins.

Both in Johannesburg, in the first Test match played on the new Wanderers ground, and in Cape Town the toss was important and South Africa were bowled out in the last innings for 72. The coincidences did not stop there, for at Newlands Russell Endean became the first batsman to be given out "handled the ball" in a Test match – and he had been the wicket-keeper hampered when Len Hutton had been out "obstructing the field" at The Oval in 1955.

Trevor Bailey, who opened the innings throughout the series with Peter Richardson, hurried South Africa to defeat in Johannesburg with five for 20 in the second innings and eight for 53 in the match. John Wardle, with the left-arm bowler's chinaman and googlies, took seven for 36 in the last innings at Newlands and 12 for 89 in the match.

The Second Test was the only one of the five in which the Springbok captain Jackie McGlew was fit to play and it was under Clive van Ryneveld that South Africa made their recovery. After an opening stand of 115 by Richardson and Bailey in Durban, England could only draw the Third Test. Needing 232 to win the Fourth in Johannesburg, they reached 147 for two but succumbed to Hugh Tayfield's nine for 113 and lost by 17 runs. On a relaid pitch in Port Elizabeth the toss was probably all-important. South Africa won it and the 164 they made in the first innings off 87 overs eventually led them to victory by 58 runs.

It had been a disappointing series for England, and to some extent for their captain, but within a few weeks Peter May was playing probably his most influential and best remembered innings. West Indies, still captained by John Goddard, had arrived in England without, so it seemed, having found fast bowlers to emulate the feats of Constantine and Martindale in the 1930s.

There was one, Wesley Hall, who had a splendid action but he was only 19 and was considered to be on an educational visit. He did not play in a Test match. The fastest was a certain Roy Gilchrist but he was wild and had the reputation of being a greater danger to the batsman's head than to his stumps. He soon dropped out of Test cricket after being sent home from India for disciplinary reasons.

Yet England were still bowled out for 186 on the first day of the First Test played at Edgbaston for 28 years. Ominously, it was by Sonny Ramadhin, the familiar menace of seven years before. As he took his seven wickets for 49 on a good pitch, the spectre of 1950 seemed to be manifesting itself again.

West Indies then made 474. Of this total Collie Smith, a tremendous all-rounder, contributed 161. An off-spinner and a quick-footed batsman bursting with strokes, he must have had a great impact on the Test cricket of the next decade but for his tragic death in a car accident in England two years later at the age of 26.

England were batting again on the Saturday afternoon and soon lost Richardson and Insole to Ramadhin. May and Brian Close batted through the last hour and the young England captain had the weekend in which to consider what was needed. He had both the technique and the determination required and he set himself to wear Ramadhin down. In Colin Cowdrey, who came in when Close was out early on Monday morning, he had an ideal partner – a batsman with a wide-ranging technique who had the skill and patience to follow the plan implicitly.

They batted through the rest of the day and it was not until Tuesday afternoon that Cowdrey, who had been playing some sparkling strokes since passing 100, was caught at long-on off Smith. Eight hours 20 minutes had passed and 411 runs had been scored since West Indies took a wicket. May went on to make 285 and was still undefeated when he declared at 583 for four. He had batted for nearly 10 hours.

The West Indian batsmen, seven of them, were then out so swiftly to Trueman, Laker and Lock that it seemed that an earlier declaration might have won the match for England. But May was not going to allow a talented batting side beginning Kanhai, Pairaudeau, Walcott, Sobers, Weekes, Smith and Worrell to recover. The rewards for the great partnership and the quelling of Ramadhin lay in the future.

The effect on Ramadhin's performance was remarkable. From

the moment that May came in at Edgbaston until the end of the five-Test series Ramadhin took only five wickets. Though in all first-class matches on the tour he took 119 wickets at 13 apiece, his 14 wickets in Test matches cost 39 each.

At Lord's, where good fast bowlers were in their element in those days, England won by an innings in three days. Trevor Bailey took 11 wickets. The Saturday crowd saw Everton Weekes make a brilliant 90 before West Indies succumbed.

At Trent Bridge England made over 600 (Richardson 126, Graveney 258, May 104). Frank Worrell carried his bat through the West Indies' innings for 191 not out but they followed on. Collie Smith then made 168 and Dennis Atkinson and John Goddard just held out for long enough to earn a draw.

At Headingley England won by an innings again, this time by just after lunch on the third day. Peter Loader, playing instead of the injured Statham, took six for 36 in the first innings and nine wickets in all, including the first hat-trick by an England bowler in a Test match this century. It was a measure of England's bowling strength at the time that a bowler of the class of Loader, with his wiry athletic frame and effective variations of pace, should be only in reserve. Not for the first or the last time the Headingley Test pitch came under scrutiny and the weather was no help to West Indies. It is still hard to believe that such a formidable batting side, with as good a batsman as Gerry Alexander at number nine, could have failed to make 150 in either innings. England made 279 (May 69, Cowdrey and Sheppard 68 each) and that was enough.

The sight of The Oval Test pitch that year must stick in the memory of those who saw it, anyhow in the memory of those with an eye for colour. The outfield was a lush green; the pitch was pink. The ball was turning on the first day but Peter Richardson, first with a new opening partner in Sheppard and then with Graveney, had the scoreboard showing 238 for one before he was bowled by Smith for 107. Graveney was always a very fine player of spin and he made it all look simple. As the ball turned, he helped it on its way and made 164 in an innings of rare artistry. Yet after failing in two Test matches in 1956 he had been left out of the touring side to South Africa.

Laker and Lock were soon bowling and by half past two on the third afternoon had bowled West Indies out twice for 89 and 86. Tony Lock took 11 wickets for 48. What part, it may be wondered, had Ramadhin played in these conditions? The answer is that though he had only taken one Test wicket since Edgbaston nearly three months before, he was still played with care. He bowled 53.3 overs and took four for 109.

Peter May's pre-eminence among the batsmen of his day continued in 1958 when he was in his second season as captain of Surrey who were champions for the seventh successive year. He headed the first-class averages with 63.74. Second was Willie Watson. Those who saw May batting at close quarters and most often, not least the umpires, would tell you that he was the best English batsman to have come on the scene since the War.

The 1958 New Zealanders under John Reid were very weak – England bowled them out five times for under 100 – and the series in a wet summer was poor preparation for England's tour of Australia that winter. There they were well beaten by a resurgent Australia under Richie Benaud.

India in 1959, captained by D.K. Gaekwad, were even less successful than New Zealand and lost all five Test matches in a beautiful English summer.

In July 1959, towards the end of a crucial Championship match against Yorkshire at Bradford in which May had played a major part, he left the field with an ailment which required an immediate operation. He did not play again for nearly six months and then, while leading England in West Indies, he suffered a recurrence and had to come home after playing in only three Tests. This time it was more than a year before he played again and even in 1961 he was so unsure of his form and fitness that he asked not to be considered for the First Test against Australia. He played at Lord's, where England lost a home Test for the first time for five years, under the captaincy of Colin Cowdrey. May only resumed the captaincy in the Third Test at Headingley.

This was a match of sudden transformations. The pitch, rightly as it proved, had been viewed with great suspicion and when Australia won the toss, they soon put themselves in what at tea seemed to be a winning position. Their score stood at 187 for two and Neil Harvey and Norman O'Neill, a handsome stroke-player on his first tour of England, were going well.

Brian Statham had dropped out through injury and Trueman shared the new ball with Les Jackson, a fine fiery fast-medium bowler with something of a slinging action whose only other Test match had been played 12 years before. He was now 40.

It proved to be a pitch on which the less expert batsmen on both sides were out of their depth. In an hour and a half after tea on that first day Australia were out for 237, Trueman bowling at his fastest to take five wickets. England passed this score with only four wickets down but had to work hard to earn a lead of 62. Neil Harvey then reached 50 for the second time in the match and, at 99 for two in mid-afternoon on the third day, Australia looked capable of setting England an unenviable task in the last innings on this pitch of varied pace and bounce.

Yet by a quarter to six the match was over. When Trueman started a new spell, Harvey mishit his third ball to cover-point. At this, May and Trueman decided that he should switch to a shorter run and bowl off-cutters. Trueman did this with improved accuracy. The effect was sensational. The remaining seven wickets fell for 21 runs and in Trueman's spell of 7.5 overs he took six wickets for six runs. England needed only 59 and won by eight wickets.

The Fourth Test at Old Trafford also fluctuated. For four days England seemed to be working slowly into a winning position as they built up a first-innings lead of 177 and by early on the last morning had taken nine wickets for 334. But the left-handed Alan Davidson hit the off-spinner David Allen for 20 in an over. Allen, who had taken the last three wickets and had hitherto conceded barely a run an over, was taken off and Davidson and Graham McKenzie, who was on his first tour at the age of 20, added 98 for the last wicket.

This made all the difference. Instead of needing around 160, England had to make 256. Only very rarely had a side made this many to win a Test in England and, with only three hours 50 minutes remaining, it would be against the clock.

It would not have been a surprise if England had approached their task cautiously, leaving the decision about going for the runs until later when they knew what wickets they had in hand. But events had soon got out of hand. Their left-handed opening pair of Raman Subba Row and Geoff Pullar made 40 in quick time and Subba Row stayed on while Ted Dexter played an innings of the utmost brilliance – 76 in 84 minutes. When he was out, only 106 runs were needed with plenty of time left. England were now committed to going on with the assault, with all the risks which that would bring on a worn pitch.

Richie Benaud had been prevented by a shoulder injury from bowling at his best on the tour but by now he had set himself to bowl his leg-spin into the rough outside the right-handers' leg-stump. Having had Dexter caught at the wicket, he bowled May round his legs first ball. May had in fact made 95 very well in the first innings but it is the misjudgement in the second innings which is remembered.

Once started downhill on a slippery slope, there was no relief for England. Australia won by 54 runs with 20 minutes to spare. Leading by 2–1 in the series, they had much the better of the final Test at The Oval, though after rain England earned a draw.

That winter Peter May retired from Test cricket, not because of ill-health, declining form or through the disappointment of having lost a Test series. He was 32 and despite his long illness had captained England in 41 Tests, more than anyone else. He had a growing family to support and was impatient to develop his career in the world of insurance. From cricket he had earned nothing but honour. He was, as it proved, to be one of the last of the amateurs.

9

Surrey's Seven Years on Top

TOWARDS the end of the 1950s big changes were on their way in English cricket. On the whole the game had adapted itself reasonably well to changing times but it was clear that more would have to be done. Nobody had expected the huge crowds of the early post-war years to continue because the counter-attractions were now so numerous. Moreover, the county grounds, mostly dating back to the last century, were badly in need of modernisation.

In 1957 M.C.C. had appointed a special committee under H.S. Altham to review the conduct of the game and its future welfare. It covered what was to become familiar ground, the lbw Law, the limitation of on-side fielders, limitation of first-innings overs, preparation of pitches and a possible knock-out competition. These, of course, were proposals only for experiment in English domestic cricket. Some were adopted by the Advisory Committee. The amendment in the lbw Law, designed to reduce padding-up, was to become incorporated in the Laws. Others, such as the first-innings limitation of overs, were tried sooner or later and, like the abolition of the follow-on, were discarded. Whatever else, the cricket administrators of that period can scarcely be accused of not experimenting, even if the counties did not always choose the right experiments to back. There was, however, still a long way to go before the idea of "marketing" the game took root.

The County Championship was not exactly a help in stimulating interest in domestic cricket, for as the 1950s neared their end there had been only one Champion County for seven years. Familiarity breeds apathy and towards the end of their extraordinary achievement, Surrey's very fine side were being taken for granted.

For the first five years the driving force had been a remarkable cricketer, Stuart Surridge, who was 34 when he took over the captaincy in 1952. He was an amateur, a director of his family firm of sports good manufacturers. Among his virtues was the priceless one of enthusiasm. He had come up through the lower levels of Surrey cricket and since the War, with help from the great coach of the day, Alfred Gover, had developed a bowling action which would not have won prizes for grace but was effective enough to have earned him the new ball with Alec Bedser. That was not all. He was a magnificent fielder close to the wicket and a powerful late-order hitter of the ball.

Under the previous captain, Michael Barton, a pre-war Oxford batsman, Surrey had been quietly developing into a promising side and had earned a half-share of the Championship with Lancashire in 1950. They had finished sixth behind Warwickshire in 1951 but in 1952 they won 20 of their 28 matches and took the Championship outright for the first time since 1914. Throughout his five-year reign Surridge had to make do with reserves when Bedser, May, Laker, Lock, Arthur McIntyre once, and later Peter Loader were required for Test matches. In 1952 May, still up at Cambridge, played in only eight Championship matches.

One always has to be careful not to imply that sides prosper through their bowlers' feats on their home pitches. Figures are usually produced showing that the bowlers took as many or more wickets on opponents' grounds. So it was with Surrey. The Oval in the mid-1950s was a very different place from the ground with the dry fast outfield and the splendid batting pitches of pre-war and immediate post-war seasons.

Now the outfield was lush and the ball kept its shine. The pitches would soon take spin with a rounded bounce and held something for good bowlers of all types. The other counties might be able to match Surrey in the first innings but it was only very rarely that they also had the spinners who could keep up with Laker and Lock in the second innings. Often it was the speed with which the Surrey bowlers ran through sides that defeated the opposition and the weather. Peter May recounts a match in 1954 when, after Worcestershire had been bowled out for 25, he and Ken Barrington had painfully raised Surrey's reply to 92 for three. At this point Surridge declared. "We thought he'd gone off his head," says May. But Worcestershire were then bowled out again for 40 and by half past twelve on the second morning Surrey had earned the points they needed to clinch that year's Championship before the unsettled weather could stop them..

What The Oval pitches undoubtedly did, weather permitting, was guarantee victory for one side or the other. Scores of 300 were rare. Yet it was on these pitches that Peter May averaged 50 or 60 in the Championship.

Much depended on the strength of the reserves on whom Surrey relied when their Test players were away. Eric Bedser, who opened the innings, was scarcely needed as an off-spinner when the side was at full strength but was an all-rounder for whom any side would have found a place.

Of the other regular players, Bernard Constable was a consistent batsman at number three or four, Tom Clark was a fine driver of the ball, Arthur McIntyre was one of the best wicket-keepers in the country and a quick-footed middle-order batsman. The first Championship was won with the pre-war heroes Laurie Fishlock and Jack Parker, then 45 and 39 respectively. By the end of the seven years, Micky Stewart and Ken Barrington were established as two of the best young batsmen in the country.

In 1952 Surrey drew away from mid-June and won comfortably. The three matches which they lost were all when their leading players were absent. They had a stiffer task in 1953 when their best players were away recovering the Ashes. Sussex, captained by David Sheppard that year, put in a determined challenge for the Championship which they have still never won and in mid-August Leicestershire suddenly appeared on top of the table for the first time ever. Raman Subba Row, born and bred in Surrey, made a lot of runs after the University season as Surrey came from behind but he had still to do his National Service and when that was over he became captain of Northamptonshire.

Surrey came from even further behind in 1954. Eighth nearing the end of July, they won nine of their last 10 matches. When they looked like being thwarted by rain at Cheltenham, Surridge hustled everyone on to the field when the rain temporarily eased and swiftly finished off the match by taking six for 31 himself before a storm soaked the ground.

In the fine summer of 1955 Surrey had the astonishing record of winning 23 of their 28 matches and losing the other five. Yet Yorkshire, now a strong bowling side, won 21 and only drew two matches. Of the two matches between them, Surrey won at The Oval but Yorkshire won a battle royal at Headingley in June. After being 102 runs behind on first innings, their fast bowlers,

Fred Trueman and the left-arm Michael Cowan, reduced Surrey to 27 for seven on the second evening in a dim light and a frenzied atmosphere which made a Test match seem all sweetness. As usual they finished the season better than anyone, even winning a match at The Oval when the Middlesex fast bowlers, John Warr and Alan Moss, had them six for four on the first day.

Though they won at Leicester by seven wickets in the middle of May they had been the sufferers from one of the most amazing pieces of bowling in cricket history. They were replying to Leicestershire's modest total of 114 and had reached 42 for one with Peter May going well when Charles Palmer, the Leicestershire captain, decided to bowl an over after tea to allow his two spinners to change ends.

In that over he bowled May, so he stayed on and with his accurate medium pace took eight successive wickets without conceding a run. Every time he passed the bat he hit the stumps. Seven of his eight victims were bowled. Surrey were all out for 77 which included a last-wicket stand of 10. Palmer finished with figures of 14–12–7–8. This was on 21 May and until then he had bowled only two overs that season.

The win in 1956 was of more than usual importance to Surrey because it was to be Stuart Surridge's last season. Moreover, no county had previously been outright champions in five successive years. In a season of many interruptions through rain Surrey's ability to dispose of opposition in quick time was decisive.

In 1957 and 1958 Surrey continued their winning run under Peter May, in 1957 by the huge margin of 94 points. They won 21 matches against the 15 of Northants who were second. The win in 1958 was gained in spite of the absence of Alec Bedser through pneumonia in the first half of the season. Peter May was in tremendous form and in the two matches in which Surrey beat the touring New Zealanders by an innings he made 165 and 116 not out. The highest New Zealand total in their four innings against Surrey was 118.

There had been no strong evidence that Surrey's seventh successive win would be the last in the winning run, especially as Yorkshire, who had always seemed to be the side most likely to dethrone them, finished only 11th. Yorkshire were not the force of other days in this difficult season which culminated with the sacking of Wardle after he had been picked for M.C.C.'s coming tour of Australia and New Zealand.

This was to prove a bigger blow to England and Peter May

than it was to Yorkshire and their new captain Ronnie Burnet. In late July 1958 the Yorkshire Committee decided that they had had enough of Wardle's allegedly disruptive presence in the dressing-room and told him that he would not be required after that season. Wardle responded with an article in the *Daily Mail* criticising Burnet and other Yorkshire players. A fortnight later the M.C.C. Committee interviewed Wardle and "after very careful consideration" withdrew the invitation for the tour.

Wardle had been no trouble on previous tours on which he had become ever more important to the side. On hard overseas pitches his wrist spin, which he had developed to a high degree of accuracy, was irreplaceable. He had been able to perfect it over the years because he was still worth his place as an orthodox left-arm spinner and an aggressive left-hand late-order batsman. In England this form of bowling was a useful sideline. In Australia it could be a major weapon.

John Wardle had finished the previous tour of Australia in 1954–5 by taking eight wickets in the last Test. In South Africa two years later he took 26 Test wickets at 13.80 each, including seven for 36 at Newlands when South Africa were bowled out for 72 in the last innings. An indication of how he might have fared in Australia in 1958–9 is provided by the fact that Australia's most successful bowler in that series was a wrist-spinner, their new captain Richie Benaud, who took 31 wickets at 18 each.

Without Wardle, England's bowling lacked variety. Their team was a strong-looking one on paper but contained several players nearing the end of their Test career and was a sitting target for a vigorous young Australia side including a dashing new batsman in Norman O'Neill.

During 1959 Surrey introduced another young batsman with a big future – John Edrich, a left-handed cousin of W.J. of Middlesex – but in a lovely summer there were signs that the Oval pitches were easing. Both home and away, the Surrey bowlers were finding it harder to bowl sides out twice. Tony Lock had returned from Australia with a changed action which offended no one and in a dry summer, and on pitches now to be covered for much longer than hitherto, was not the destroyer of previous years.

Yet the biggest factor in Surrey's decline was the loss of Peter May who on 21 July left the field in Bradford after ensuring that Surrey had won their second victory of the season over Yorkshire. It was to be 21 months before he was fit again to play for Surrey.

Alec Bedser was an admirable deputy captain but May's batting was inevitably missed.

Much of Yorkshire's success in 1959 was owed to Raymond Illingworth's performance with both bat and ball, and Fred Trueman had one of his best seasons. When they needed 215 in 105 minutes at Hove to win the Championship, two young bats-men – Brian Stott, a left-hander, and Doug Padgett – did them proud and they raced home by five wickets with seven minutes to spare.

It was, above all, a triumph for Ronnie Burnet in the second and last year of his captaincy. In the previous year he had been brought in at the age of 39 to bring order to the dressing-room. Though he had not previously played in a first-class match, he had been highly successful with the Yorkshire second eleven, the Minor County Champions in 1957. In 1959 his particular brand of discipline and encouragement did the trick again at the higher level.

Surrey were not to win the Championship again until 1971 but Yorkshire were entering a prosperous period in which they were Champions seven times out of 10, yielding only to Hampshire in 1961 and Worcestershire in 1964 and 1965. It was no coincidence that this period of success ended soon after the introduction of the instant registration of overseas players. This helped to spread the honours round counties who had seldom or never won the Championship previously but it put Yorkshire at a serious disadvantage.

10

The Gentlemen become Players

BY the early 1960s events in England were moving towards the abolition of amateur status in English first-class cricket. This had not been recommended by the Duke of Norfolk's committee in 1958. There was certainly not yet a dearth of good amateurs, even if several counties now had professional captains and England had been led successfully by a professional, the now Sir Leonard Hutton, knighted in 1956.

Gentlemen and Players had remained an attractive fixture and the last in the long line, in 1962, had had an extra interest; the M.C.C. captain in Australia and New Zealand was about to be announced.

There were three candidates, Ted Dexter, Colin Cowdrey and the Reverend David Sheppard who was shortly to be taking a sabbatical and would be available for his second and last tour of Australia. Any of the three would have graced the job. In the event, Cowdrey was ill and unable to captain the Gentlemen. Sheppard played a fine innings of 112 on the first day and at the end of the second day Dexter was announced as captain in Australia.

A far bigger surprise was the announcement of the 16th Duke of Norfolk as the tour manager. He had been President of M.C.C. five years before and had taken his own team of first-class players to West Indies. To some who did not know him it may have seemed a quaint appointment in this day and age, but the Duke was liked and respected by first-class cricketers, many of whom had played on his beautiful ground at Arundel. For some years he had entertained visiting teams there for a one-day practice match soon after their arrival in England, a happy tradition carried on after his death in 1975 by his widow, Lavinia, Duchess of

Norfolk and the Friends of Arundel Castle Cricket Club.

In Australia M.C.C. had Alec Bedser as assistant-manager and when the Duke's duties as Earl Marshal required his return home for a short time in mid-tour, it was agreed that Billy Griffith, the new Secretary of M.C.C., should stand in for him.

The Duke's appointment lent a considerable fillip to the tour, not least in Australia where the public was greatly intrigued by the presence in a visiting cricket team not only of an Anglican priest in David Sheppard but of a real live duke who was the leading Roman Catholic layman in the United Kingdom.

While the tour was in progress, the Advisory Committee, mostly comprising the first-class counties, the precursor of the Test and County Cricket Board, voted to do away with amateur status and to make all first-class players just cricketers.

The times when amateurs came out of different gates from professionals and stayed at different hotels were past. Only on a few grounds was there still a separate dressing-room for amateurs. But many of those who voted for the abolition must have done so with a heavy heart. No one lamented the end of the amateur more than the old type of professional who had seen how valuable to the game the independent status of the amateur was. An amateur county captain was an important link between players and committees. The amateur played with a spirit and enthusiasm which brought a breath of fresh air to first-class cricket.

Since the War Oxford and Cambridge, especially the latter, had gone on supplying England with Test players such as May, Sheppard, Cowdrey, Bailey, Dexter and Warr. Admittedly some had to retire when still in their prime. Peter May left the Test arena at 31. Subba Row was only 29 when he retired after making two hundreds in the 1961 series against Australia. John Warr was still taking a lot of wickets when he left Middlesex for a full-time job in the City in 1960. All three were destined to reach the highest levels of cricket administration but had reached the point where if they wanted to prosper in their various businesses they would have to stop playing and give them full-time attention.

Unlike most other games, such as rugby union, which did not allow their players to be paid for writing books, even after their retirement from playing, cricket's definition of the amateur was delightfully simple. He was an amateur if he was not paid for playing. It was this simplicity which became its great weakness. When some of the best players in England were amateurs, there was nothing to stop the commercial interests, which were beginning to realise the advantages of linking their products with cricket, from engaging amateurs to advertise their wares.

This was clearly a recipe for ill-feeling. Professionals understandably regarded advertising as their legitimate "perks". A situation in which amateurs would make more out of the game than professionals was clearly intolerable. There was only one solution – make them all just "cricketers".

Amateurism in cricket had always been a peculiarly English arrangement born of the relative shortness of the season and the concentrated nature of English first-class cricket. Other cricket-playing countries had climates which allowed them to play for seven months of the year or more if they wished. Matches were spaced out and players did not have to absent themselves totally from their jobs during the cricket season.

A quarter of a century later, the effects of abolishing the amateur had to be seen in conjunction with social and educational changes and with the growth of sponsorship. There were more players coming into first-class cricket from the breeding-grounds of the former amateurs, the independent schools and the universities, because they had the facilities, the coaching and the encouragement not found at state schools. The clubs had done a splendid job by setting up or expanding youth sections and now there were Test players in England who had not played organised cricket at school. Moreover, the players from the seats of learning which supplied the old type of amateur were now often more commercially-minded than those with fewer "A" levels. The I.Q. of some county cricketers was now alarmingly high to some who wrote about the game and whose academic achievements fell some way short of those of the classical scholars about whose cricket they were writing.

Many players now have degrees or qualifications from sixth form colleges, universities, or teacher training colleges before they become full-time cricketers. With these behind them, they have been able to delay taking up their chosen profession for a few years and have taken the opportunity to see something of the world by accepting winter coaching and playing jobs in South Africa, Australia, New Zealand and South America.

There was one other event in the early 1960s which was to have long-running after-effects – the withdrawal of South Africa from the Imperial Cricket Conference of which it had been a founder-member with England and Australia in 1909. This was necessitated when South Africa left the Commonwealth in 1961.

Rule 5 of the Imperial Cricket Conference (I.C.C.) provided that membership of the Conference would cease should a country cease to be part of the British Commonwealth.

This archaic rule, which in effect was a hindrance to the expansion of the game, was entirely against what M.C.C. stood for – encouraging cricket and cricketers wherever they played.

However, the wording was clear enough and South Africa, closest of all to England through the prowess of cricketing Rhodes Scholars at Oxford and through the engagement of English coaches in their cricket, left the I.C.C. At the time this was not the heavy blow it might have seemed, for the I.C.C. was mainly a forum for discussion on technical matters. In the days before air travel became commonplace the more distant member countries did not always send their administrators to the annual meetings at Lord's but were represented by expatriates or friends resident in the United Kingdom. Moreover, though Test matches involving South Africa would now nominally be unofficial, they were still Test matches and sternly fought.

Why, it may be asked, did Pakistan not have to drop out of the I.C.C. when it left the Commonwealth in 1972? The answer is that by then, in 1965, the I.C.C. had changed its name to the International Cricket Conference, had changed its rules of membership and had begun enlarging itself by giving associate membership to countries such as Denmark and Holland who had never been in the Commonwealth.

11

Boost of the Tied Test

WHILE English cricket was seeking ways of modernising itself further, the game in Australia received an immense boost by the visit of West Indies under Frank Worrell. In two previous tours of Australia, one before the War and one after, West Indian teams had not been seen at their best and had lost each series 4–1.

More recently, in 1955, the Australians had gone straight to the Caribbean after losing at home to Len Hutton's England team and had no difficulty in restoring their confidence by winning three Test matches and drawing the other two. Though they lost in England in 1956, they had recovered the Ashes in 1958–9 and were entitled to fancy their chance against the West Indian side which arrived in October 1960.

By contrast, West Indies had a modest recent record. Two years before they had lost a series in Pakistan 2–1 and earlier in 1960 England had beaten them 1–0 in the Caribbean despite the illness of their captain Peter May who had handed over to Colin Cowdrey for the last two Tests. It had not been a particularly happy series, having been marred by a riot and much short-pitched bowling. There had been some unrest concerning the captaincy of Gerry Alexander, a splendid batsman-wicket-keeper who had been in the Cambridge University side of 1952 with Peter May. He had also won an amateur international cap for England at football.

The West Indians arrived in Australia with Frank Worrell as captain, as it were by popular demand. The other two "Ws", Weekes and Walcott, had retired and though they had two young players of the highest class in Sobers and Kanhai and one of the best fast bowlers in the world in Wesley Hall, there was still plenty to prove to Australian crowds. Gary Sobers' record Test score of

365 not out against Pakistan in Jamaica two and a half years before was an interesting statistic but it had not yet quite sunk in that the same young man, still only 24, was also capable of winning matches as a left-arm fast-medium bowler, a left-arm spinner in both orthodox and unorthodox styles and as a superlative close fielder of lightning reactions.

The preliminaries scarcely flattered West Indies, for Western Australia beat them and New South Wales beat them by an innings. Yet the Test series was given a magical start. The First Test in Brisbane was a tie, the first in Test history – and from this spectacular launching pad the series took off.

On the first day of this great match West Indies recovered from a start of 65 for three, initially through a brilliant 132 by Sobers. Worrell, Solomon, Alexander and Hall each made fifties in a total of 453. Australia's innings of 505 owed most to Norman O'Neill's 184.

When West Indies had been bowled out for the second time, largely by the left-arm fast-medium Alan Davidson who took 11 wickets in the match, Australia needed 233 to win. They had just over five hours left or, as it proved, 69 eight-ball overs. They were soon in trouble against Hall and were 92 for six.

At this point Richie Benaud joined Davidson and they played so well that with 12 minutes left, only seven runs were still needed. The story goes that hereabouts some New South Welshmen, satisfied that Australia were safely home, left the ground and flew back to Sydney.

Davidson and Benaud had run between the wickets as boldly as they had batted and with excellent judgement. The West Indian fielding had proved far from infallible under pressure, the throwing especially wayward. Suddenly everything changed as the batsmen embarked on what did not appear to be a very hazardous single and Solomon threw down the stumps from mid-wicket to run out Davidson. He had made 80.

Wally Grout came in and took a single off Sobers, so that only six runs were needed from three wickets as Hall began what proved to be the last over.

Off the first ball to Grout the batsmen ran a leg-bye. Five needed and Benaud, who had made 52, with the strike. The second ball of the over was a bouncer which Benaud, hooking, touched to the wicket-keeper. Meckiff played the third ball back to the bowler and they ran a bye to the wicket-keeper off the fourth ball.

With four needed, Grout hit the fifth ball to a great height. As

a posse of fielders and the bowler hovered underneath, the out-
come was predictable. The ball escaped, the batsmen ran a single
and three runs were needed from three balls. Meckiff banged the
sixth ball away on the on-side and they ran two. They then went
for the third run which would have won the match but Conrad
Hunte fired in the perfect throw and though Grout dived full
length, he was run out.

There only remained Kline who played the seventh ball on the
on-side. Meckiff was running hard but Solomon repeated his
throw of a few minutes earlier from square-leg. The wicket was
hit again, the world was full of jumping West Indians and history
was made. The match was tied.

Even without this result, it had been a match of splendid cricket.
What the tie did was to capture the imagination of a much wider
audience and to the immense credit of all concerned this lasted
throughout the series.

Australia won the Second Test in Melbourne over the New
Year. Heavy rain penetrated the covers and West Indies had to
follow on after being bowled out for 181. In Sydney where, not
for the last time, the pitch took spin, West Indies won by 222
runs. Eight wickets apiece were taken by the off-spinner Lance
Gibbs and Alf Valentine, one of the two spinning heroes in
England more than 10 years before.

The Fourth Test in Adelaide was a somewhat improbable draw,
for when Australia's number 11, Lindsay Kline, came in to join
the ever-adhesive Ken Mackay, an hour and 50 minutes remained.
They were still there at the end and Australia still led 2–1 in the
series.

"Slasher" Mackay served Australia well as an all-rounder for
some years. A spidery unathletic figure with a loping gait which
was a frequent source of amusement to spectators, he was an
obdurate left-handed batsman who was no joke to bowlers and a
useful medium-paced bowler.

His last stand in Adelaide was not the only unusual event in the
match. Lance Gibbs performed the hat-trick in Australia's first
innings, the first against Australia since J.T. Hearne's feat at Leeds
in 1899. Rohan Kanhai made a hundred in each innings and the
West Indies wicket-keeper and former captain Gerry Alexander
contributed 63 not out and 87 not out. He made 50 or more in
each Test – 108 in Sydney – batting at number seven or eight and
averaged 60 in the series.

The series had been played in such an atmosphere of sustained excitement that it was hard to believe that it would be blessed by a worthy final Test. Yet there was no sense of anti-climax for the 274,404 who watched the Fifth Test in Melbourne, a world record 90,800 of them on the second day, the Saturday.

By early on that second day West Indies, having been put in by Benaud, had been bowled out for 292, after which Bobby Simpson and Colin McDonald put Australia in a strong position with an opening stand of 146. This stand ended in a remarkable piece of bowling. Gary Sobers came on in one of his slower methods half an hour before tea on the Saturday. He bowled to the close of play by which time Australia were finding the going harder. On the Monday morning he took the new ball and bowled until lunch and for an hour afterwards. In all, he bowled 41 successive eight-ball overs from one end and took five wickets, being relieved only when Australia were 335 for nine.

West Indies were only 64 runs behind on first innings and by the end of the third day were 62 ahead with eight wickets standing. Another palpitating finish was in sight.

This was the heyday of Australia's great left-handed all-rounder Alan Davidson and he took five wickets to bring his tally in only four Tests up to 33.

Australia needed 258 to win with time irrelevant, for the two sides had agreed to play an extra day rather than let the series end in anti-climax. In fact, a sixth day was not needed. The pitch was taking some spin now but Bobby Simpson, having played some brilliant strokes against Hall and the new ball, stayed to stop Gibbs and the other West Indian spinners from breaking through. His 92 was a match-winning innings. One of the great mysteries of this era was how Simpson had to wait for another three and a half years before making his first Test hundred. It eventually came at Old Trafford when he was captaining Australia. Less surprising was that he went on in that innings to make 311 and over the next few years added nine other Test hundreds.

Through Simpson's innings in Melbourne Australia always looked the likelier winners though, in a series in which a dramatic change had been frequently just around the corner, the fifth-day crowd of 40,000 could never relax.

Nor did the match die quietly. When Australia were 254 for seven, needing just four more runs, Grout played a late cut to a ball from Valentine and while the West Indian wicket-keeper pointed at a fallen bail, the batsmen ran two. The umpires conferred and, without revealing how the wicket had been broken, allowed the runs to stand. Still to come was Grout's departure and the dropping of a straightforward catch at mid-on before Australia scrambled home by two wickets.

Not since the Olympic successes of Betty Cuthbert in this same arena four years before had Australian enthusiasm run so high. But this time it embraced the opposition as well. Two days later, Melbourne stopped work as the West Indian players drove in open cars through densely packed streets in the city centre.

Cricket had been re-established in Australia. To those who had feared for the game only four years before when Australia were losing at cricket and winning in many other fields, it was something of a miracle, even allowing for the traditional resilience of Australian cricket and indeed the nation's games-playing flair.

In the Melbourne Olympic Games Australians had tended to laugh at their team's participation in the hockey tournament, for the game was not widely played in their country. By the 1980s they were the world champions. They can compete and often beat the best in the world at rugby union football, though they have only New South Wales and Queensland from whom to pick and then in the shadow of the immensely popular rugby league game.

After the tremendous series of 1960–1 a trophy was instituted for competition between Australia and West Indies and subsequent series have been played for the Frank Worrell Trophy. Sadly Sir Frank himself, knighted in 1964, died in 1976 aged 42.

In the early 1960s the state of cricket in England was causing some concern, not least at the money-making end of it. The problem was not so much that England lost both to Australia in 1961 and to West Indies two years later but that in other years they were winning too easily. New Zealand, India, South Africa and Pakistan had not been able to avoid heavy defeats and five-day Test matches which might finish halfway through the third day were becoming difficult to sell to a public which would go to see England beaten by Australia and West Indies but were disappointed by a mis-match in other years. The days when England would lose at home in successive series to India, New Zealand, Pakistan, West Indies and Australia were still a quarter of a century ahead.

There proved to be a solution to this imbalance – a half-season tour. The then President of M.C.C., G.O. (later Sir George) Allen, and the Secretary, Billy Griffith, travelled round the world in order to put the idea of the half-season tour without causing offence. Some countries might have seen the proposition as a slight on their national honour but in fact in New Zealand and South Africa it was highly popular. Few of their players were full-time professionals and there was often difficulty in getting them leave from their jobs for a tour of over five months. A tour of barely three months presented much less of a problem. In New Zealand the proposed change was also attractive because it would allow them more frequent tours to England. Ideally, young players on one tour should profit from the experience gained on it and be all the better for it on their next tour. But when nine years elapsed between tours, as had happened to New Zealand between 1949 and 1958, this seldom materialised.

It was proposed that England's oldest opponents, Australia, should continue to come for a whole season. In due course, West Indies also returned to full-season tours. The influx of immigrants from the Caribbean meant that West Indies were almost playing home matches in England. One might not see many of their supporters in other years but when West Indies were the visitors, they turned out in their tens of thousands.

The new programme of tours was scheduled to start in 1965 with half-season visits from New Zealand and South Africa.

At the same time ways were being sought to make the County Championship and England's domestic first-class cricket more popular. For some time this had been done by public exhortations to batsmen to play more strokes. This merely made more people think that the game could not be worth watching. The main reasons for the diminishing crowds were twofold: one was that it was part of the inevitable decline from the high levels of the immediate post-war years when there were few counter-attractions; the other was that, as in almost every other sport, television had increased the public interest in the big events, at the expense of the minor ones.

For some years a knockout single-innings competition of a limited number of overs had been mooted and eventually on 20 December 1961 the counties voted to launch it in 1963. Sponsorship was almost unknown but the Advisory Committee accepted a block grant of £6500 from Gillette for this new venture and the Gillette Cup was born.

Some predictions at the time were accurate, some well wide of the mark. It was feared that limited-over cricket would produce an orgy of medium-paced bowling, which it did. There was also some idea that amateurs or recently retired players such as Peter May and Denis Compton would be able to take one day off from the office whereas they could not manage longer. However, it was soon realised that the best preparation for the hurly-burly of one-day cricket, with its need for furiously run singles and athletic fielding, was not sitting at an office desk.

The Gillette Cup, originally of 65 overs a side, was an instant success in 1963. The final at Lord's on the first Saturday in September was still an increasingly lucrative sell-out when it became the NatWest Trophy in 1981. It was followed in 1969 by the John Player League – of 40 overs a side on Sunday afternoons – which became the Refuge Assurance League in 1987 and in the following year involved the first four finishers in semi-finals and a final at Edgbaston. The Benson and Hedges Cup was founded in 1972 with the ration of 55 overs a side as a competition for the first half of the season, part round robin, part knockout.

Limited-over cricket was slower to take a hold overseas but by the 1980s it was flourishing at the expense of conventional cricket and Test matches, notably in Australia and India.

In England the most successful exponent of the one-day game in its first years was the great theorist, Ted Dexter, who was also the outstanding stroke-player in the country. Dexter worked out what was required with the resources at his command in Sussex and twice led his side to victory in the first two years of the Gillette Cup. Much of their success came from having Dexter himself and another dashing stroke-player Jim Parks at the wicket when the time came for acceleration.

It did not take long for the full possibilities of defensive cricket in the one-day game to be realised; indeed when Worcestershire were threatening Sussex's score of 168 in the first final Dexter had most of his fielders distributed round the boundary and Sussex won by 14 runs.

Limited-over cricket has one fundamental weakness – that bowlers do not have to bowl the other side out. The knockout format and the likelihood of a definite result in a day were attractive to the public, especially in a country in which county loyalties die hard. This form of cricket did have one advantage: the rules of it could be tinkered with. Whereas the conventional game had to abide by the Laws of Cricket which are only changed after long and earnest worldwide consultation, the limited-over game was so artificial anyhow that another rule to meet the development of a bad habit was no problem. Hence the calling of a no-ball to a delivery slanting only just outside the batsman's legs and the adoption of a "circle" within which four fieldsmen plus the wicket-keeper and bowler must be placed at the moment of delivery.

The limited-over game undoubtedly attracted a new public to grounds and was acceptable to television companies. It was to become a deeply rooted topic of controversy as to how much this was a good thing. How, for example, could a coach impress on a young player the virtues of playing straight when the young man could see the best batsmen in the country stepping back and cutting off the leg-stump? More people might come to watch that type of cricket but if this was achieved by a lowering of standards, by reducing the variety of the game and changing its character, it was undesirable. When in the late 1970s it was decided in Australia that players should be dressed in different coloured "pyjama" clothes, in daylight as well as under lights, the game's rather pathetic wanting to be liked held it up to ridicule.

Crowds in England were spared such sartorial excesses and indeed floodlit cricket. One post-war experiment in the County Championship using the late daylight of midsummer evenings quickly established that if there is one thing worse than watching cricket on a cold damp afternoon, it is watching it on a cold damp evening.

This was undoubtedly a great age for experiments, one of which was a revival of the single-wicket game which had been popular in the early nineteenth century. It was an entertaining two-day novelty when played at Lord's in the mid-1960s but did not survive the extension of limited-over cricket.

Another experiment rather earlier had been with a smaller ball. When it was tried out in the nets at Lord's Ray Lindwall happened to be present and was invited to use it. He swung it so much that he told the Committee that if they brought it into use, he would postpone his forthcoming retirement for some years.

Another experiment took place at Lord's when the lbw Law was under consideration, not for the first or last time. Three parallel lines were chalked between the stumps at one end and those at the other and bowlers of various types were invited to take part. This was long before the slow-motion instant replay and some of those sitting on top of the pavilion were surprised to see that, unless a right-arm bowler delivers from very close to the stumps, almost every ball which pitches on a line between the wickets will miss the leg-stump.

Thus the only modification of the lbw Law since the War – designed to stop padding-up – has been that which rules that if the batsman makes no genuine attempt to play the ball, he may be out lbw even if his leg is outside the off-stump.

All this – and the settlement of one of the most difficult issues carried over from the 1950s, throwing.

12

Chuckers Out

THROUGHOUT cricket history there have been periods when the illegal actions of bowlers have caused concern and periods when they were not an issue at all. By the mid-1960s the game was emerging from one of the periods of concern which had dawned as far back as 1952.

The difficulty of identifying an illegal action or throw or chuck and then knowing what to do about it is considerable. The identification would be easier today because of videos and the slow-motion instant playback of television. In the 1950s the authorities had to set up their own cameras on days when the suspect was certain to be bowling and presumably did not know that he was the focus of attention.

Often the suspicions were not brought out into the open for one of five reasons. One was that the alleged offender was a slow bowler who did not endanger life and limb by his throwing. A second was that he was not a good enough bowler to worry about. A third, which must have often been in the minds of English umpires, was that to call a bowler for throwing might be to take away his livelihood. A fourth was that if a bowler in a side touring England was called, there might be international repercussions. A fifth was that a bowler offended only occasionally. One fast-medium bowler, never called, said that he did not know when he was going to throw but always knew when he had. Presumably this was when he fired off his faster ball.

For one reason or another the no-balling in 1952 of Cuan McCarthy by Paddy Corrall at Worcester and of Tony Lock by Fred Price at The Oval was not followed up. McCarthy had toured England with the 1951 South Africans and was only up at Cambridge for one year. He would not be playing regular first-class cricket afterwards. Lock was a slow bowler, though he had a well-disguised faster ball which on the uncovered pitches of the day could be unplayable. It was Doug Insole who, after being bowled by Lock, jovially asked the umpire if he had been bowled or run out.

Though there was some murmuring about Lock's action, it seemed to be passed by the umpires and indeed by spectators, for Fred Price was showered with abuse after his calling of Lock at The Oval. There were certainly many who thought that any umpire who no-balled a bowler for throwing was a publicity-seeker and a "stirrer".

Lock carried on with much success until towards the end of the M.C.C. tour of Australia and New Zealand in 1958–9 when he was shocked to see a film of himself bowling. He changed back to something like his original pre-1952 action and played first-class cricket for another 12 years, first for Surrey and then for Leicestershire and Western Australia, both of whom he captained with great enthusiasm. He became a better bowler on hard pitches than he had ever been before and as late as March 1968 was summoned from Australia to the Caribbean when England lost a spinner, Fred Titmus, through injury.

It was the M.C.C. tour of Australia in 1958–9 which hastened official action. From their first matches in Perth and Adelaide the England players saw bowlers whose actions surprised them. At their first meeting with Ian Meckiff they thought he was too wild to be dangerous but they soon had to change their mind about that when in the second innings of the Second Test in Melbourne he took six for 33 and rushed them to defeat after a fairly even first innings.

That M.C.C. team, losers in the Test series 4–0, was not well placed to complain about anything. However the captain, Peter May, and the manager, Freddie Brown, were so dismayed by what they saw as a plague spreading that they felt it was their duty to do something. The problem was exacerbated by "drag". Gordon Rorke was a 20-year-old giant fast bowler who, in the process of delivery, put his rear foot down behind the bowling line as required but then dragged it so far that when the ball left his hand the batsman must have been barely 17 yards away. He then received a ball banged in from a great height.

There were draggers in English cricket too. They were a nightmare for the umpires who usually marked out a line a yard or more behind the bowling crease and told the bowler that it would be a no-ball if his rear foot was put down beyond that.

The Law was eventually changed so that the legitimacy of the ball is decided, not by where the back foot is put down behind the bowling crease but where the front foot is placed relative to the popping crease. Australia does not agree with this change and though it may correct the drag, it certainly has two big disadvantages. It seems to produce an excessive number of no-balls and it does not give the batsman time to adjust his stroke to hit a no-ball, even when the bowler is a slow one. Thus the batsman cannot have the free hit at the ball which used to enliven the proceedings and was popular with spectators.

Before leaving Australia in February, Peter May and Freddie Brown told Sir Donald Bradman that they would be mentioning the increase in throwing in their report. That there were Australians who were uneasy about the situation was confirmed subsequently by the title of Jack Fingleton's book on the tour – *Four Chukkas to Australia*. Ray Lindwall, picked for the last two Tests at 37, was said to have described himself as the last of the straight-arm bowlers. But the Australian Board of Control had denied more than once that there was a throwing problem.

In 1960, however, Sir Donald was one of the Australian Board's two delegates to the I.C.C. meeting at Lord's. The Board's chairman, W.J. Dowling, was the other.

The subject of throwing had just had an airing in England because the South Africans had arrived with a young bowler, Geoffrey Griffin, who had broken his elbow in an accident at school and could not straighten it in the normal way. He had had his 21st birthday while playing in the First Test, his first, and was picked again for the Second Test at Lord's. He had been called twice in South Africa and three times already on the tour. At Lord's one of the senior umpires, Frank Lee, called him 11 times from square-leg, but before the England captain Colin Cowdrey declared at 362 for eight, Griffin earned the singular distinction of becoming the first bowler to perform the hat-trick in a Lord's Test match. Having had M.J.K. Smith caught at the wicket for 99 off the last ball of an over, he bowled Peter Walker for 52 and Fred Trueman with the first two balls of his next over.

Soon after lunch on the fourth day South Africa had lost by an innings. To entertain the big crowd and provide some cricket for the Queen and the Duke of Edinburgh who were due to arrive shortly, an exhibition match was played. This time it was Syd Buller who was at square-leg and he called Griffin four times out of five. Griffin finished the over bowling underarm. That was the end of his Test career, though he stayed in the tour party playing as a batsman.

The confusion which surrounded throwing and what action to take about it had been illustrated in a match at Derby in which Griffin had been passed but Derbyshire's young fast bowler, Harold Rhodes, had been called six times for throwing by umpire Paul Gibb.

A tall wiry young man, Rhodes was probably the unluckiest player involved in a throwing controversy, for he was dogged by it throughout his career and then was cleared. Derbyshire always maintained that he was not a thrower and he played in two Tests in 1959 against India. There must have been times subsequently when the England selectors wanted to pick him again but did not risk him in the prevailing climate. Eventually in 1968 a thorough investigation revealed that he suffered from a "hyper-extension" of the arm. Whether this would have made any difference to his Test career if discovered earlier is doubtful, for he did look to many eyes as if he was throwing, even though he was not.

In 1960, while the sad episode of Griffin kept the topic of throwing in the public mind, there were unfounded mutterings that the Australian tour to England in 1961 might be marred by bowlers with doubtful actions and might even not take place. Many hours were spent over the definition of a throw. There was talk of a moratorium and a truce was agreed for the first seven weeks of the Australian tour.

Effectively it was the work of Sir Donald Bradman and G.O. Allen which eliminated the throwing in their respective countries. The throwers in Australia began to disappear, none came to England in 1961 and the tour passed harmoniously, helped by Richie Benaud's flair for public relations.

The problem of how county administrators, umpires and selectors should handle cases of suspected throwers lingered on into the 1960s. There remained a few special cases, notably those of Ian Meckiff and of Charlie Griffith who came to England with the West Indian team of 1963.

There was still the potential for discord which might damage future international tours, for bowlers who were widely considered to be "chuckers" had still never been called or only on isolated occasions. This was partly because umpires were not convinced that any action which they took would be supported by the Board. And if the bowlers had not been called and were taking a lot of wickets, the Test selectors might have to pick them.

Meckiff, widely regarded as the most blatant chucker, came in this category. He was still around in 1963–4, partly because he had not always been fit and partly through loss of form. In 1962–3 he played twice for Victoria against Ted Dexter's M.C.C. touring team and with 47 wickets at 19 apiece he played a big part in Victoria's winning of the Sheffield Shield that season. It was clear that if he retained his form, he would have to be picked against the visiting South Africans in 1963–4 and that what happened then might be decisive. The Australian Board of Control had instructed the State Associations to urge umpires to deal firmly with bowlers with doubtful actions and assured them that they would receive full support. There were several cases of bowlers having been called in minor cricket.

It so happened that the South Africans, captained by Trevor Goddard, did not play Victoria before the First Test in Brisbane but Meckiff took 11 wickets in Victoria's first two Sheffield Shield matches, including the first five against Western Australia. He was duly picked for Brisbane and umpires, administrators and, not least, the Australian captain Richie Benaud prepared for "High Noon".

Australia batted first and it was the second afternoon before Goddard and Eddie Barlow opened for South Africa and Meckiff bowled his fateful over. Umpire Colin Egar no-balled his second, third, fifth and ninth deliveries.

Benaud was said to have approached Meckiff with the words: "Brother, we've got problems," which was abundantly clear, not least to Meckiff. Benaud took him off and shortly afterwards he retired from first-class cricket, aged 28.

Crowds love a victim of authority and at the end of the day's play Meckiff was carried off shoulder-high. On subsequent days extra police were summoned in case the umpires, selectors and Benaud needed protection but the weather was all against demonstrations and this was clearly the end of Meckiff as a player. He was an amiable character and 20 years later was a well-regarded commentator on the game.

In 1962 India had lost their captain Nari Contractor, a sound left-handed opening batsman, who was seriously injured by a ball which lifted to hit him just above the right ear. The bowler was Charlie Griffith who later in the same match between Barbados and the Indians was no-balled for throwing. Contractor had a fractured skull and needed an emergency brain operation. This was said to have saved his life but though he did play cricket again, he did not play in another Test match.

In 1963 the powerfully built Griffith was a highly effective partner for Wesley Hall on West Indies' tour of England. There was an unease throughout the tour based on doubts about the legality of Griffith's shorter, faster ball but nothing happened to stop his triumphant progress through a summer in which he took 119 first-class wickets at 12 apiece.

When M.J.K. Smith's M.C.C. team arrived in India later that year they were surprised to find that the first question which they were asked was: "Why did your umpires not no-ball Griffith?" The Indian players had been sure that English umpires, in whom they had implicit faith, would not tolerate Griffith's action. In fact, he was no-balled only once in England and that was not until 1966 when Arthur Fagg called him in the West Indians' match against Lancashire.

Elsewhere the throwing controversy rumbled on, though there was no longer fear that young cricketers might imitate illegal actions. The Law was hard to interpret with consistency. In New Zealand Gary Bartlett had an action which always bothered the purist but he played in 10 Test matches as a fast-medium bowler over a period of six years and certainly did not upset New Zealand's tour of South Africa in 1961–2, which was said to have been a model of what a tour should be. The New Zealand captain was John Reid and the manager Gordon Leggat, a leading attorney in New Zealand and an outstandingly able cricket administrator. It was a great loss to the game – and not only in New Zealand – when he died suddenly in 1973 aged 47.

In England throwing receded into the background again. Watchfulness was still required because there was always a chance that illegal actions might be ignored because they belonged to not very good bowlers. There is evidence, too, that when a case did crop up it was dealt with swiftly and with little publicity.

One county took on a young bowler from local club cricket with an action which was a great surprise to the senior players when they gathered for the new season. The young man played in an away match and was watched intently by the square-leg umpire. Next morning, by a strange chance, the same umpire was standing in a match involving the same county 200 miles away. He twice no-balled the offender who was taken off after three overs and was not seen again.

13

Springboks' Rise to Obscurity

WHEN the 1960 South African team under Jackie McGlew arrived at London Airport there had been a small demonstration at the gates. It was Easter, the Aldermaston marchers were staging nearby and the Campaign for Nuclear Disarmament had shown its versatility by sending a detachment under a jack-booted commander to make unfriendly noises. It caused mild surprise, especially to those old enough to have known the hospitality and generosity shown by South Africans during the War. Cricket, amongst other games and sports, had reason to be grateful, for the great coaching centre at Lilleshall had been built with money from the South African Aid to Britain Fund.

If this small demonstration was a straw in the wind, there were others pointing in a very different direction – to the rise of South African cricket from its low in 1960 to the pinnacle of 1970.

More than a hint of this was dropped by a private team, the Fezela, whose short tour in 1961 included three first-class matches. They beat Essex by six wickets and Gloucestershire and the Combined Services by an innings. The counties were at full strength, or very near it.

That team was captained by Roy McLean and impressed those who saw them by playing in the same dashing way as McLean. Fezela included Kim Elgie, well known in Britain as a centre three-quarter who had played eight times for Scotland while at St Andrews and London Universities. Otherwise, the names were mostly unknown in England, though it did not take a very lively imagination to foresee that it would not be long before Eddie Barlow, Denis Lindsay, Colin Bland, Peter Pollock and Peter van der Merwe changed this. All were in their early 20s and it was mentioned in passing that Pollock had a 17-year-old brother who

140

really was a bit unusual.

Within a few months most of these were playing under Jackie McGlew against the visiting New Zealanders and sharing the series 2–2. By then South Africa, having left the Commonwealth, had had to withdraw from the Imperial Cricket Conference, as it then was. Hitherto, cricket had been a game for the English-speaking population and the Afrikaner took no great interest in it. There were pessimists who thought that in an Afrikaner-run republic it would fade away.

Exactly the opposite happened. Cricket had been brought to South Africa by British soldiers and sailors as far back as the early 1800s. The first Test matches had been played in 1888–9 against an England side captained by C. Aubrey Smith, the famous Hollywood actor of later years. The game was too deeply rooted to fade away.

There were two other reasons for its increasing popularity. One was that the break with the British Commonwealth brought a greater unity between English- and Afrikaans-speaking residents through a feeling that "we're all in the same boat now". The other was the arrival of players such as Eddie Barlow and the Pollock brothers who played in a way to catch the imagination – and were successful with it.

Thus while English cricket administrators were having to think up new ways of kindling interest in the first-class game and of improving its public relations, cricket was climbing to new heights of popularity in South Africa. There were days when Afrikaans newspapers led both their front and their back pages on cricket. It was a refreshing experience to leave a public grown cynical about modern cricket and to arrive in a country where it was being talked about with a new excitement.

Captained by Trevor Goddard, the South Africans had been to Australia and, like their equally underestimated predecessors 11 years earlier, had come away with a draw, this time 1–1.

The way in which the draw had been earned had been even more remarkable. Though Australia had made nearly 350 in each innings in Adelaide, South Africa in between had made 595 and they won by 10 wickets. It was said that even hardened Australian cricket-watchers were on their feet cheering as, from 70 for two, Barlow and the 19-year-old Graeme Pollock, who had already made his first Test hundred in Sydney, put on 341 for the third wicket in less than four and three-quarter hours. Barlow made 201 and Pollock 175.

Barlow, in his first bowl of the match, broke the Australian resistance in the second innings by taking three wickets in a few minutes. This was to be a speciality for him. At a medium pace which was sometimes quicker than the batsman expected he moved the ball about and would turn a match in a short inspired spell. For good measure he was also a brilliant slip catcher.

Eddie Barlow was sturdily built of medium height, a batsman who combined soundness with an ever-present desire to attack if given the slightest opportunity. The left-handed Graeme Pollock was tall and powerfully built even as a teenager, a marvellous timer of the ball blessed with an effortless majesty at the wicket. He reminded many of Frank Woolley who, as an active octogenarian, was to be seen watching him on winter visits to South Africa.

In the final Test of 1963–4 in Sydney South Africa led by 100 on first innings and were only stopped from winning by a dogged last-wicket stand between Tom Veivers and Neil Hawke which added 45 runs and, more important, occupied 75 minutes.

In the following Southern summer South Africa were hosts to an M.C.C. team under M.J.K. Smith's captaincy. Ted Dexter, who had been the England captain for much of the previous three years, was in the team but missed the start of the tour through contesting a Cardiff seat at the General Election against the future Prime Minister, James Callaghan.

England won the 1964–5 series 1–0 but from a point three-quarters of the way through the Second Test, there was not much doubt that South Africa were the stronger side.

For several years the off-spinner Fred Titmus had been treated with infinite respect by England's opponents at home and overseas. He had pinned down many of the best batsmen with variations administered with great control. With another fine off-spinner, David Allen, he was mainly responsible for bowling out South Africa twice in the First Test in Durban on a pitch which was taking spin by the second evening.

England had batted with some care for 190 overs and Ken Barrington (148) and Jim Parks (108) were still together in an unbroken stand of 206 when Smith declared at 485 for five.

For much of the Second Test in Johannesburg England maintained their superiority. Dexter made a brilliant 172 and Ken Barrington 121. The left-handed Bob Barber, that amiable eccentric whose career as an England opener was far too brief, had been not far short of making a hundred on the first morning.

South Africa, having been tied down by Titmus, followed on 214 behind and by the fourth evening looked destined to become two down. But there was still Colin Bland, a magnificently athletic batsman who, using his feet superbly, played a highly significant innings of 144 not out. It marked the end of the beginning. For the rest of the series England were hanging on to their lead but looking second best.

Within a few months South Africa were in England for a three-Test series in the second half of the 1965 season. In the first half, England had beaten New Zealand with some ease.

By now the Springboks were fast developing into a formidable side, even without their highly skilled opening batsman and swing bowler Trevor Goddard, who was not available for the tour. He was succeeded as captain by Peter van der Merwe.

The First Test at Lord's, after many fluctuations, could have gone either way when it was left drawn. England, needing 191 to win, were then 145 for seven.

The Second Test at Trent Bridge belonged to the Pollock brothers. Peter, the fast bowler, took five wickets in each innings. Graeme, the batting genius, still only 21, made 125 and 59 in a low-scoring match. His 125 was one of the great match-winning innings of the post-war era.

On an unlovely, overcast, typically English first morning South Africa were 16 for two when Pollock came in. Soon afterwards the score was 43 for four and his partners were suffering all sorts of discomfort, especially against the medium pace of Tom Cartwright. Until lunch Pollock assessed the alien conditions without favouring them with his full range of strokes. After lunch in 70 minutes he made 91 out of 102 with an effortless brilliance which few of those present would forget. He gave no chance until he was caught at second slip off Cartwright, having made his 125 out of 160 in only 140 minutes.

He had done enough. South Africa were always just on top and eventually won in four days by 94 runs.

The Third Test at The Oval was not unlike the First in its evenness. The English climate has a lot to answer for and the thunderstorm which broke on the final afternoon ended a splendid match which was moving towards a fascinating climax. England had begun the last innings needing 399 to win, a target which they had never before come near in home Tests. Yet when the storm burst they had reached 308 for four, needing only another 91 in 70 minutes. Colin Cowdrey was going well at 78 and the

Springboks still had to shift batsmen of the calibre of Mike Smith and Jim Parks.

However, it was generally accepted that the South Africans were well worth their 1–0 win, not least for the enthusiastic way in which they had played against the counties. One of the great attractions of the side was the fielding of Colin Bland.

The weather in what was then Rhodesia allowed outdoor practice even in the close season and Bland, a superb mover, had practised picking up and throwing when off-balance until he achieved almost incredible accuracy.

In Durban where the sub-tropical grass off the square at that time acted as a brake, Bland seemed to be covering almost all the off-side from cover-point. Those who saw him in action at Canterbury, where he was asked to give an exhibition during a match against Kent, still talk about the way in which he could pick off one stump from 30 yards. In the Lord's Test Ken Barrington and Jim Parks, both of whom were well aware of the danger when the ball went anywhere near Bland, were still run out when he hit the stumps from unlikely positions.

By showing what could be done in the field and making fielding an entertainment, Bland, of Scottish grandparents, had made a considerable contribution to the game. Yet three years later he was turned back at London Airport for having a Rhodesian passport. Rhodesia by then had declared independence. Considering some of the characters who are allowed into the United Kingdom, it seemed a bit hard, as it must have done to others a few years older who had fought in British regiments during the War.

The political clouds were gathering but as yet were not affecting Australia who went on two tours of South Africa in 1966–7 and 1969–70. The first was under the captaincy of Bobby Simpson.

Australia had never before lost a match in South Africa but though they lost their second first-class match to the Transvaal, they did so with honour. After the Transvaal captain Ali Bacher had made 234 in the second innings, the Australians, needing 490 to win, went down by only 76 runs.

They lost again in East London to a South African XI which included the 21-year-old Barry Richards, who made a hundred, and Mike Procter, aged 20. These two had been the outstanding batsmen in a Nuffield Schools tour of England in 1963, since when Procter had become a fast bowler with an unusual action. His arm came over slightly earlier in the final stride than is normal.

The presence of these young players promised a lot for the future and underlined the current strength of South African cricket at the top, for Richards was not called on in the series and Procter not until the third of the five Tests.

There had been heavy rain in Johannesburg until just before the First Test and South Africa, having chosen to bat, were soon 41 for five and in sore trouble against Graham McKenzie, Australia's main fast-medium bowler of the 1960s. But this was to be the series of Denis Lindsay, South Africa's wicket-keeper-batsman. He was remembered in England for hitting the leg-spin of Bill Greensmith for five successive sixes to finish off Fezela's match with Essex. Yet he was more than a spectacular hitter and had sometimes opened the innings on tours.

His sixth-wicket stand with "Tiger" Lance added 110 to the score of 41 for five but he was caught at the wicket when hooking at the fast bowling of Dave Renneberg and South Africa were all out at tea for 199. By the end of the first day Simpson and Bill Lawry had made 99 without mishap. Next day, Christmas Eve, Australia passed the South African total with only one wicket down, well in control, so it seemed.

However, Trevor Goddard gave little away – 39 runs in 26 overs – and Barlow had one of his spells in which he had Redpath, Cowper and Stackpole all caught at the wicket, the last two for nought. In the end, the Australian lead was only 126.

The Wanderers outfield was becoming ever faster as it dried and the pitch was not without pace. On Boxing Day Graeme Pollock played a classical innings of 90 but when the fifth wicket fell, South Africa only led by 142.

Hereabouts the catches were not sticking and Australia were not helped by being refused one which they did seem to have made. Soon the floodgates opened as van der Merwe settled in and supported Lindsay in a seventh-wicket stand of 221. Lindsay hit five sixes, a five and 25 fours. In the match he made 69 and 182 and by the time Australia succumbed by 233 runs on the fifth day he had also taken eight catches, including a record-equalling six in the first innings.

Over the New Year Australia won the Second Test in Cape Town. Bobby Simpson made 153 and Keith Stackpole 134. Even a marvellous 209 by Graeme Pollock – made almost entirely on the back foot because of a pulled muscle – did not stop the South Africans from following on.

Lindsay had found a strange way to be out. Aiming a specula-

tive hook at Renneberg, he hit the ball on to his forehead whence
it rebounded to the gratified bowler who dived and caught it.
Lindsay was knocked out and had to be carried off.

This second mishook was not lost on the Australians and they
tended to bowl short to Lindsay subsequently. He was in general
a fine hooker and after his 81 in the second innings at Newlands,
he accommodated himself with 137 in Durban in the Third Test
and, the best of the lot, 131 in Johannesburg in the Fourth.

Rain limited play to 14 hours in the Fourth Test but when a
storm ended the match at tea on the fifth day Australia were
within two wickets of losing by an innings. Lindsay had come in
on the second day when the other batsmen, in answer to
Australia's 143, had struggled for three and a quarter hours to
reach 120 for four. In 105 minutes that evening he made 111 out
of 146 with no trouble at all.

South Africa did not quite win that match but they did win the
Third and Fifth Tests and took the series 3–1. It was the first
which they had ever won against Australia who had first played
them in 1902–3. Lindsay had made 606 runs in the series, nearly
all at a great pace, and had taken 24 catches. He only played a
defensive stroke as the very last resort. The rest was all quick-
footed attack – and yet the ball was seldom struck with anything
but the middle of the bat.

The cricket played in this series led to even greater enthusiasm
for the game in South Africa and the visit of M.C.C. in 1968–9
was keenly awaited. However, there were clearly going to be
problems ahead, the most imminent provided by the increasing
success of Basil d'Oliveira, a Cape Coloured, in English cricket.

English professionals coaching in South Africa had long talked
about his great natural ability and when he came to England in
1960 to play for Middleton in the Central Lancashire League, he
was immensely successful with both bat and ball, as he was for
Kidderminster in the Birmingham and District League in 1964
during his year's qualification for Worcestershire, who that year
were winning the County Championship for the first time in their
history.

They won again in 1965 when d'Oliveira marked his arrival in
first-class cricket with 1500 runs and 35 wickets. A year later he
was playing for England in three Test matches against West
Indies. He was 34 or, as *Wisden* decided at a later date, 37.

As a batsman d'Oliveira hit the ball very hard with great
strength of forearm and was especially effective on pitches which

required improvisation. As a bowler he moved the ball about at medium pace and was seldom as straightforward as batsmen would think. In 1967 he made his first Test hundred against India at Headingley under the captaincy of Brian Close but was not needed to bowl much.

That winter d'Oliveira was in the M.C.C. team to West Indies but had little success. In England he played in the First Test of 1968 but was one of five dropped after Australia's victory at Old Trafford. Later in the series Roger Prideaux, the Northampton-shire captain, came on the Test scene and was picked again for the final Test at The Oval which England had to win to square the series.

In the previous week Colin Cowdrey, the reigning England captain, had played at The Oval for Kent and, while making a hundred, had been surprised by how much the ball was swinging. He was uneasy that he and the other Test selectors had not picked anyone to "wobble" the ball about. Thus when Prideaux dropped out through illness, Cowdrey asked not for the agreed reserve batsman but for Basil d'Oliveira who, though not making many runs for Worcestershire, had been taking wickets.

In the event d'Oliveira, dropped at the wicket when 31, made 158 and bowled only nine overs, though he took a vital wicket when England were pressing for victory on an extraordinary last day. This was the day when spectators helped the ground staff to mop up after a lunchtime deluge and Australia just failed to hold Derek Underwood off on a pitch which became very awkward as it dried.

That night, after England's victory with six minutes to spare, the selectors sat down to pick the team for the tour of South Africa. Political considerations were not for them. It had always been accepted that if a player was not to be picked, perhaps on disciplinary grounds, the decision would be made by M.C.C. who would inform the selectors, as had happened with Wardle in 1958. Otherwise their choice would be made purely on cricketing merit. So it was that Douglas Insole, the chairman, Alec Bedser, Peter May and Don Kenyon, augmented by G.O. Allen, Arthur Gilligan and the captain Colin Cowdrey went about their task.

They were reasonably well stocked with batsmen at the time and to many the surprise was not that they could not find a place for d'Oliveira but that Colin Milburn was not chosen. As the chairman said, d'Oliveira was considered "from an overseas point of view as a batsman rather than as an all-rounder". They already had a bowler of similar type in Tom Cartwright, though he had had a nagging shoulder injury for much of the season.

At this stage it was by no means certain that South Africa would have rejected d'Oliveira's inclusion. In reply to M.C.C.'s soundings in April, the Prime Minister, John Vorster, had said that visiting teams of mixed race would be able to tour the country if they were teams from countries with which South Africa had "traditional sporting ties" and "if no political capital were made of the situation".

The non-selection of d'Oliveira provoked a furore, especially from the non-cricketing public who refused to believe that his omission was not for political reasons. A group of 20 members of M.C.C. asserted their right to call a special meeting of the club.

As the row simmered the *News of the World* announced that it had engaged d'Oliveira to report the tour in South Africa. As a move likely to exacerbate the trouble, this took a lot of beating and predictably enraged the South African Government.

The next move came in the second half of September when a medical report reversed a previous assurance that Cartwright would be fit for the tour. In his place the selectors named the player who had been pencilled in as cover. This was d'Oliveira.

Just as the anti-apartheid forces in England had refused to believe that the original selection had not been influenced by political issues, so the South African Government was not going to be persuaded that d'Oliveira's selection now was not the result of political agitation. Those who knew the long-standing role of Test selectors in England believed that the choice was wholly on cricketing grounds but to others Mr Insole's original statement that d'Oliveira had been considered only as a batsman was now invalidated by the choice of him to replace a bowler.

Next day Mr Vorster, speaking in Bloemfontein, not the most liberal part of his country, said that South Africa was not prepared to accept a team forced on it by people "with certain aims". The harshness of his words offered no hope of understanding. It was a formality for M.C.C. to cancel the tour.

There was a gap of 18 months before the Springboks were due to tour England in 1970. In the meantime they received another visit from Australia, now captained by Bill Lawry. After 12 days in Ceylon and two and a half months in India the Australians arrived in South Africa for a four-Test series early in 1970. Of their five Test matches in India they had won three and, on a turning pitch in Delhi, had lost one.

It was nearly three years since the South Africans had played a Test match and there was a school of thought which held that they would be too rusty or past their best. On the other hand, their enthusiasm and the class of many of their players were such that even in the nets at Newlands before the First Test they gave the impression that they were now even more talented than three years before.

Ali Bacher was now captain, Barry Richards was installed to open the innings with Trevor Goddard, allowing Eddie Barlow to bat around number five and Mike Procter, now one of the world's best all-rounders, was not required to bat higher than number eight. For the first two Tests, Denis Lindsay, the record-breaker of 1966–7, had to yield to Dennis Gamsy who was the wicket-keeper in form but Lindsay was back for the last two and made 43 and 60 in the last.

The margins by which South Africa won the four Tests speak for themselves – 170 runs in Cape Town, an innings and 129 runs in Durban, 307 runs in Johannesburg and 323 runs in Port Elizabeth. Only one Australian innings out of the eight exceeded 300. Procter took 26 wickets at 13 apiece, Peter Pollock 15 at 17 each, Barlow 11 and Goddard nine. They were supported by fielders who caught anything which came near them.

The batting, with Lee Irvine, a left-hander who had just spent two successful seasons with Essex, at number six, stretched a long way down to the highly competent Peter Pollock at number nine or ten. Its most memorable moments came in Durban where Barry Richards was only just robbed of a hundred before lunch on the first day by a certain Australian leisureliness in the field. The hour after lunch when he and Graeme Pollock batted together and made 103 provided batting of the very highest quality and a memory to treasure in the empty years to come. Richards made 140, Pollock 274. They were aged 24 and 25 respectively.

The only department in which this South African side was not proved to be of the highest class was in slow bowlers. They included two in Cape Town, the off-spinner Kelly Seymour and Grahame Chevalier, slow left-arm. They both took wickets as did Athanasios Traicos of Rhodesia who played in the other three Tests. Traicos, then at the University of Natal, showed himself to be yet another brilliant close catcher but on the pitches of the day was not often needed as a bowler. He was to survive in international cricket longer than any of his contemporaries. He captained Zimbabwe in the World Cup of 1987.

It was a sad spring for English cricket in 1970. The Springboks' rugby tour had taken place but amid violent scenes on many grounds and cricket was in every way more vulnerable to disruption than rugby. It mattered not to demonstrators that the South African players whom they would be attacking were themselves laying the foundations of non-racial cricket.

The South African Cricket Association, as it was then, had already announced that all teams would be chosen on merit in future. Yet in England, the fact that non-white cricketers needed experience and encouragement more than any others was brushed aside in the desire to disrupt.

The Cricket Council, newly formed as the governing body of cricket in England, kept re-asserting that the tour, though shortened, would still go ahead. The political scene was further complicated by the imminence of a General Election.

Eventually on 21 May the Home Secretary, James Callaghan, invited the Chairman of the Cricket Council, Maurice Allom, and the Secretary, Billy Griffith, to see him in his office and there asked them to cancel the tour "on the grounds of broad public policy". The cancellation came next day and within a few days was replaced by a tour by a Rest of the World team captained by Gary Sobers, managed by Freddie Brown and Leslie Ames and including five South Africans, Barlow, the Pollock brothers, Richards and Procter.

While still intending to stage the South African tour the Cricket Council had informed the S.A.C.A. "that no further Test tours between South Africa and this country will take place until South African cricket is played and teams are selected on a multi-racial basis in South Africa".

Within five years a mixed South African team was playing at Newlands, within 10 years all the conditions had been met and the S.A.C.A., reconstituted as the South African Cricket Union, had an Indian President, Rashid Varachia. Within 20 years the S.A.C.U. was engaged in a massive programme of bringing cricket to the underprivileged, which put other countries to shame.

All this was dismissed as "window-dressing" by delegates to the I.C.C. who refused, or were not allowed by their governments, to go to South Africa to see for themselves. The implied commitment of the Cricket Council's statement of 1970 went unhonoured.

14

A Levelling-Out of Talent

WHILE standards in South Africa had been rising in the 1960s to a level never reached there before, Australian and English cricket could be said to have been marking time. Since recovering the Ashes under Richie Benaud in 1958–9 Australia had won 2–1 in England in 1961, had drawn a home series in 1962–3 against the England team of Ted Dexter and the Duke of Norfolk and had won 1–0 in England in 1964.

Penetrative bowling was in short supply but what there was on the Australian side came from Graham McKenzie and Neil Hawke. Fred Trueman, though 33, was still England's main fast bowler.

Australia won the 1964 series with their seven-wicket victory in the Third Test at Headingley. This was a closer match than it sounds, for at one time Australia's first-innings score in answer to England's 268 stood at 178 for seven. They were being plagued by Titmus who bowled 50 overs in the first innings and took four for 69. The match turned when Dexter, given a difficult decision, rested Titmus and took the new ball, at the sight of which the robust Peter Burge leapt into action and, with support from Hawke and wicket-keeper Wally Grout, gave Australia a first-innings lead of 121. Burge made 160 out of the last 265.

Rain interfered with much of this 1964 series but the Fourth Test at Old Trafford testified to the friendliness of the bowling of both sides on a good batting pitch. In his 30th Test match the Australian captain Bobby Simpson, having reached a first Test hundred which was remarkably belated for so fine a player, batted on into the third day to made 311 in nearly 12 and three quarter hours. He declared at 656 for eight, after which Ken Barrington made 256, Ted Dexter 174 and England mustered 601.

On the way home the Australians played three Test matches in India, winning one and losing one, and drew one against Pakistan in Karachi where Bobby Simpson made a hundred in each innings.

In many ways the tour of M.J.K. Smith's M.C.C. team in Australia in 1965–6 was one of the most entertaining, for it included the finest hours of the left-handed Bob Barber's career. He was 30 now and while playing for Cambridge and Lancashire had been known as a fairly dour batsman who was not the worst leg-spinner if ever allowed to bowl. This seemed to change with his move to Warwickshire.

By the time he found himself on reliable Australian pitches he was making life very difficult for bowlers of all types whose only hope was that he was hitting so outrageously across the line that it could not last for ever. Opening the innings with the sound and painstaking Geoffrey Boycott, Barber slogged his way round Australia with remarkable consistency. His innings of 185 in under five hours on the first day of the Third Test in Sydney was a great joy to watch, though the crowds who went to see an England side which batted with considerable aggression were well down on former years.

The England batting stretched a long way down and David Allen at number ten made 50 in Sydney. The pitch there was taking spin by the third day and England, with two accurate and dissimilar off-spinners in Titmus and Allen, were far better equipped for it.

Australia's two slow bowlers, the leg-spinner Peter Philpott and David Sincock, left-arm chinaman and googly, lacked the required control. Spectators from England, accustomed to much tight bowling at home, must have rubbed their eyes as they watched a Test match between Australia and England in Sydney, the very pinnacle of competitive cricket, one would think, and saw more slow full tosses and long-hops than they would see in several seasons at home.

Barber averaged 50 in all matches. It might have been double that figure if he had exercised a little restraint. He was far more often out to one of his own excesses than to the bowler's skill.

England won in Sydney by an innings but their lead was short-lived. Australia won in Adelaide, also by an innings. England were severely punished for one bad match, though a drawn series was probably a fair result.

Bobby Simpson, who had been prevented from playing in

Sydney by illness, resumed in Adelaide the captaincy of a side which suffered a last-minute change of great significance. When Graham McKenzie had been unfit to play in Brisbane, Peter Allan, the tall Queensland fast bowler, had deputised. Since then, he had taken all 10 Victorian wickets in Melbourne and for the Fourth Test in Adelaide the selectors preferred him to McKenzie, who had been a regular choice for five years. However, on the first morning in Adelaide Allan had to drop out through injury. McKenzie was reinstated and in his opening overs took the wickets of Barber and John Edrich. When Neil Hawke removed Boycott, England were 33 for three.

This was a start from which England never quite recovered, though as the pitch soon lost its early liveliness Barrington and Cowdrey seemed to have the situation in hand. Then Cowdrey, the non-striker, apparently mistaking a call when Barrington played a ball straight to mid-on, advanced down the pitch and *in absentia* was run out at the bowler's end.

Simpson (225) and Lawry (119) passed the England score in their opening stand of 244 and Australia never lost the grip on the match which McKenzie had given them. Allan never played in another Test match.

In the final Test in Melbourne the left-handed Bob Cowper, who had been dropped by Australia after the Third Test, was restored on his home ground and made 307. Bill Lawry made his fifth hundred of the season against the touring team and his third in Test matches. It was calculated that he had batted for more than 50 hours against the English bowlers.

During the rest of the 1960s the England captaincy passed from Mike Smith to Colin Cowdrey, thence to Brian Close, back to Cowdrey, for one match when Cowdrey was unfit to Tom Graveney and eventually to Raymond Illingworth. While Australia were short of top-class bowlers, England were strengthened by the improving John Snow and Derek Underwood. One of England's strengths had been Jim Parks who was a talented batsman to have coming in at number seven. As a batsman-wicket-keeper he was soon followed by Alan Knott who was a brilliant young wicket-keeper and a consistently effective batsman.

Thus when Bill Lawry's Australian side arrived in 1968 and suffered one of the wettest Mays on record, there was some confidence among the natives that this was the series in which England could win back the Ashes lost nearly 10 years before. But it was widely agreed that the England selectors did not have a great

match when the series began at Old Trafford. Having assembled
14 players, they left out three good bowlers, David Brown, Tom
Cartwright and Derek Underwood. Remaining were only three
regular bowlers, John Snow and Ken Higgs, both fast-medium,
and the off-spinner Pat Pocock. To augment them were Bob
Barber and Basil d'Oliveira who so far that season had taken only
seven wickets between them. England duly lost the toss and the
match by 159 runs.

Thereafter England's contest was largely with the weather. At
Lord's the playing time was cut by half and though Brown, Snow
and the Essex all-rounder Barry Knight bowled Australia out for
78, the weather which helped them to do this prevented them
from doing much more. At Edgbaston rain on the last day ended
the match after England had looked to be in a winning position.
This was the 100th Test match for the England captain, Colin
Cowdrey, who marked the occasion by making 104. Few could
remember having seen him play better than for his first 50. Then
he pulled a muscle, an injury which put him out of the next Test
at Headingley.

Lawry was also unable to play in the Fourth Test and there
were two deputy captains, Tom Graveney and the wicket-keeper
Barry Jarman, directing affairs in a fairly even match. Only an
hour's play was lost at Headingley but when a storm broke at
The Oval on the last morning of the final Test, it looked as if
England were yet again to be frustrated by rain.

They had made 494 (Edrich 164, d'Oliveira 158) and led by
170 on first innings, though Bill Lawry had made the only
Australian hundred of the series. England batted vigorously in the
second innings and Australia started the last innings on the fourth
evening, needing 352 to win. In the last 35 minutes they lost
Lawry to David Brown and Ian Redpath to Derek Underwood. It
looked as if England would win comfortably on the last day.

Over the past three seasons England had had a valuable new
bowler in Underwood, still only 23. Left-arm and only just below
medium pace, he bowled usually round the wicket with great
accuracy and numerous subtle variations. He was seldom mastered, certainly in England, and on a wet turning pitch could be
next to unplayable. On the last morning at The Oval he was
working his way steadily through the Australian batting with
Raymond Illingworth shutting up the other end. When the storm
broke just before lunch, Australia were 85 for five.

In that era of partial covering, pitches were still left open if rain fell during the hours of play and The Oval pitch was flooded. The storm passed, the sun came out again and spectators swarmed on to the ground to help the ground staff in their mopping up. The Australians accepted with a good grace the unusual sight of spectators equipped with brooms and buckets.

Play restarted with 75 minutes left but English fears that the pitch might for a time be too sodden to be of much use to the bowlers were soon being justified. Brown, Snow, Underwood, Illingworth and d'Oliveira all tried with a ring of close catchers in attendance but John Inverarity, who had opened the innings, remained unmoved. Forty minutes passed before d'Oliveira bowled Jarman. The ball had started to do enough from the pavilion end for hopes to be revived. Cowdrey promptly switched d'Oliveira to the other end and replaced him with Underwood.

As the pitch began to dry, Underwood was in his element and poised for a swift execution. In four and a half overs he took the remaining four wickets, the last of them that of John Inverarity who had held out for four hours. Underwood was in what would probably have been his last but one over when Inverarity played no stroke to a ball which did not turn and was lbw giving Charles Elliott one of the easier decisions of his umpiring career. England had squared the 1968 series with six minutes to spare.

Before England next went to Australia in 1970–1, events seemed to suggest that this would almost certainly be when the Ashes were recovered. Ably captained by Illingworth, who took over when Cowdrey tore an Achilles tendon early in 1969, England had comfortably beaten West Indies, the last time this was to happen for many years. Though losing 4–1, they had not done badly against the Rest of the World team which at short notice took over the fixtures originally allotted to the South Africans in 1970. England's most recent overseas tour – to Pakistan with the team intended for South Africa in 1968–9 – had not established much except that Pakistan at that time was not a suitable country for a cricket tour. The tour did not last until its scheduled end.

The most significant recent series had been that played by Australia in South Africa where they had lost all four Tests by vast margins.

England at this time were well equipped for a tour of Australia. In John Snow they had a bowler of strong wiry physique who was at the peak of his career. In his early days for Sussex he had finished his run-up with a stride to the left away from the stumps.

This limited the variations open to him. He worked on eliminating it and became a much more complete bowler, fast and accurate, giving the batsman little rest. Peter Lever, though nearly 30, had not played for England until 1970 but looked to be still improving. Bob Willis, who joined the team in November replacing the injured Alan Ward of Derbyshire, was only 21 and not the fast bowler of later years but he still took 12 wickets. Underwood, benefiting from being in a supporting capacity, took 16.

This was not a great England side but it was well handled by Illingworth and quite capable of looking after itself. Boycott and Edrich were seldom shifted easily. Brian Luckhurst had played 13 seasons for Kent without being considered a batsman of Test calibre but when his chance came at the age of 31 in 1970 he took it well. In Australia he made five hundreds, two in Test matches.

The middle batting of d'Oliveira, Fletcher, Knott and Illingworth was usually productive. If another batsman was played, it was John Hampshire or Colin Cowdrey.

It was a sad tour for Cowdrey, his fifth of Australia and his fourth as vice-captain. He had recovered well from his serious injury of May 1969 and made a lot of runs on a private tour of West Indies in the following winter. He headed the Kent batting averages in 1970 when he led them to their first Championship since 1913. But at 38 he seemed to be in the evening of a Test career of 22 hundreds. He did not play in the two Tests in Sydney which England won.

It was not an entirely happy tour. The New Year Test in Melbourne was washed out but the tour programme was rejigged to include an extra Test in Melbourne later. This was not popular with the England players who saw their programme made still more arduous for the benefit of the Australian Board's finances.

However, they won the Fourth Test in Sydney handsomely, Boycott making 77 and 142 not out and Snow taking seven for 40 in the second innings. The Fifth and Sixth were high-scoring draws but there was always hope on the English side that the Sydney pitch for the final Test would suit England well and give the stronger side an excellent chance of winning.

In fact, England had to go into the match without Boycott who was averaging 93 in the Test series. By the end of it they had also lost their most successful bowler, Snow. That they still won was a mark of their superiority and of the somewhat shaky state of Australian cricket that season.

For the last Test the Australian selectors made an extraordinary selection. They dropped their captain, Bill Lawry, who had not been in the form of other years but still averaged 40 in the series. In the second innings of the previous Sydney Test he had made 60 not out, carrying his bat through the Australian innings of 116. They replaced him with another Victorian left-hander, Keith Eastwood, who had made a lot of runs in the Sheffield Shield recently when deputising for Lawry, including 201 not out in Sydney, but had not had a regular place in his state side. He was, at 35, a year older than the man who had been so difficult to dig out throughout the 1960s.

In the event Eastwood made five and nought and Australia lost, by 62 runs, a match which could well have been won with a batsman of Lawry's experience and application. The pitch was never straightforward.

This last Test of 1970–1 was Ian Chappell's first as captain of Australia. It was the second Test of a young fast bowler with a fine action called Dennis Lillee. He was only 21, a West Australian who had already had the gruelling experience of bowling in Perth to Barry Richards, who was playing that season for South Australia. On the first day Richards had made 325 in five and a half hours, extending it to 356 next morning.

England, with their 2–0 win over Australia, had entered the 1970s in good order. Australia were in recession and West Indies' improvement of the early 1960s had not been sustained. India and Pakistan had been at war and had not played each other for 10 years. Both of them, like New Zealand, had been comfortably beaten on their latest visit to England. South Africa were almost certainly stronger than any of them but that was not to be proved.

Without reaching the forbidding heights of the 1980s when four fast bowlers would grind opponents into submission, West Indies had been highly successful in the early 1960s, first under Frank Worrell and then, from 1965 when Australia were beaten in the Caribbean, under Gary Sobers.

The 1963 tour of England, Worrell's last before his retirement and knighthood, was a triumph despite reservations about the bowling action of Charlie Griffith. West Indies won three Tests and England, under Ted Dexter, won at Edgbaston where Trueman (seven for 44), Derek Shackleton and Dexter himself bowled West Indies out for 91 on a windy last day. But the most memorable of the five Tests was the one drawn at Lord's.

West Indies, leading by only four runs on first innings, would have been in serious trouble in the second innings but for a brilliant 133 by Basil Butcher in a total of 229. Only two other batsmen reached double figures against Fred Trueman, who took 11 wickets in the match, and Derek Shackleton, whose accurate medium pace pinned down so many of Hampshire's opponents between 1948 and 1969. On the fourth morning the last five West Indian wickets fell for 15 runs in six overs.

England thus needed 234 to win in nearly two days. But there were complications. Nearly two hours' play was lost through bad light on the fourth evening and rain delayed play on the last day until 2.20. England resumed at 116 for three but had lost Cowdrey who had been playing well when he had a bone in his left forearm broken. Barely 14 overs an hour were being bowled by Hall and Griffith, mostly short on a pitch still retaining some life.

Worrell kept Hall going from the pavilion end throughout the three hours 20 minutes' play on the last afternoon. Griffith bowled all but five overs from the other end. The batsmen acquired bruises almost as fast as runs. Only 18 were scored in the first hour for the loss of Barrington who had led the recovery from 31 for three.

By now England's affairs were being conducted by Brian Close who, not for the last time in a Test career running intermittently from 1949 to 1976, seemed to thrive on physical discomfort. As a left-hander he had some slight advantage against the short fast ball and with a characteristic display of raw courage he kept the score moving up until only 15 runs were needed in 19 minutes. For some time Close had been varying stalwart defence with charges at the fast bowlers and it was on one such sortie that he was caught at the wicket off Griffith. He had made 70 and was eighth out.

David Allen and Derek Shackleton picked up what runs they could but eight were still needed when Hall began the last over. Off the fourth ball Shackleton was run out and Colin Cowdrey had to come in with six runs needed off the last two balls. If required to bat he had been intending to take up a left-handed stance to protect his left arm, but in fact Allen had the strike and played the last two balls safely.

West Indies, with their thousands of supporters now resident in the United Kingdom, had become such an attraction that in the changed plan of future tours they were scheduled to come again

in 1966 when cricket would be in competition with the football
World Cup to be staged in England in midsummer.

The 1966 West Indies team in England, captained by Gary
Sobers, was not quite the force of 1963 but neither were England.
The weather, too, was less co-operative. England had three captains during the series, the first, Mike Smith, being dropped after
an innings defeat in three days at Old Trafford. Sobers won a
highly important toss there and the off-spinner Lance Gibbs took
10 wickets.

With Colin Cowdrey as captain England did have a sniff of victory on the fourth morning at Lord's. West Indies, 86 behind on
first innings, were 98 for five in the second innings. Then Sobers
(163) and his cousin David Holford (105) dug in for the rest of
the day and were still together in an unbroken sixth-wicket stand
of 274 when Sobers declared on the last day.

West Indies won the next two Tests comfortably but foundered
in the last at The Oval when England appeared under their third
captain of the summer, Brian Close.

By then West Indies, three up, may have been somewhat
relaxed but everything came off for Close. Tom Graveney, who
had been recalled to Test cricket after a three-year gap, had
already made one hundred and a 96 in the series and here he
made 165 as England, in reply to West Indies' 268, recovered
from 166 for seven to reach the heights of 527. Graveney was run
out after an eighth-wicket stand of 217 with John Murray, the
wicket-keeper. Murray, an elegant batsman who had always
looked capable of making runs at the highest level, went on to
make 112 and the numbers ten and eleven, Ken Higgs (63) and
John Snow (59 not out), completed a bizarre innings by adding
128 for the last wicket.

The new England captain provided one particularly golden
touch. Having instructed Snow to bowl Sobers a bouncer first
ball, Close took up his position at short-leg and was given a gentle
catch off the glove when Sobers mishooked. England won by an
innings and 34 runs.

The continuing weakness of some visiting teams in conditions
alien to them raised numerous problems apart from the obvious
ones of reduced income and of poor preparation for a winter tour
against tougher opposition on hard pitches. In the lovely summer
of 1959 Colin Cowdrey had come under fire for not enforcing the
follow-on at Old Trafford with a lead of 282. Of the previous
three Tests England had won the first in four days and the next

two in three days. Before the third day's play in the Fourth Test started it became known that England would bat again, thus guaranteeing a full day's cricket for the Saturday crowd and some play after the weekend.

Well meant though it was, this decision of Cowdrey's, not to press for victory at the earliest possible time, was seen as devaluing the Test match. In the event, it almost backfired, for after a somewhat meaningless second innings in which England increased their lead to 547, India batted very much better. Abbas Ali Baig, an Oxford freshman who had joined the touring team after the University Match, made 112 before being run out, the more robust "Polly" Umrigar made 118 and it was the fifth afternoon before the Indian innings ended at 376.

In 1965, the England selectors had begun the series snorting fire and fury at unenterprising batting and they soon found a victim. In the First Test against New Zealand at Edgbaston Ken Barrington batted seven and a quarter hours for 137 and was dropped from the next Test. In his defence it was said that he was out of form and had few runs behind him for Surrey that season. The selectors took the view that spending an hour, and 20 overs, in the 80s without scoring and, after reaching 100, hitting an off-spinner for 14 in an over, was carrying rehabilitation too far. Barrington, much liked by all and a mainstay of the England batting almost throughout the 1960s, accepted the selectors' action philosophically. When he was brought back at Headingley he made 163 and shared in a lively second-wicket stand of 369 with John Edrich who made 310 not out.

The selectors again took action over slow batting in 1967. When Geoffrey Boycott batted throughout the first day of a series against India for 106 not out on a pitch which started slightly damp, he came under the hammer and was left out of the next Test. It was not easy to explain to the uninitiated how he came to be dropped after making 246 not out. Moreover, after following on 386 behind, India batted so well – their young captain, the Nawab of Pataudi, making 148 and his side 510 – that the match was in the last afternoon before England won by six wickets.

In 1967 England beat India 3–0 and Pakistan 2–0. The visiting teams from the sub-continent were still not doing themselves justice in English conditions but the new arrangement of twin tours avoided one-sided five-Test series. It seemed a pity that India, in particular, could not show the British public how hard they were to beat at home, especially with spinners of the calibre of Bedi,

New Zealand *v* Pakistan at
Edgbaston in the Prudential
World Cup in 1983. A neutral
umpire, Barrie Leadbeater,
formerly of Yorkshire, remains
unmoved by Abdul Qadir's
impassioned appeal against
Geoff Howarth. *KK*

Two of the best and most appreciated overseas players in English cricket, both
from South Africa, meet in the NatWest Final of 1985 when Essex narrowly
beat Nottinghamshire. The all-rounder Clive Rice led Notts to two
Championships in the 1980s; Ken McEwan, the non-striker here, was an
attractive batsman of great value to Essex for 12 years. *KK*

Essex recruited the Australian captain Allan Border to succeed Ken McEwan and while his stock was rising at home he also became a popular figure in English domestic cricket. *KK*

Though not required by England for Test matches after 1977, Dennis Amiss continued playing for Warwickshire for another 10 years and in 1986, against Lancashire at Edgbaston, made his 100th first-class hundred. *KK*

Richard Hadlee, a model of economy and accuracy among fast-medium bowlers, had much to do with Nottinghamshire's two Championships in the 1980s, during which he also became the biggest taker of wickets in Test history. *KK*

In 125 Test matches Sunil Gavaskar broke many batting records and rounded off his career with 188 runs of high quality in the M.C.C. Bicentenary Match at Lord's. *KK*

Fifty years on. Sir Leonard Hutton
at The Oval on the anniversary of
his 364 against Australia in August
1938. *JW*

Russell Cobb of Leicestershire
coaching in South Africa in March
1989, an 'offence' which, if
repeated, after 1 April, 1989 could
bring him severe penalties from the
T.C.C.B. as a result of the I.C.C.
agreement of January 1989. *JW*

Alan Knott, seen here in his familiar search for suppleness, was one of the world's best wicket-keepers for more than a decade. *JW*

Keith Fletcher's playing days with Essex lasted 26 years during which he made 63 hundreds, played in 59 Tests and, as captain for 13 seasons, brought Essex from near the bottom of the Championship table up to their position as the most consistently successful county of the 1980s. *KK*

David Gower, the most elegant of left-handers, played many fine innings for Leicestershire and England and did so with charm in an age when this was in short supply. *KK*

Ian Botham and Bob Taylor after their extraordinary success in the Golden Jubilee Test match of the Indian Board in February 1980. Botham made 117 and took 12 wickets. Taylor took 10 catches, a Test record, and made 43, sharing in a sixth-wicket stand of 171 with Botham. *JW*

Boycott in defence against Lillee at Lord's in 1981. England, having lost the
First Test, drew this one and at the end of it Botham resigned the captaincy.
Mike Brearley was brought back in haste and, whether by coincidence or not,
Botham's form in the next three improved dramatically. England won them all.
KK

Terry Alderman, an Australian success
of the 1981 series in England. As a
swing and seam bowler he took 42
wickets at 21.2 in the Tests.
KK

Glenn Turner, a sound and prolific opening batsman for Worcestershire and New Zealand, was not short of strokes when the occasion demanded. In 1973 he made 1000 runs before the end of May and here, in 1982, he is making his 100th hundred at Worcester against Warwickshire, extending it to 311 not out. *KK*

Mike Brearley in September 1982 interviewed after his last first-class match, having led Middlesex to the Championship for the fourth time in the last seven years. *KK*

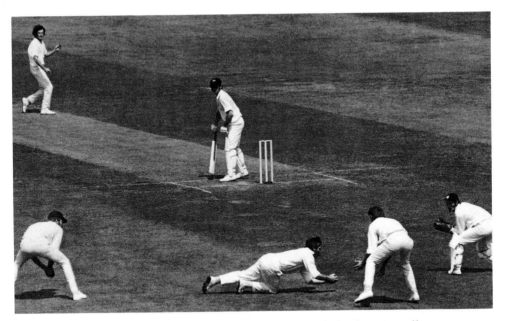

Peter Parfitt, a brilliant fielder anywhere, catches the left-handed Bob Massie off John Snow at Trent Bridge. Parfitt, 35, had been recalled to Test cricket after a three-year interval but retired for business reasons that winter. *KK*

Varying degrees of disappointment are registered by an England side already severely shaken. In the Prudential World Cup semi-final at Headingley in 1975 they had been bowled out for 93 largely through Gary Gilmour's six for 14 but had reduced Australia to 39 for six. At this point Frank Hayes (nearest camera) narrowly missed the stumps at the bowler's end and Gilmour, upside down, recovered to make the remaining runs with Doug Walters. *KK*

Vandalism at Headingley. The pitch on what should have been the last day of a closely fought Test between England and Australia – and, outside the ground, evidence of what prompted it. *JW*

A sight hard to believe. Eden Gardens, Calcutta, 15 minutes after the Second Test of 1976–7 ended. The last day's play might have lasted for only three balls but though India were certain to lose, as they did within an hour by 10 wickets, 70,000 still turned up. *JW*

After a self-imposed absence of three years Geoffrey Boycott returned to Test cricket in 1977. He made 107 and 80 not out against Australia at Trent Bridge where England went two up and, to immense local satisfaction, added 191 at Headingley with what was his 100th first-class hundred. Two former Yorkshire and England opening batsmen, Herbert Sutcliffe, in wheelchair, and Sir Leonard Hutton, who made 149 and 129 hundreds respectively, were present. *KK*

Boycott and the England captain Mike Brearley coming out on the last day of the Second Test against Pakistan in Hyderabad, Sind. They saved the match by batting together almost all day. Brearley's headgear was the first hint of helmets to come. *JW*

Packer cricket began in the soulless surroundings
of the Victorian Football League ground in Melbourne
but later prospered with a massive marketing operation,
floodlights and the eventual availability of genuine
cricket grounds. *JW*

Amid the wealth of talent from overseas from 1968
onwards were several English-born players of
comparable achievement. Bob Willis first played for
England in Australia in 1970–1 and had his finest hour
in 1981 when his eight for 43 finished off Australia
at Headingley. *JW*

▲

Umpire Dickie Bird mounts guard on the pitch
after a bomb scare causes spectators to leave
the stands on the Saturday of the Third and
last Test at Lord's in 1973. *KK*

The young Nawab of Pataudi, eventually to ▶
be known as Mansur Ali Khan, came to the
captaincy of India from Winchester and
Oxford despite losing much of the sight of one
eye in a car crash in 1961. *JW*

Barry Richards, perhaps the most complete batsman of his time, played for Hampshire for 10 years. In this match against Warwickshire the West Indians Alvin Kallicharran *(left)* and Rohan Kanhai are in the opposition. *KK*

By the mid-1970s nearly all the world's best players were registered for English counties. When India and Pakistan began playing each other again after a gap of 18 years, the respective captains, Bishen Bedi and Mushtaq Mohammad, had spent the previous English season playing for Northamptonshire. *KK and JW*

Gordon Greenidge came to Hampshire from Berkshire junior cricket and can scarcely have suffered through finding himself opening the innings with Barry Richards while still in his teens. *KK*

Gary Sobers played for Nottinghamshire for a few seasons but the County Championship was too great a strain for all his varied talent to be of service in a congested season. *KK*

Clive Lloyd – here addressing himself to the England bowling at Trent Bridge with Alan Knott and Chris Old at close quarters – began a long association with Lancashire. His immense power made it peculiarly difficult for a captain to set a field to him. *KK*

Bob Massie played in only six Tests for Australia but in the first of them, at Lord's in 1972, he performed a feat of which any of the world's great bowlers would have been proud. On a ground not usually considered helpful to swing bowling, he swung the ball late and a lot, taking eight wickets in each innings. *KK*

Prasanna, Venkataraghavan and Chandrasekhar. But their day was coming.

West Indies had been to India in the previous winter of 1966–7 and had won two of the Tests. They had also had to survive a nasty riot in Calcutta where the authorities were said to have made the predictably inflammatory misjudgement of selling the same seats twice.

England's visit to West Indies in 1967–8 was preceded by an unfortunate controversy over the captaincy. Brian Close had been in office since the last Test of 1966 and had led England through the successful summer of 1967. In August, however, just as the England selectors were going to announce Close as their captain in West Indies, he directed a delaying action at Edgbaston when Warwickshire had to score 142 in 100 minutes to beat Yorkshire. These tactics, which Yorkshire, the likely champions, scarcely needed, were considered to be deliberate time-wasting and to exceed the bounds of fair play.

The M.C.C. Committee were put in a dilemma. Time-wasting was something on which they had taken a well-publicised stand in recent years and now they were being asked by the selectors to confirm as captain, of a touring team in an always sensitive part of the world, one whom they were about to censure for just such an offence. They told the chairman of selectors, Doug Insole, to think again.

Mike Smith, captain in three recent tours to India, South Africa and Australia, hastily announced his retirement from first-class cricket and the selectors fell back on Colin Cowdrey. For nine years Cowdrey had captained England in odd matches as a deputy for the reigning incumbent but had never before been put in command for a whole tour. With Leslie Ames as manager, he handled this tour efficiently, batted extremely well himself, averaging 66, and to the general surprise returned triumphant.

Only one match in this 1967–8 series was not drawn and that was the Fourth Test in Trinidad which England won by seven wickets, Cowdrey making 148 and 71, Boycott 62 and 80 not out. It was one of the very few Test matches won after the losers had declared. Sobers had declared West Indies' second innings with only two wickets down, leaving England to make 215 in two and three-quarter hours. They won with eight balls to spare.

Some of the gloss was rubbed off the England victory by the fact that it was made possible by Sobers' declaration, variously described as cavalier or ill-judged. But it could be argued that

England would have won the Second Test in Jamaica but for a riot which interrupted play on the third afternoon when they looked to be winning comfortably.

A year later, in 1968–9, West Indies were beaten 3–1 in Australia which was surprising because, with batsmen of the calibre of Seymour Nurse, Gary Sobers and Clive Lloyd at five, six and seven, it was not clear how Australia were going to bowl them out. Yet it was done with ease by the fast-medium bowlers McKenzie, Connolly and Freeman with variety provided by John Gleeson, a right-arm, mainly leg-spin bowler who propelled the ball with a bent middle finger and could be difficult for batsmen to read.

West Indies also lost two of the three Test matches in the first half of the 1969 English season. Only five of the 1966 side remained. The top-class fast bowling of Hall and Griffith had not been replaced yet. There was no great depth of batting. Too much depended on Sobers, who was below his best and probably stale, and on the quick-footed but determined Basil Butcher.

In 1969 England, under Illingworth, had one of their stronger sides of that era, probably second only to South Africa's. Boycott was meticulous in the technique of batting, as he was in throwing and in dress. He did not always present himself in the kindliest of lights, for his reputation was of self-centredness, but he was immensely valuable. His opening partner at that time was John Edrich – small, tough and left-handed. Edrich had no great range of strokes but never seemed to run out of opportunities to accumulate off his legs and square on the off-side. In the Lord's Test three Yorkshiremen made hundreds, Boycott, John Hampshire in his first of only eight Tests, and Ray Illingworth. After 18 years with Yorkshire, Illingworth had, only a few weeks before, embarked on a highly successful second career as captain of Leicestershire.

The wickets fell mostly to Snow, David Brown, a tall enthusiastic fast bowler who was nearing the end of a Test career in which he had served England splendidly since 1965, and Barry Knight, who by now had moved from Essex to Leicestershire. Knight, a highly competent stroke-playing batsman to have coming in at number eight, strengthened the middle batting, as did Alan Knott, now accepted as the world's outstanding wicket-keeper.

Yet times were changing, largely under the influence of air travel which gave players more experience of conditions outside their own country. In the early months of 1971, while England were recovering the Ashes in Australia, the Indians arrived in West Indies with a new 21-year-old opening batsman, Sunil Gavaskar, who had recently been making a lot of runs in Bombay. He stood barely five feet five and, despite his technical proficiency, doubts were expressed about his ability to handle fast bowling on West Indian pitches. He was kept out of the First Test in Jamaica by a finger injury but India, having been 75 for five, were sustained by another batsman from Bombay, Dilip Sardesai, who for 10 years had been a sound and reliable player in Indian Test sides. Here he made 212 of a total of 385 and West Indies, bowled out by the two off-spinners, Prasanna and Venkataraghavan, had to follow on before earning a comfortable draw.

Gavaskar played in his first Test in Port of Spain on a pitch which took spin. This was a considerable help to the Indians, who knew all about spin bowling. West Indies produced a 35-year-old off-spinner, Jack Noreiga, who had not played first-class cricket for eight years before that season. He took nine wickets for 95, but was outgunned. Sardesai made 112. Gavaskar's contribution was 65 and, when India were making the 124 needed for victory, another 67 not out. Their seven-wicket win was their first against West Indies in 25 Tests.

In a high-scoring Third Test in Guyana Gavaskar made 116 and 64 not out. This was drawn and so was the Fourth in Barbados in which Sardesai patched up a start to the innings of 70 for six with 150. Gavaskar suffered his first, and last, failure of the tour, mishooking a bouncer when he had made only one. He put this right with 117 not out in the second innings and rounded off an extraordinary first Test series with 124 and 220 in the last Test, in Port of Spain. This guaranteed that India would not lose their 1–0 lead and in the end they were not far off winning the match. In four Tests Gavaskar had made 774 runs and averaged 154.80. Sardesai averaged 80 and the next Indian batsman only 37.

All this was watched with keen interest in England where the Indians were due during the second half of the 1969 season. For this tour the Indian team included a bowler, Bhagwat Chandrasekhar, who had played his first Test matches against England seven years before aged 18 but whom for some reason they had not taken to the Caribbean. He was tallish, with a very quick right arm, a leg-spinner but of medium pace. His bowling arm was withered as a result of polio in his youth. In the field he threw with his left arm. He was difficult to play and on certain types of pitch could win matches. Many of his wickets were taken when the ball stopped and lifted more than expected.

Pakistan were the touring side in the first half of the 1971 season and provided ample evidence that they were beginning to come to terms with English conditions. Though they lost to Northamptonshire and by 10 wickets to Cambridge University, who were captained by a Pakistani, Majid Khan, this did not stop them from making 608 for seven when they were up against the full might of England in the First Test at Edgbaston. After a spectacular innings of 274 by the tall, bespectacled Zaheer Abbas, two other talented batsmen, Mushtaq Mohammad and Asif Iqbal, made a hundred apiece. The last two had been gaining experience playing for English counties, something on which to ponder as England followed on and were almost certainly spared further embarrassment by rain on the last day.

The Second Test at Lord's was ruined by rain and England only won the last at Headingley by 25 runs after being led on first innings.

Under Illingworth, England had beaten West Indies 2–0, performed respectably though losing 4–1 to the multi-talented Rest of the World side in 1970, had recovered the Ashes that winter in Australia and now had beaten the much improved Pakistan.

In 1971 they were out of luck in that Boycott, who was having one of his most prolific seasons, suffered an injury which kept him out of the last two Tests against India. They may also have been unlucky when rain ended the first Test at Lord's at tea on the last day. India, needing 183 to win, were 145 for eight. And England were having much the better of the Second Test at Old Trafford when rain prevented play on the last day.

At The Oval in the last Test they led India on first innings by 71 runs and it was only on the fourth afternoon that they suddenly found themselves in a losing position. The ball was turning slowly, too slowly for the England slow bowlers, Illingworth and Underwood, but not for Chandrasekhar. With Venkataraghavan at the other end, he swept through the England batting, taking six for 38, and England were out for 101.

India needed 173 to win, which was a lot in the conditions. It seemed even more when Gavaskar was lbw to Snow for nought – in this series the young prodigy had averaged only 24. His seniors had been more successful and the captain Ajit Wadekar and Dilip Sardesai kept their heads now. When they were out, Farokh

Engineer, the Lancashire wicket-keeper-batsman, steered India home with four wickets to spare for their first victory in a Test match in England.

It had taken them 39 years.

15

Years of Change

IN the late 1960s there were several major changes in the conduct of cricket in England, which sooner or later reached other countries. One was the continued growth of sponsorship which led to the increase in limited-over cricket. Another was the reorganisation of the administration of cricket in England.

The game had got along well enough previously under M.C.C. The Committee included cricketers, former cricketers and cricket-lovers. Many were distinguished in other walks of life. In 1967, within three years of his Prime Ministership, Sir Alec Douglas Home had been President of M.C.C. As his successor, he had nominated a former England captain, Arthur Gilligan. The Presidency was no sinecure, as Field-Marshal Lord Alexander had discovered in the 1950s.

Since 1962, when he succeeded Ronald Aird, the Secretary of M.C.C. had been S.C. Griffith, who had kept wicket for Cambridge University, Sussex and England. He carried an increasingly heavy burden. The President held office for only a year and the one continuing role among the unpaid administrators was that of the Treasurer of M.C.C., at this time G.O. Allen. The Secretary was responsible for the running of the first-class game, for the development of non-first-class cricket, for the I.C.C., for which M.C.C. had always provided the secretariat, and for the M.C.C. as a private club, at this time with nearly 10,000 members.

When Billy Griffith went to Australia and New Zealand in 1965–6 as manager of the M.C.C. touring team captained by M.J.K. Smith, his position as Secretary meant that he was in frequent consultations with administrators over the future of the game while coping with the day-to-day duties of a touring manager. It was an exhausting role.

The huge range of the Secretary's responsibilities was such that he needed two Assistant Secretaries. Donald Carr, recently captain of Derbyshire, looked after first-class cricket, Jim Dunbar dealt with the other levels of cricket and the running of Lord's, the most famous cricket ground in the world. Yet there was still a gap in the administration. This was the age of public relations and another Assistant Secretary was recruited in Jack Bailey, formerly a fast-medium bowler for Oxford University and Essex. He became Press Liaison Officer not only for M.C.C. but for the first-class game in general.

During discussions with the Sports Council, the Department of Education and Science and the Minister concerned with sport in the Labour Government, Denis Howell, M.C.C. were told that a private club could not be the recipient of public money and that the administration of cricket should be separated from M.C.C.

Cricket was not likely to be a major recipient of government money but it had to make provision for the future in which youth cricket would need all the help it could find. Thus the M.C.C. Council, soon to become the Cricket Council, was formed as the overall governing body of cricket in England, comprising representatives of the game at all levels. Under it came the National Cricket Association which had been in existence for some years. Its Secretary would be Jim Dunbar, though he remained on the secretariat of M.C.C. The Advisory Committee, through which the counties had run first-class cricket, would be replaced by the Test and County Cricket Board which would be another component of the Council. M.C.C. would become just a cricket (and squash and real tennis) club with its representatives on the Council. By popular demand M.C.C. retained its responsibility for the Laws of Cricket. It also differed from the ordinary private club in that it was the owner of Lord's.

The eventual distribution of responsibilities was only decided after long consultations. The N.C.A. gave birth to a litter of County Associations unrelated to but, it was hoped, working in collaboration with existing county clubs.

There were obviously areas where the separate parts of the Council would be inter-dependent and demarcation lines were not easy to draw. The N.C.A. had little money, the T.C.C.B. was the money-maker and in time would be distributing huge sums annually. Its biggest single money-making source was Lord's, owned by M.C.C. Here was staged not only the most lucrative

match of a Test series but the final of the Gillette Cup which had
been a sell-out since the inauguration of the competition in 1963.

Billy Griffith retained the secretaryship of M.C.C., the I.C.C.,
the Cricket Council and the T.C.C.B. which had absorbed the
Board of Control of Test matches at home. This enabled the new
organisation to function harmoniously to the extent that Mr
Griffith was unlikely to have a serious row with himself. There
were also former players who had served on several committees
and could be said to have a tent in various camps.

By tradition M.C.C. had always provided the secretariat for the
I.C.C., and the President of M.C.C. in his year of office had been
Chairman of the I.C.C. With the increase of international cricket
and attendant politics the I.C.C. became very much more than the
forum for discussion on the game founded in 1909 by England,
Australia and South Africa.

M.C.C. continued to provide offices at Lord's for the Cricket
Council and its other component parts. Until 1977 England teams
going abroad were still called M.C.C. touring teams, though it
was the T.C.C.B. which sent them.

It was when Billy Griffith retired at 60 in 1975 that the difference between the various bodies became clearer. Again, there
were long consultations. Advice was sought from experts on management. As a result Mr Griffith's roles were split in two. Donald
Carr became Secretary of the Cricket Council and the T.C.C.B.;
Jack Bailey became Secretary of M.C.C. and the I.C.C.

Not surprisingly the T.C.C.B., as the body with the money,
played an increasingly prominent part. They had succeeded
M.C.C. in funding the N.C.A. and their representatives took an
increasingly tight grip on the Council at the expense of M.C.C.
When, in 1983, a revision of the Council's constitution brought
changes, the original intention that no two of the constituent
bodies could outvote the others was laid to an uneasy rest. One of
the M.C.C. members on the Council, G.O. (later Sir George)
Allen, resigned from the Council which he had done much to set
up. There was concern that the game should be controlled by the
tiny minority involved in the professional side of it.

In the early 1970s, however, the administrative changes seemed
to have been weathered. On the field limited-over cricket had
proved so popular – with the public though not with all the players – that in 1969 a Sunday afternoon league of 40-over matches
was set up under the sponsorship of John Player and Sons.

For some years a team of former players called the International Cavaliers had played televised matches. In those days there was little professional sport on a Sunday and the counties had held their hand until it was established that the ancient Sunday Observance Act could be circumvented. If a fine was incurred it was a small one and was cheerfully paid.

In 1972 the Benson and Hedges Cup was launched with a format which provided for four groups of counties plus the Minor Counties and Universities to play on a round robin basis in the early part of the season. The first two in each group qualified for the knockout rounds with a final at Lord's in July.

Apart from the financial benefit, these new competitions spread the chances of success round the counties. The County Championship of three-day matches was still the most valued honour in the players' estimation but now a county had four chances of glory – and that in an age when the acquisition of talented overseas players was reducing the gap between the strongest counties and the weakest. By 1988 every county had been in a Lord's final, the last of them Hampshire, winners in that year of the Benson and Hedges Cup. The first Benson and Hedges Cup winners in 1972 were Leicestershire who had played in the County Championship since 1895 without winning it.

This wider distribution of honours was admirable in its way but it was not long before the value of limited-over cricket was being questioned, especially in England. Elsewhere it had been slower to take root but when it did become established, it posed a greater threat to the traditional game than it did in England. Its basic weakness – that bowlers did not have to bowl the other side out – led to a defensiveness which could be highly skilled but was not a desirable quality to hand on to cricketers of the future.

After the initial successes of Sussex in the Gillette Cup there was a period from 1970 to 1976 when Lancashire were in the final six times in seven years, winning four times. They also won the John Player League in the first two years of its existence. Under Jack Bond and later David Lloyd they fielded brilliantly and were seldom short of runs. Their massive left-hander Clive Lloyd, soon to captain West Indies, played many devastating innings. But the most refreshing contribution which they made was through their employment of two slow bowlers who were often the most effective of their bowlers and a welcome change from fast-medium.

Jack Simmons did not play for Lancashire until he was 27. A burly off-spinner, he was also a powerful hitter in the lower order, as was David Hughes, the left-arm spinner. Though their role was a defensive one they bowled their overs more swiftly than those with a longer run-up and they made the point that on many types of pitch, especially in England, bowlers to whom batsmen had to make a positive move could be more effective then their faster colleagues.

Simmons and Hughes kept the ball well up to the batsman, slanting it in to his legs at a brisk pace so that he found it difficult to hit the ball anywhere but in an arc between midwicket and the bowler. In that arc three of Lancashire's most athletic fielders were deployed and were seldom passed. In their first Gillette final of 1970 Simmons and Hughes bowled 24 overs between them for 61 runs and took four of the most valuable Sussex wickets. Nineteen years later – when Hughes was the Lancashire captain and Simmons was in his last season before retiring aged 48 – they were still a considerable force and in the previous year when the Refuge Assurance Cup was first played for by the first four finishers in the League, Lancashire were the first winners.

Hughes indeed had long been a legendary figure in the history of the limited-over game for his innings in 1971 against Gloucestershire at Old Trafford when the semi-final finished in semi-darkness. Earlier the match had been interrupted by rain and the lights were on all round Old Trafford when Hughes found his way to the crease at number nine. Neither he nor Jack Bond, his partner, can have fancied their chance in that light of making the 27 runs still needed off the fast bowling of Mike Procter. But Hughes addressed himself to the off-spinner John Mortimore who was bowling from the Stretford end and hit him for 24 in an over – two sixes, two fours and two twos. Bond made the winning run at 8.50 p.m.

This famous finish may have illustrated that when it is really dark it is the fielding side which is at the greater disadvantage. The batsman must have a rough idea of the direction from which the ball is coming. The fielder may have no idea at all.

However, this does not detract from David Hughes's feat and as if to show that he was equally at home in broad daylight, he launched a no less remarkable attack in the 1976 Gillette final against Northamptonshire. Lancashire, batting first, had struggled to 169 for seven in 59 overs when Bishen Bedi, at the time considered just about the best left-arm spinner in the world, began the last over. Hughes hit him for 26 in it, two of his three sixes being struck off the last two balls.

This was not enough to stop Northants from winning the first trophy in their 98-year history – with a team which included two Pakistani Test players, Mushtaq Mohammad and Sarfraz Nawaz, as well as the Indian captain, Bedi. The levelling-out of the counties' strengths had been greatly assisted in November 1967 when they voted in the Advisory Committee by the required two-thirds majority to allow the instant registration of one overseas player per county. No qualifying period was required provided that the county did not already have two overseas players specially registered under existing regulations. Provisions were made to stop a "transfer system" which had long been the great bogey of English cricket administrators, though the qualifying period for registering overseas players had been reduced from two years to one.

One worthy object of instant registration of the best overseas players was to raise the standard of English county cricket. In time, however, it was realised that there had been cases where the development of young English-born players was being held up through overseas players taking their places. There were also to be cases where counties saw the promise of a young overseas player and signed him up before he had played Test cricket. Malcolm Marshall was signed by Hampshire when he was 20 and had not played in a Test match. The success of West Indies teams in England in the 1980s owed much to the experience of English conditions gleaned by their players while in county sides.

Not every county picked wisely and obvious domestic problems arose when an overseas player was taken on, probably at an inflated salary, and was not as successful as the county's senior home-bred players. This was a sure recipe for domestic discord.

In the short term the best acquisition was probably made by Middlesex much later when they signed a bowler who never played in a Test match, Vintcent van der Bijl.

However, in the long term some counties found that overseas players, after contributing wholeheartedly to the county's welfare while playing, went home when they retired and were not on hand to advise as recently retired senior players often are. Moreover, the original dispensations in the rules of registration which allowed overseas players, if resident in England for five years, to be regarded as in the same category as an English-born player, meant that the new instant registration of the late 1960s was not all it seemed. Counties could have several players in their side who were not qualified for England but who were counted for registration purposes as English. Thus Mushtaq Mohammad, who in the mid-1970s was captaining Pakistan, was also captaining Northants. It could be argued that there was much to be learnt from seasoned overseas players. Another no less persuasive view was that they were stopping young English cricketers from gaining experience, not only as players but as captains. It was a difficult balance to strike.

Yorkshire could be absolved. They had last been champions in 1968 but they stuck to their proud tradition of playing only Yorkshire-born cricketers and clearly suffered for it. Between 1890 and 1968 they had only twice finished worse than eighth in the Championship and in the 10 seasons since Surrey's monopoly finished in 1959 they had won it seven times. In the next 21 years after the introduction of instant registration of overseas players, there were only seven seasons in which they finished eighth of the 17 or better – and in 1983 they were bottom.

Not all of the decline could be attributed to their lack of overseas players. There were domestic differences usually involving their one great player of the age, Geoffrey Boycott. This, too, was an age in which young cricketers of ability were not content to wait in their county second eleven until they were nearly 30, as had happened before the War. Young players, marrying earlier than their fathers and grandfathers, were restless to be off to other counties who had room for them. Yorkshire had always had first-class players to spare and they must have suffered even more now from this seepage of talent.

By 1978 it was clear that the door opened wide to overseas players 10 years before needed to be partially closed again. The Cricketers' Association asked the Board if the two overseas players allowed could be reduced to one. The Board acted on this before the 1979 season but there were difficulties, not least with the legal position and possible charges of restraint of trade. Thus the reduction did not apply if a player had been signed, or if negotiations had been taking place, before 28 November 1978. For three seasons counties could still play two overseas cricketers but from 1982 only if both had been signed, or were negotiating, before the 1978 date. Otherwise they would be limited to one.

The object of this was to safeguard the jobs of 44 overseas players then under contract to the counties. It reduced the number of players not qualified for England in county sides but meant that for the next decade or more there would still be more than one such player in some county sides. Even then some counties found it convenient to have two overseas players on their staff, though they were only allowed to play one of them in competitive matches. This was an effective way of ensuring that they had a relatively fresh bowler available. In the mid-1980s Surrey could choose between two West Indian fast bowlers, Sylvester Clarke and Anthony Gray, Derbyshire between John Wright, the reigning New Zealand captain and opening batsman, registered in 1977, and the West Indian fast bowler Michael Holding who had been with them since 1983.

The counties had also been tapping for some years a new source of English-qualified players. Derbyshire were well served by Ole Mortensen, a fast-medium bowler from Denmark. Hampshire found a medium-fast bowler from Holland in Paul-Jan Bakker, who in 1989 took 77 wickets for them at 22 apiece.

The need to do what was fair to the individual player, to the county who wished to register him and to English cricket overall made registration a continuing problem. There were conflicting loyalties. What the members wanted for their respective counties was not necessarily what was best for English cricket. But in May 1977 a vast new problem had erupted, affecting not only England but the other Test-playing countries as well. Mr Kerry Packer had arrived on the scene.

16

The Advance of Tony Greig

ENGLISH cricket had suffered a cruel blow in 1969 when Colin Milburn, a bulky, well-loved, jolly character, lost his left eye in a motor accident. He was 27 and beginning to fulfil the great promise as a stroke-playing opening batsman which he had shown since coming to Northamptonshire from his native Durham.

His injury came only two months after he had been summoned to Pakistan by M.C.C. as a replacement. He came from Perth where he was averaging 62 for Western Australia in the Sheffield Shield. After a journey of nearly 40 hours to Dacca he was too late to play in the Second Test but, opening the innings in the last Test in Karachi, he played a superb innings of 139 in the Test match abandoned through rioting on the third morning.

Milburn had made a hundred in one of his previous eight Tests but his immobility in the field was against him and the selectors had preferred his county captain Roger Prideaux when picking the team for this tour which was originally to be of South Africa. Milburn had just started the home season of 1969 with 158 against Leicestershire when he had his accident. Though he made a gallant effort to resume his first-class career in 1973 and played in 15 Championship matches, the handicap was too great and he turned to coaching and commentating. He died early in 1990, much mourned.

Also in the Midlands at this time but utterly different from Milburn, especially in physique, was the young New Zealander Glenn Turner. A slightly built, far from robust figure, he had qualified for Worcestershire in 1968 before he was 21, before instant registration and before he played in his first Test match. He soon became one of the most prolific opening batsmen in the world, well equipped with strokes though these were usually subordinated to the less ambitious side of a sound technique.

When the New Zealanders went to the West Indies in 1971–2, Turner carried his bat through the first innings of the First Test for 223 out of a total of 386. In all, he made four double hundreds on the tour, two in Tests. Bev Congdon, soon to take over the New Zealand captaincy when Graham Dowling was forced to retire through injury, was not far behind him and neither side had the bowlers to prevent all five Tests from being drawn.

In the middle 1970s Turner himself succeeded to the captaincy but he was not always at one with the New Zealand Board in those days when he was the ultra-professional from a country of part-time cricketers where there was little money in the game. He played for Worcestershire until 1982, latterly captaining them. One of his last innings, in which he made his 100th hundred, was his 311 not out in only five hours 43 minutes against Warwickshire at Worcester. In his last match he made 118 and 66 against Kent at Hereford before appendicitis ended his last season prematurely.

He had exceeded Don Kenyon's 70 hundreds for Worcestershire and as early as 1970 had broken the county's record of nine hundreds in a season set by C.F. Walters in 1933. In the penultimate home match of the season against Lancashire he was as close to making the 10th as it is possible to be without succeeding, being run out by Clive Lloyd's throw when only inches short of his 100th run. Undeterred by this infuriating near-miss, he put the matter straight in the remaining match at Worcester against Warwickshire.

After the cancellation of a tour which should have been made by South Africa in 1971–2 Australia did much as England had done in 1970 and played a Rest of the World side. The series was marked by an innings of 254 in Melbourne by Gary Sobers which Sir Donald Bradman described as "probably the best ever seen in Australia". However, the most significant feat for Australia was the fast bowling of Dennis Lillee who had played in his first Tests in the previous Australian season against England.

In England in 1972 Lillee confirmed his quality by taking 31 Test wickets at 17 apiece, though it was another bowler, Bob Massie, who was responsible for one of Australia's wins in a series drawn 2–2. Massie's previous experience of conditions in the United Kingdom had been gleaned in the Scottish League while playing for Kilmarnock two years earlier. There he must have learnt the value of bowling a full length, for in his first Test match he swung the ball prodigious amounts on a ground, Lord's, not usually considered an accommodating one for swing bowlers and took 16 wickets for 137 runs.

Briefly at Trent Bridge in the next Test he looked capable of carrying on in this vein. Having taken four for 48 in the first innings, he bowled the left-handed John Edrich who played no stroke because the ball started so wide outside his off-stump. But the magic somehow wore off. Massie took only two more wickets in the remaining two Tests and only ever played in two Test matches after this tour.

This was a weird, inexplicable interlude but did not divert attention from the genuine revival which Australia were making through the batting of the Chappell brothers and the fast bowling of Lillee.

That winter England toured India for the first time for nine years. Illingworth was not available but the side was well led by A.R. Lewis, the Glamorgan captain who had looked a batsman of class since his days at Cambridge in the early 1960s.

Tony Lewis made a superlative start, being top scorer with 70 not out in the First Test which England, to the general surprise, won by six wickets on Christmas Day. They lost, though only by 28 runs, in another low-scoring match in Calcutta and lost again on a turning pitch at Chepauk in Madras which was ideal for the Indian spinners. Lewis himself made a fine hundred in the Fourth Test in Kanpur and there were two more well-made hundreds by Keith Fletcher and Tony Greig in Bombay, but the series was won 2–1 by India.

Though Greig, six and a half feet of him, had a most successful tour with bat and ball, the England batting was not at its strongest. Boycott had missed much of the last home series through injury and had medical reasons for not touring India. However, hereabouts there was a marvellous transformation in the career of another batsman, Dennis Amiss.

For some years Amiss had been looked on as a young batsman of high promise but when he had been picked for England he had done little except to suggest that he had limitations against fast bowling. However, he was now opening the innings for Warwickshire after being dropped early in the 1972 season and had done enough to earn a place on this tour in the absence of Boycott. But he was no more successful in India and after the Third Test he was dropped.

After a week in Sri Lanka during which Amiss made two fifties operations switched to Pakistan and a three-day match in Peshawar in which not a ball was bowled. A good start was urgently needed in the First Test which followed and despite the shortage of practice and Amiss's ill-health since arriving in Lahore, a good start was duly forthcoming. Lewis won the toss, the pitch had more bounce than any in India and Amiss, having shared with Mike Denness in an opening stand of 105, made 112.

This and the other two Tests which followed, in temperatures mounting towards the end of March to around 105 degrees, were drawn. In Hyderabad Amiss made 158 and in Karachi he was one of the three batsmen in the match who were out for 99 – Majid Khan and Mushtaq Mohammad being the others. Yet it was his 62 not out in the only other match in Rawalpindi which will live longest in the memory of those present, for it was played on a soft turning pitch of unpredictable bounce against two excellent spinners called Nazir – Nazir senior, left arm, and Nazir junior, off-spinner – and it won M.C.C. a match which had seemed likely to have been lost with the toss.

Quiet and reserved of manner, Dennis Amiss was an unostentatious cricketer, basically sound but with strokes off the front foot through the covers which were of high quality. Like most other batsmen he did not look as if he enjoyed playing the best fast bowling on unreliable pitches but he made a better hand of it than most.

In England during 1973 he made 138 not out against New Zealand at Trent Bridge and was one of the more successful batsmen – with Boycott and Keith Fletcher – in the short series which West Indies won 2–0. In West Indies a few months later he made 669 runs in the five-Test series, averaging 82. Among his hundreds in the Caribbean were three in Test matches. In Jamaica he made 262 not out and batted nine and a half hours to save a match which England had seemed certain to lose. In just over a year since going to the wicket in Lahore, having made only 348 runs in 12 Tests spread over seven years, he had made 1450 in Test matches. He was not finished yet, for he made 188 in the Lord's Test of 1974 against India and 183 at The Oval against Pakistan. In the calendar year of 1974 he scored 1379 runs in Test matches.

Lillee and Thomson put a brake on his rush of runs as they did on those of other England batsmen, but when he was brought back to play in the last Test of 1976 at The Oval against West Indies, he batted five hours 20 minutes and made 203 against Michael Holding and three other fast bowlers. On predictable pitches he had found ways of coping with the fastest bowling.

Until 1976 West Indian Test teams had been given variety by the presence of Lance Gibbs, an off-spinner of the highest class. Until the 1970s they had also had Gary (now Sir Garfield) Sobers who brought variety to any side in which he played. After the retirement of Gibbs, they sacrificed variety for victory and unfortunately for the spectator they were good enough to get away with it. Four and even five bowlers of fast and fast-medium would hammer away hour after hour, inevitably at a slow over rate so that the batsman lost the rhythm and confidence acquired by feeling the ball in the middle of the bat.

The West Indian selectors were in the blissful position of not having to worry too much if the fast bowlers could not bat because a new batting genius had appeared in Antigua in Vivian Richards. At about the same time Gordon Greenidge came on the scene, less exotically, from Reading. If these failed, there was still the new captain, Clive Lloyd, at number five to repair the damage. Lloyd was a tall left-hander whose violent but judiciously played strokes had such power that the mishit could go for six and normal field-setting was unavailing.

During the brief captaincy of Rohan Kanhai West Indies had been to England in the second half of the 1973 season and had won 2–0. They followed the New Zealanders who had lost 2–0, a result which did the losers less than justice. At Trent Bridge they made 440 in the fourth innings (Bev Congdon, the captain, 176, Vic Pollard 116) and only missed a record-breaking win by 38 runs. At Lord's they declared at 551 for nine with a first-innings lead of nearly 300 but England earned a draw fairly comfortably and made better use of an unpredictable pitch at Headingley.

The same could not be said of the England bowlers against West Indies in the second half of the season, not surprisingly perhaps because Boyce (Essex), Julien (Kent), Sobers (Notts), Vanburn Holder (Worcestershire) and Gibbs (Warwickshire) all had several years' experience of bowling in English conditions. Indeed in the Second Test, at Edgbaston, all 11 West Indians were or had been on the staff of English counties. Sobers was captaining Nottinghamshire but was released for the three Test matches.

At Lord's in the last Test of 1973 West Indies declared at 652 for eight – Kanhai 157, Sobers 150 not out, Julien 121 – and won by an innings. That was not all – just after lunch on the Saturday there was a bomb scare which caused the stands to be vacated during an 85-minute hold-up. At that time the I.R.A. was active in London and with so many people packed together the luckless Secretary of M.C.C. Billy Griffith, whose decision it was, could not rely on its being a hoax, which it was.

Earlier in 1973 the Australian resurgence had continued with a win in the Caribbean which was remarkable because it was achieved almost without any contribution from the two bowlers who had performed so well in England in the previous year. Lilliee was having serious back trouble and though he played in the First Test did not take a wicket and did not play in the other four. Bob Massie found that the ball would not swing for him and he did not reach the Test team. Max Walker, a strongly built medium-fast bowler of boundless stamina who had come on the Test scene when Australia were winning all three Tests at home against Pakistan, took 26 West Indian wickets at 20 each.

The financial difficulties of staging a Test series in West Indies were underlined in this series. When Australia came to the last Test in Port of Spain already 2–0 up, barely 7000 turned up in the five days – and this on the island usually given two Tests as being the most lucrative.

The next visitors to the Caribbean were England, only five months after they had been well beaten by West Indies in a short series at home. Raymond Illingworth's overall successful captaincy had ended with that series and he was succeeded by Mike Denness, an elegant batsman from the West of Scotland who had followed Colin Cowdrey as captain of Kent. Denness's side had unexpected success after an unpromising start in Trinidad where they lost the First Test by seven wickets and created an outsize rumpus through an incident at the end of the second day's play.

The last ball of the day was played to Tony Greig at silly point and while batsmen and fielders started to move off, Greig, in an excess of competitiveness, threw to the non-striker's end from which Alvin Kallicharran had departed with all the inner peace of mind of a batsman whose score stands at 142 not out. On Greig's appeal umpire Sang Hue, not having called "over", gave Kallicharran out.

This made for angry crowd scenes and two hours of diplomatic discussion before it was announced that the appeal had been withdrawn and that Kallicharran would resume his innings next morning. This incident was especially unfortunate because Greig was beginning to play an increasingly valuable part in the England side with his medium-fast bowling delivered from a great height, consistent middle-order batting and close fielding in which his reach enabled him to cover more ground than others.

The 82 which Amiss averaged in the series was nearly twice that of Greig, Boycott and Knott, but it was Boycott's 99 and 112 in a low-scoring match that put England in a winning position in the final Test in Port of Spain. The pitch was slow and took spin but was not of much help to Derek Underwood, though he bowled 49 overs for 76 runs. It was Greig who levelled the series by turning to off-spin and taking 13 wickets for 156 runs.

This feat raised hopes that Greig would be equally effective on slow turning pitches elsewhere but somehow he could never repeat anything like it. Yet the match may have had one long-term consequence. Geoffrey Boycott was said to have felt that in the prevailing euphoria his two very fine innings had been over-looked. Perhaps they had – but in a way which was a tribute to his own consistency. Press and public were accustomed to his making runs. A performance such as Greig's was much rarer, especially when the bowler was operating in a method to which he was not accustomed.

This was later given as a reason for Boycott's decision in May 1974 to withdraw from Test cricket at the height of his powers. He had previously opted out of a tour of India for health reasons. His reason for dropping out this time was not entirely clear. His explanation, that he had not got over the pressure and tension of international cricket and was not confident of being able to stand up to a long Australian tour, was hard for the public to under-stand. Some thought that he coveted the England captaincy and took no great pleasure from making runs which led to bouquets being showered on the reigning captain.

Unfortunately events in Australia in the following winter of 1974–5 left many people in no doubt that his main reason was that he did not wish to face the often fearsome fast bowling of Lillee and Thomson. In hindsight, he was deemed to have been shrewd but unpatriotic.

This may have been the easy interpretation but it was not a fair one. Despite the eye weakness which caused him to play first in glasses and then in contact lenses, Boycott was wont to handle fast bowling better than most and with no lack of courage. Moreover, no one could have expected that the attack of Lillee and Thomson would be as frightening as it often was.

Dennis Lillee had not played first-class cricket for many months while he fought to recover full fitness after an operation on his back. Those who had had a similar injury and many others were adamant that it was impossible that a fast bowler could recover his full pace and control after such an experience. They reckoned without the progress of medical science and Lillee's determination to get himself fit again.

Another factor in forecasts about the coming tour by Mike Denness's side was that not a lot was known about Jeff Thomson who had the reputation of being wild with a slinging action. Lillee apart, the fast bowlers produced recently by Australia had been less than lethal and their opponents may have been lulled into a false sense of hope.

In the event, Lillee gradually built himself up until he was bowling as well as ever. Thomson proved more controlled than forecast, and very fast. Walker gave little away as an admirably steady third bowler; and the pitches, except on the Melbourne Cricket Ground, were quick enough for their slight unevenness to make batting a matter of courage as well as technique. Ian Chappell's usual practice was to start with Lillee, downwind, and Thomson. After about an hour Lillee would come off and Thomson would replace him. Thereafter Lillee and Thomson would alternate in three- or four-over spells with Walker at the other end. There were occasions when Lillee and Thomson, having bowled for the first hour, would start to bowl faster, a development which batsmen tend to find particularly depressing. If a few overs were needed from someone else before the new ball was taken, Ashley Mallett, the off-spinner, or another slow bowler would bowl them economically and perhaps pick up a wicket or two from batsmen who in their relief were over-ambitious.

Unfortunately on most of the pitches that season Lillee and Thomson were downright dangerous. The same two umpires, Tom Brooks and Robin Bailhache, stood throughout the series. The England captain and manager, Mike Denness and Alec Bedser, were accorded the usual courtesies in the selection of umpires and presumably were satisfied that these two were better than the others whom they had seen.

The Australian public were justifiably glad to see the Ashes return and to some extent England brought their suffering on themselves. The first short-pitched bowling came from England in the first innings of the series in Brisbane when Bob Willis and Peter Lever took five wickets through mishooks. It was no excuse to say that they did this not to intimidate but because they were bereft of other ideas and bowled short to trap the batsmen into mishooks. It was all too clear that when Lillee and Thomson bowled short, their extra pace was such that batsmen hooked at their peril.

Uncommitted spectators can have taken no pleasure from seeing batsmen walking out to bat knowing that they were in danger. The helmet had not yet come into usage but, if anything, it increases the number of bouncers fired off by bowlers who persuade themselves that the batsman will come to no harm. In a television interview on the eve of the First Test in 1974–5 Lillee said that his policy was to aim at the b 'sman's ribcage, a statement which did not do justice to his bowling o win him many new admirers.

The only relief for Denness and his side, which since the First Test included Colin Cowdrey, was in the two Tests played in Melbourne where the pitch was slower. In the Third Test it was Australia, already two up, who surprisingly settled for a draw when needing only another 16 runs to win in three eight-ball overs with three wickets, including Rodney Marsh's, in hand.

Cowdrey had been summoned, shortly before his 42nd birthday, on the strength of some stirring efforts in the past against very fast bowling. He had played a full season for Kent in 1974 but it was nearly four years since he last played in a Test match. It was asking a lot for his reflexes to be as sharp as they had once been and though he usually spent quite a time at the crease, his 41 in the second innings of the Second Test in Perth was his highest score in a Test during that tour. A few days before, he had been working in the City of London but had to be thrown into battle soon after his arrival in Perth because of injuries to Dennis Amiss and John Edrich.

In Sydney, Denness was so dissatisfied with his own batting that he stood down from the Fourth Test and England were captained by Edrich. Cowdrey was not in fact the oldest player in the side. Fred Titmus was a month older. When he had made 61 with great fortitude in the second innings in Perth he had been playing in his first Test match since losing four toes in a boating accident in the West Indies nearly seven years before.

Australia won comfortably in Sydney, thus recovering the Ashes, and won particularly well in Adelaide. The normal dry, very hot weather of Adelaide in late January was for once replaced by wind and rain. The match started a day later after a cover had been blown off leaving a wet patch at one end. When Denness won the toss, he put Australia in and set Underwood to work on the sort of pitch on which he had had many successes.

On this occasion Underwood was thwarted by an innings of

great skill by Ian Redpath who made only 21 runs but stayed until the going had become easier. Of the 15 Australian wickets which fell in the match, Underwood took 11 and the faster bowlers, Willis and Arnold, only three, but the Australian fast bowlers were as effective as ever, especially Lillee. Though Thomson, having damaged an ankle playing tennis on the rest day, could not bowl in the second innings, Walker and Mallett helped Lillee to tidy up.

Anything less predictable than an England victory in the last Test in Melbourne by an innings was hard to imagine but the *dramatis personae* and the setting were different. Thomson's injury prevented him from playing. Lillee bowled only six overs before retiring with a bruised foot. The humid conditions on the first day were also different, for Peter Lever, swinging the ball and hitting a damp patch at one end, took six for 38 and with Chris Old and Tony Greig had Australia out for 152. By then the pitch was playing comfortably and on the second morning the stage seemed to be set for a last big innings by Colin Cowdrey on the ground where he made the first of his 22 Test hundreds 20 years before. Indeed, before the ground was converted into the main stadium for the 1956 Olympic Games. However, in what was to be the last of his 114 Test matches he was soon out to Walker.

This time the other batsmen took their chances. At last they were batting on an easy-paced pitch with their two tormentors gone and from 18 for two Edrich (70), Denness (188), Fletcher (146) and Greig (89) built up a huge lead. Denness, who had made only 130 runs in his previous eight innings in the series, played most handsomely to make the highest score of his career and the highest by an England captain in Australia.

He followed it with 181 in Auckland in the First Test against New Zealand, sharing in a fourth-wicket stand of 266 with Keith Fletcher who made 216, but England's victory by an innings was marred by a distressing accident to Ewan Chatfield, New Zealand's new fast-medium bowler. Playing in his first Test match at the age of 24, Chatfield deflected a ball from Lever on to his head causing a hairline fracture of the skull. Bernard Thomas, the M.C.C. physiotherapist, raced out to him and though Chatfield's heart momentarily stopped beating, was successful in reviving him. This appalling accident no doubt brought the wearing of helmets nearer, though it did not lead to any lessening of short deliveries bowled to late-order batsmen.

In Chatfield's case a happy and remarkable future lay ahead.

He was still playing Test cricket in 1988–9 when everyone else in the match had dropped out of it.

In 1975 the first World Cup was played in England, founded largely to provide associate member-countries of the I.C.C. with an income. Whether the title "World Cup" was strictly honest is doubtful, for one of the strongest cricketing countries, South Africa, was excluded. It was contested by the six other Test-playing countries plus Sri Lanka and East Africa. They played in two groups of four from which the first two went forward to semi-finals with a final at Lord's to follow.

The tournament began with a mystical display by India at Lord's after England had made 334 for four in their 60 overs. India's reply was 132 for three, Gavaskar having batted doggedly through the innings for 36. Having decided presumably that they had no chance of winning, he and the other batsmen must have decided to treat themselves to batting practice on a very good pitch. It seemed that the Indian captain, Venkataraghavan, and other members of his side were not in agreement with this policy. Nor was the 20,000 crowd.

England reached the semi-final but then went down to Australia in extraordinary conditions at Headingley. The pitch was damp and green, the atmosphere heavy and Australia's left-arm fast-medium bowler Gary Gilmour was next to unplayable. Bowling a full length and swinging the ball vast amounts, he took six for 14 in his 12 overs. Australia needed only 94 to win and though they were 39 for six, Gilmour came in on what was clearly the day of his life and with a few boisterous strokes and assistance from Doug Walters settled the match. Only 65 of the 120 overs available had been needed.

With not a slow bowler in sight the final between West Indies, who had beaten New Zealand at The Oval by five wickets in the other semi-final, and Australia lasted until 8.43 on a glorious summer's evening. West Indies, under their new captain Clive Lloyd who made 102, always looked the likelier winners, though in a final fling by Thomson and Lillee 41 runs were added for the last wicket before Thomson was run out in the 59th over and Australia were beaten by 17 runs.

The Australians stayed on for the second half of the 1975 season for a tour including four Test matches. This was rather too soon for England after their rough handling by Lillee and Thomson a few months before. Denness began by putting Australia in at Edgbaston. With rain forecast, this was dangerous.

The rain came soon after Australia's innings ended on the second day. Unfortunately for England it stopped in time for them to continue their innings that day, with an hour added to make up for time lost. On a lively pitch Lillee, Thomson and Walker went to work once again and Australia won by an innings.

This was the sort of situation in which captains are sacked. Denness was no exception and Tony Greig took over for the Second Test at Lord's. The selectors also produced David Steele, a dour, unexciting batsman from Northamptonshire who played very straight and who was known as a good player of fast bowling. Prematurely grey at 33 and batting in glasses, he was an unlikely looking hero but he proved a staunch competitor, making 50 and 45, 73 and 92, 39 and 66, and caught the public imagination to such an extent that by the end of the year he was being voted B.B.C. Television's Sportsman of the Year.

The last three Tests were all drawn and England might even have won at Headingley but for an unprecedented occurrence which made play impossible on the last day.

Though England had made only 288 they found themselves with a first-innings lead of 153, largely through the left-arm spin of Philippe Edmonds who took five for 28 in the first innings of his first Test. They increased this to 444 but at the end of the fourth day Australia were 220 for three and the pitch was playing well enough for them to nurse some hope of making the 445 to win which would have broken all Test records.

The pitch was not so good next morning. During the night vandals had worked their way under the covers and had dug holes in the pitch with knives, adding a gallon of crude oil for good measure. Slogans painted around the ground indicated that this had nothing to do with cricket but was part of a campaign to secure the release of a citizen from the East End of London who was serving 17 years for armed robbery. The two captains, Tony Greig and Ian Chappell, decided that the best thing was to abandon the match as a draw. It might well have been one anyhow, for there was some rain during the day.

The next English summer of 1976 has gone into history as one of the sunniest of the century. The visitors were West Indies who had just had a rough time in Australia where they had yet to win a series. Greg Chappell, taking over from his brother who still played in the side, made a hundred in each innings in his first match as captain. Lillee, Thomson and Gilmour took 76 wickets between them. West Indies lost 5–1 but in England a few months later they resumed their advance towards the all-powerful position which they were to occupy in the 1980s. It was not until the Third Test at Old Trafford that they won the first of their three victories in the series and the circumstances of that did not endear them to everyone.

Gordon Greenidge made a hundred in each innings, the first a brilliant 134 out of a total of only 211. England were bowled out for 71 (Michael Holding five for 17), but when they began the last innings with 80 minutes of the third day's play left and with 552 needed to win, they were submitted to what most of those present that Saturday considered was grossly intimidatory bowling by Holding, Roberts and the 20-year-old Wayne Daniel.

As it happened, England's opening pair in this match were two left-handed batsmen renowned for their courage, John Edrich and Brian Close. It was 27 years since Close had played in his first Test match on the same ground. Now, at 45, he was playing in what proved to be his last and he could not have gone out in a more honourable way.

As left-handers, he and Edrich had a slight advantage in that the fast bouncer was usually slanting away from them and was thus more easy to avoid than if they had been right-handed. But it was a disgraceful exhibition of bowling which should have been stopped by the umpires, if not by the West Indies captain. Lloyd Budd, a much respected Hampshireman, was standing in his first Test and must have been reluctant to take action when his more experienced colleague was taking none. Bill Alley did eventually warn Holding but as a rugged Australian may not have done so earlier because the bowlers were getting nowhere against the resolute Edrich and Close. The two heroes came in bruised but with wickets intact.

The unusually unanimous condemnation of this piece of bowling had its effect. On the Monday the fast bowlers kept the ball up to the bat and a start of 54 for no wicket became 126 all out.

In the last Test on a good pitch at The Oval Holding, the fastest through the air, bowled an admirably full length and took 14 wickets for 149 runs, remarkable figures for a fast bowler on an easy-paced pitch.

Tony Greig came through the series with reputation unblemished, having by most estimates done as well as captain as could be reasonably expected. He had made a hundred in the Headingley Test, batting at number six, and against the fast bowling menace of the past two years had been the most successful batsman.

His extra inches allowed him to play the lifting ball with greater safety and confidence than the others, though Alan Knott, with improvisations such as stepping back and tipping the lifting ball over the slips' heads, coped better than most.

Greig's career had not been without controversy but the selectors, and almost everyone else, were prepared to take a chance that his many good points would prevail. He was a fine all-rounder of many parts and those who had seen him in India on England's last tour four years before were hopeful that he might become the first England captain to lead a winning side there since Douglas Jardine in 1933–4.

There was no suggestion that his birth and education in South Africa would be held against him. Indeed he had established an extraordinary rapport with the huge Indian crowds. This was not for want of trying on Greig's part and some of the methods and gestures which he employed were not exactly compatible with the dignity of a future England captain. But the crowds were clearly fascinated by this blond giant and in many ways this eased the passage through India of his team.

It was a remarkable Test series from the start. Dennis Amiss, though far from well, batted throughout the first day's play in Delhi and for eight and a half hours in all to make 179 out of England's total of 381. But the major contribution came from John Lever in his first Test match.

Lever had been picked for the tour not only because, as a left-arm fast-medium bowler, he brought some variety to the attack but because he had the rare merit for a fast bowler of being always fit. His virtues were not known to include batting, yet coming in at number nine, one or even two places higher than that in which he was accustomed to bat for Essex, he made a most valuable 53 in his first Test innings. He was also not renowned for swinging the ball, yet in Delhi, after a change of ball in the 11th over of India's innings, he swung the replacement so much that he took seven wickets in the first innings and 10 for 70 in the match, which England won by an innings.

While England were in the nets on the day before the Second Test at Eden Gardens, Calcutta, they were surprised to see the ground staff scrubbing hard at what had been a well-grassed pitch. Next morning, New Year's Day 1977, Greig lost the toss but after Chris Old in the gully had taken a spectacular catch from Gavaskar in the first over, Willis, Lever, Old and Underwood bowled India out for 155.

This did not seem a bad score when England were 14 for two but Amiss and Derek Randall in his first Test helped the score along slowly until Greig came in at 90 for four. He joined Roger Tolchard, the reserve wicket-keeper who was playing here as a batsman. He was known as an excellent player of spin.

Greig soon played an off-drive which flew uppishly past mid-off and then, accepting on the strength of this that the utmost care was required on this pitch, settled in to add 142 with Tolchard in four and a half hours. Greig's 103 was an innings of great self-discipline which eventually, after a timely piece of left-handed slogging by Chris Old, led to a first-innings lead of 166.

The disadvantage of batting second had been overcome and early on the fifth day England won by 10 wickets. The match only just lasted into the fifth morning and could have finished in three balls but, though India had no chance of winning, the usual crowd of 70,000 turned up, an oriental phenomenon if ever there was one.

There was a surprise in Madras where, since the development of the once rather attractive Chepauk ground into a concrete stadium, the Indian spinners had been wont to prosper. Now the mud pitch was found to be hard and bouncy, a rarity on the sub-continent. England were always in control but became involved in a bizarre international incident before they won the match by 200 runs and with it the series.

India were looking like being about 100 behind on first innings when during lunch on the third day John Lever mentioned to the England physiotherapist Bernard Thomas that in the humid heat he was having difficulty in keeping sweat out of his eyes. Bernard Thomas suggested that he should try a piece of gauze round his brow and, to make it stick, rubbed in some ointment which he had been given in Calcutta. Lever tried it but soon found that it did not work and after a few minutes, as he prepared to bowl an over, he put the strip down behind the stumps right under umpire Reuben's eyes.

In no time the matter was reported to the Indian Board, suggestions of cheating were in the air and after Ken Barrington, the manager, had explained what had happened he was left in the dark as to what was going on. Telephone communications with London were never at their best when this sort of incident occurred but eventually the Indian Board said that they could not decide whether the intentions of the bowler were deliberate or not and they referred their findings to the T.C.C.B. in London.

This suggested that the Indian Board did not accept the word of Lever, Bernard Thomas and the England captain who, though not involved himself, was highly articulate in defence of his bowler to the Indian Press. However, the T.C.C.B. quickly announced that it was satisfied with the explanation given by captain and manager and that was the end of it. The ridiculous incident had been a help undoubtedly in some quarters in glossing over the fact that India were 3–0 down in a five-match series.

England lost the next Test in Bangalore and drew the last in Bombay before going on to Sri Lanka and then to Melbourne to play a match to mark the Centenary of England–Australia matches. Of the modern heroes, Dennis Lillee took 11 wickets, Rodney Marsh made 110 not out and Derek Randall contributed a memorable 174 to England's last innings of 417.

The original match ended on 17 March 1877 with Australia winning by 45 runs. By an amazing fluke the five-day Centenary Match ended 100 years later to the day – with Australia winning again by 45 runs.

It was a splendid match. Goodwill abounded, old friends met again and a sense of tradition was in everyone's mind. The game seemed to be starting on the second century of international cricket with friendship and understanding as strong as ever.

Not for long.

17

Enter Mr Packer

Sunday 8 May 1977 was the date when the full meaning of the arrival of Kerry Packer in the world of cricket became clear. Previously rumours circulating in South Africa had been taken as heralding another tour there, such as those made by the International Wanderers and the Derrick Robins' XI, tours which did not clash with the players' official commitments for their counties or states and for their countries.

The announcement in Australia giving the names of 18 Australian cricketers and 17 from other Test-playing countries who had signed contracts was in general a shock. It had been a well-kept secret.

England's share at first was only four but they included the captain. Tony Greig had just led a successful tour of India but he appeared to be one of the convenors of the pirate operation. Alan Knott had scarcely missed a Test match in the last 10 years, Derek Underwood was not far behind him and though John Snow was 35, he had played in three Tests against West Indies the year before. Geoffrey Boycott, who had been showing signs of offering himself for Test selection again, had been approached, it was said, but had not signed.

Few grudged the best players of the day being paid more, especially at a time when the best footballers were known to be commanding huge sums. But there was great indignation in the English cricketing public that somebody outside cricket could step in and buy the allegiance of some of the best players for what was called World Series Cricket. The supporters of an English county tended to expect the players of that county to have as strong a sense of loyalty for it as they themselves had in supporting it. Moreover, though the rest of the Test-playing world was affected,

190

it was an Australian problem arising from the resurgence of Australian cricket in the 1970s and the desire of Mr Packer's Channel Nine to acquire the television rights of Test cricket. The Australian Board refused to give these as it already had a long-standing if less lucrative arrangement with the Australian Broadcasting Commission. Mr Packer's response was to buy up the players.

The number of "renegades" grew as players worked out what abandoning their existing role would entail at a time when inflation was rising fast. The English players approached fell roughly into four categories:

1 The senior players who were near the end of their Test and perhaps first-class careers and were bound to find the idea of a well-rewarded final fling attractive.

2 Some younger players, perhaps recently married, who did not want to join W.S.C. but found it hard to make their wives understand that tradition was more important than the money which might buy them a house.

3 Some players who did not want to join W.S.C. at all and hoped that their county would make them an offer which with other sources of income would narrow the gap between what they had been earning and what they were being offered.

4 Players with good winter jobs outside cricket which they hoped would develop into a long-term job for the future when they retired from the game and worked full-time.

In some cases it was a hard decision for a young man to have to take and could create a divisiveness which was alien to the friendship and humour of the cricket world.

Of the players from other countries who joined W.S.C., the West Indians were obviously in favour of it. There was so little money in West Indies cricket that they must have welcomed a new market for their talents, though it could lose them their jobs with English counties if the T.C.C.B.'s proposed ban came about. New Zealand and India were little affected, but several of the leading Pakistanis went. It was conceded that the best South Africans, barred from other international cricket, could scarcely miss the chance of playing with the best in the world. In 1975, Boon Wallace, the liberal and much respected President of the South African Cricket Association, as it was then, had twice been refused a visa by the Whitlam Government when invited by the Australian Board to watch a Test match in Melbourne and report on South Africa's move to non-racial cricket. Mr Packer and the

Government agreed that South African players who had been on the staff of an English county and had played first-class cricket for that county should be allowed in, though Graeme Pollock, who had only played for Sussex Second XI, had to return home without playing.

Others who had signed contracts with W.S.C. had to withdraw when it was found that these would clash with contracts which they had signed elsewhere. Two of them were Jeff Thomson and Alvin Kallicharran. They had been signed up by David Lord, who had been on the fringe of Australian cricket for some time but who in financial weight was to Kerry Packer what a mouse might be to an elephant. It was a year before Thomson could be taken into the Packer fold.

The furtive way in which players had been signed up during the Centenary Test in Melbourne was not widely admired, especially as the state captains had recently thanked the Board for what was being done for them. In England the T.C.C.B. was accustomed to working on matters affecting players in collaboration with the Cricketers' Association, a reputable body which before long was warning the Board against raising fees to Test players too much because it made too big a gap between Test and other first-class cricketers.

The tension in England in May 1977 was heightened by the fact that the Australian side under Greg Chappell was already in the country at the start of a tour during which they would play five Tests in defence of the Ashes. Whether or not they were weighed down by events, they certainly appeared to play as if their minds were on other matters. Thirteen of the 17 had signed for W.S.C., all except Kim Hughes, Craig Serjeant, Gary Cosier and Geoff Dymock.

Mr Packer went to London at the end of May. He asked for exclusive television rights from the Australian Board from 1981 when their contract with the A.B.C. ran out. The I.C.C. was not having this and at an emergency meeting laid down conditions on which his programme should be run. It should be at a time not clashing with official tours, the players should be available to their countries and to their states or counties, the sides should not be labelled Australia, England, etc. and the programme not to exceed six weeks.

Mr Packer was uncompromising and underlined the strength of his position by mentioning that he now had more than 50 of the world's best players under contract. His lawyers were of the same calibre. In July the I.C.C. banned from Test cricket players who took part in matches arranged by Mr Packer and his company, Richie Benaud and his company or associated companies or persons after 1 October 1977. In August the T.C.C.B. extended this to include competitive county cricket in England.

By then Mr Packer had announced that he would apply for an injunction and damages in the High Court against the I.C.C. and T.C.C.B. with a similar action against David Lord. The bans on players thus were subject to any High Court ruling which might follow.

The hearing began on 26 September before Mr Justice Slade and lasted 31 days. The judge allowed three players, Greig, Snow and Procter, to argue that the new rules of the I.C.C. and T.C.C.B threatening the banning of players were in restraint of trade.

Until this summer it is probably fair to say that few, if any, meetings had taken place at Lord's with the possibility in the minds of the participants that the proceedings might be examined in a court of law. Mr Packer's lawyers, on the other hand, were ready with anything the least relevant.

It was often evident during the 31 days that the T.C.C.B. and I.C.C. officers were not arguing from strength but the judgement when it came was a shock in the completeness of the defeat. In footballing terms it was as if they had expected a close match and had lost 9–0.

Mr Justice Slade spoke for five hours, dealing with nine principal questions which had to be answered. With a show of stamina which impressed even the losers, he found in favour of the Packer team on every count. The costs were £200,000, a huge sum for cricket to bear at that time, especially if the best players were not going to be available.

However, one advantage of living in the Northern Hemisphere is that its cricket season does not clash with any other and during that summer the T.C.C.B. had been paid £150,000 by Channel Nine for the England–Australia Test series.

The series cannot have provided very stimulating viewing in Australia. The touring team was under closer than usual scrutiny and it was not hard to deduce some coolness between the "Packer 13" and the other four players. No one envied the Board's manager, the former wicket-keeper Len Maddocks.

England were better off. At an early stage the T.C.C.B. announced that Tony Greig would not captain England, as he would be contracted elsewhere during the coming winter, but

there was no bar on him as a player in home Tests or on anyone
else. In fact, the choice was wider than for three years, as Boycott
had decided to end his self-imposed exile. Of the 16 chosen for
England that season, only five – Greig, Knott, Underwood, Amiss
and Woolmer – had signed or were to sign for W.S.C.

Australia had come without Ian Chappell and Lillee and they
did not always have Thomson fully fit, though he took 23 Test
wickets. Their problem, for once, was a shortage of runs. For
this, a lot of the credit went to the England bowlers under the
direction of the new captain Mike Brearley, who may not have
been quite of Test quality as a batsman but had a brain which
defeated the examiners in other walks of life and was no less
effective on the cricket field.

There had been several high-class bowlers around for some
years but they had seldom all been fit. Between 1976 and 1978
Bob Willis, Chris Old and Mike Hendrick were at their best.
Derek Underwood, though only 32, had already played in nearly
80 Test matches and could be relied upon to shut up one end even
if not taking wickets. Greig's great height made him slightly different from the other fast-medium bowlers.

England's batsmen had an easier passage. Not long before, Bob
Woolmer had been batting around number nine for Kent to
whom he was often most useful for his tidy medium-fast bowling.
He and Underwood were adept at subduing batsmen in limited-
over matches in the middle of an innings when there should have
been an acceleration. He had always looked a well- organised
batsman and when he was elevated to open the Kent innings, he
took his chance. He had already saved a Test against Australia in
1975. Correct and painstaking, he batted at number three in
1977, making 79 and 120 in the First Test at Lord's, the Jubilee
Test, and 137 in the Second Test at Old Trafford which England
won by nine wickets.

The selectors had not rushed to bring back Boycott but waited
until a place became vacant. A loss of form by Amiss provided
this and Boycott returned to Test cricket in the Third Test at
Trent Bridge. He was 36.

He did not commend himself immediately to the
Nottinghamshire crowd because of his part in the running-out of
the local hero, Derek Randall, but he was suitably contrite. After
fighting hard for more than three hours for 20 runs, he was
dropped at second slip. By then, however, Alan Knott was batting
with characteristic fluency and they shared in a sixth-wicket stand

of 215 which turned the match. When England needed 189 to win, Boycott and Brearley made the operation painless by their opening stand of 154 and England won by seven wickets.

This match was also notable as being Ian Botham's first in Test cricket. It was three years since, as a formidably built 18-year-old, he had come in at number nine in a Benson and Hedges quarter-final and had turned what looked to be a Hampshire victory into a one-wicket win for Somerset.

In 1977, though clearly an all-round cricketer of great talent, he was especially effective as a fast-medium swing bowler with a fine action. On his first day in Test cricket he took five Australian wickets for 74.

At Headingley, amid Yorkshire rejoicing, Boycott became the first batsman to make his 100th first-class hundred in a Test match. In all, he made a fine 191, Botham took five wickets again in the first innings, this time for only 21 runs, and England won by an innings. Their lead in the five-match series was 3–0 and the Ashes had been recovered. The last Test at The Oval was ruined by the weather.

England had won handsomely but celebrations were muted. It was feared that this might be the last time for many years that England and Australia met in a proper Test match at full strength. A similar sadness existed among the counties who, if the T.C.C.B. ban came into force, would be losing their best and in some cases most popular players. Nowhere was this felt more acutely than in Gloucestershire where the South African Mike Procter had become a folk hero. Over the years he had performed some marvellous feats with bat and ball and in 1977, his first year of captaincy, it looked as if he was going to lead Gloucestershire to their first Championship for exactly 100 years.

Since the advent of instant registration of overseas players in 1968 and since Yorkshire had won the last of their seven Championships in 10 years, eight different counties had won in eight years – Glamorgan, Kent, Surrey, Warwickshire, Hampshire, Worcestershire, Leicestershire (for the first time) and Middlesex. In the late summer of 1977 Gloucestershire were promising to make a ninth. They had been strong challengers before and three times since the War had finished second but to find them as champions one had to go back to 1877 when Dr W.G. Grace was in his prime and there were only eight other counties in the field.

They were still leading on the last morning of the season at Bristol. If their previous home match at Bristol against Yorkshire

had been played, they would doubtless have been champions by
now but that had been rained off without a ball bowled. So had
one against Northamptonshire at Gloucester in June. Thus they
still needed to beat Hampshire to make the Championship safe.

For two days they had slightly the better of a close match.
Procter made 115, more than half his side's first-innings total,
and 57. In between, he took six wickets, varying his normal fast-
medium with spells of off-spin. Hampshire needed 271 to win but
the pitch eased, catches were dropped and, with nothing to lose,
Gordon Greenidge and the other Hampshire batsmen rattled off
the runs with 80 minutes to spare.

For the large crowd which had gathered to hail a long-awaited
triumph for the West Country it was an acute disappointment
and sentiments ran high as the very popular Procter made a
speech which, under the T.C.C.B.'s existing ban on Packer players, could have been his farewell. As a South African already
ruled out of Test cricket, he was not seen as having been disloyal
to his country and his devotion to Gloucestershire cricket was
well known.

As it was, Middlesex, captained by Mike Brearley, beat Lancashire at Blackpool that afternoon to finish five points ahead of
Gloucestershire and Kent won by 27 runs at Edgbaston to share
the Championship with them. Middlesex probably considered
themselves the unluckiest of all not to be champions outright, for
in the low-scoring first innings in which only the 20-year-old
Mike Gatting reached 50, they had missed a batting bonus point
by just two runs.

Four days after this remarkable day of county cricket,
Hampshire suffered a tragic loss which made the disappointments
of the other counties seem trivial. Desmond Eagar, who from
1945 had rebuilt Hampshire cricket as captain and secretary, died
suddenly on holiday in Devon.

It was a melancholy autumn indeed in English cricket, though
the High Court judgement did at least relieve the fears of those
counties who thought they would lose their Packer players in
1978. That winter the England team touring Pakistan and New
Zealand under Mike Brearley dropped the M.C.C. label which
touring teams had kept in deference to the past but which, now
that M.C.C. had almost nothing to do with it, was causing confusion.

Pakistan were now captained by the wicket-keeper Wasim Bari,
having lost Mushtaq Mohammad, Zaheer Abbas, Asif Iqbal and

Imran Khan to W.S.C. The tour passed unremarkably – if one overlooked fighting between police and rioters in Lahore during which tear gas was used and the 21-year-old Mudassar Nazar made the slowest Test hundred of all time in nine hours 17 minutes – until just before the Third and last Test in Karachi. Then, at the start of a one-day match against a Sind XI, Mike Brearley was justifiably surprised by a ball which bounced more than almost any other for weeks. It broke his left arm. He flew home that night, leaving Geoffrey Boycott with the captaincy and the team in mounting indignation at rumours that three Packer players were being sent from Australia to play for Pakistan. This gave Mr Packer the standing of a Test selector and was a severe blow to the "loyal" Pakistan players, especially those who would be replaced.

Mushtaq, Zaheer and Imran duly arrived in Karachi but did not mix with the other Pakistanis at the nets. The England team held a long meeting, from which the manager Ken Barrington was excluded. It seemed that they would refuse to play, though they could not discover whether the Pakistan Board wanted the three to play. It is possible that the Pakistan Board did not know either.

However, relief was on the way. On the evening before the match the Chief Martial Law Administrator, as the future President Zia was then known, flew down from Islamabad. The Board announced that the three would not play and the match went ahead on its unexciting course to the usual draw.

England went on to draw a three-match series in New Zealand 1–1. The New Zealand victory in a high wind and on a rough pitch in Wellington was their first over England in the 48 Tests which the two countries had played against each other in nearly 50 years. It was well earned and was one of Richard Hadlee's earlier triumphs, 10 for 100 in the match.

Meanwhile India, captained by the guileful but unathletic left-arm spinner Bishen Bedi, had been to Australia for a five-match Test series which, as counter to the Packer propaganda, must have exceeded the Board's highest hopes. Bobby Simpson was recalled as captain, a role from which he had retired at 31, 10 years before. He presided over a team containing only Kim Hughes, Craig Serjeant and a reluctant Jeff Thomson of the touring side in England a few months earlier but a splendid series was watched by more people than had attended previous visits by India. Australia won the first two Tests in close and exciting finishes. India won the next two comfortably. The final match, over

six days in Adelaide, was a spectacular contest which Australia
won by 47 runs after India made 445 in the last innings. Simpson,
who had contributed 176 to his side's win in Perth, made 100 and
51 in the decider.

All this compared favourably with the cricket being played by
W.S.C. before Channel Nine cameras on large but sparsely popu-
lated football grounds. However, through sheer weight of propaganda and marketing skill, the crowds grew. W.S.C. had been
kept off grounds over which the Board or state cricket associations had control but cracks began to appear when the New
South Wales and Queensland governments decided to legislate
that the Sydney Cricket Ground and The Gabba in Brisbane
should be put on a commercial basis. This led to the erection of
pylons on the Sydney Cricket Ground, which scarcely enhanced
the rather old-world charm of a ground with great character, and
led to the inauguration in the following season of the day-night
matches.

Still under Bobby Simpson, the Australians went to West Indies
in mid-February 1978 for a thoroughly ill-fated two-and-a-half
month tour. The W.S.C. season was over and though the
Australians did not include one Packer player, the West Indies
Board saw no reason to ignore players who had not yet refused to
play for their "country", if one can so name a geographical area
of many individual countries.

The first two Tests were predictably one-sided, Simpson and his
young side foundering against the fast bowling of Andy Roberts,
Colin Croft and Joel Garner. After two Tests, however, the West
Indies Board, aggrieved that their younger players were now joining the others by signing for W.S.C., asked the players to confirm
by a given date their availability for a tour of India and Sri Lanka
later in the year. Receiving no answer to what was considered by
the players to be a provocative request, the Board replaced three
players in the side for the Third Test.

At this, Clive Lloyd resigned the captaincy. Other W.S.C. play-
ers joined him. The Board picked a new team, retaining only
Alvin Kallicharran, now made captain, and the off-spinner Derek
Parry.

This made for more even matches, each side winning one of the
next two Tests, but the bitterness was too deep for harmony to be
restored. There was a flying visit from Mr Packer himself, a meeting between the players and Jeff Stollmeyer, the Board President,
charges, counter-charges, complaints about umpiring decisions

and intimidatory bowling, accusations of bowlers throwing, crowd protests and finally a pitch invasion which ended the last Test in Kingston when Australia were on the verge of winning it.

Official Test cricket was not helped by the fact that after England's tour of Pakistan and New Zealand, the players returned home for the 1978 season – to meet Pakistan and New Zealand.

Pakistan were weakened more than England by the loss of their Packer players and England, still under Brearley, won 2–0 with the Third Test beaten by the weather. Botham's progress was advertised by his 24 wickets at 14 apiece. He had made 108 at Lord's and had taken eight for 34 in the second innings there. It was clear that an all-rounder of rare ability had arrived and for once he was English – born in Cheshire, educated in Somerset, briefly on the Lord's staff and still only 22.

The New Zealand series threw up one piece of unfairness which was to hasten a change in the playing conditions for Test matches in England. Test cricket elsewhere was played on pitches fully covered against the elements. In England, if play had started, they were not covered again until play finished or was abandoned for the day.

At Trent Bridge the unfortunate effect of this, on umpires as well as players, was starkly illustrated on the third morning. England had made 429 but the pitch was so mild and true that New Zealand looked capable of making a lot of runs despite a start of 35 for three on the previous evening. But when the players came out, it was clearly about to rain. The umpires had to go by the conditions at the scheduled time of starting and at that moment the light was adequate, the rain had not yet started and so the first ball was bowled.

Botham bowled one more ball before the rain arrived and fell for some hours on an unprotected pitch. New Zealand were bowled out that evening for 120 and did not do much better when following on. Reluctantly, because the worthy purpose of leaving pitches uncovered had been to add variety to the game, full covering was introduced for the 1979 season.

That winter the scheduled tour of Australia by England was carried through. Inevitably it was seen as being in competition with the W.S.C. programme and the Australian public was not exactly encouraged by the fact that the official Australian side lost 5–1 to England. To some extent England were unlucky to go down in history as having beaten an Australian "second XI".

They themselves were four or five players below full strength, missing Greig, Amiss, Knott, Underwood and Woolmer, but they had filled the gaps well and, as in the previous summer at home, had a set of excellent bowlers who were not only at the height of their prowess but at the peak of fitness. For once the faster bowlers did not have to take all the wickets, for the two off-spinners Miller and Emburey took 39 wickets between them. Two other bowlers who had had their successes at Test level, Old and John Lever, were scarcely needed.

The absence of Alan Knott meant that England had at last been able to bring in Bob Taylor, who had long been considered one of the world's best wicket-keepers. A loyal and uncomplaining deputy to Knott, he had played in only one Test match – in New Zealand eight years before when Knott stood down for him. When he went to Pakistan and New Zealand in 1977–8 he was 36 and planning for his retirement. In fact, he found himself launched on a new career in which he played in 56 Test matches in the next six years.

By April 1979 the Australian Board saw no future in a contest with opponents who were prepared to spend endlessly and held so many strong cards. A major outlay had been on equipping the Sydney Cricket Ground with floodlighting and big crowds turned up for one-day matches between lunch and about 10.30 p.m. The S.C.G. was not a place for the squeamish on those nights, as anybody trying to persuade a taxi to fetch him from it usually found.

Having bowled bouncers at each other round much of Australia, W.S.C. Australia and W.S.C. West Indies adjourned to the Caribbean between February and April 1979. The tour was said to have been a financial success, which was of vital importance to the West Indies Board, though it had some turbulent days. There was a riot in Georgetown when the crowd became tired of waiting for play to start. The captain of W.S.C. Australia, Ian Chappell, was fined in a magistrate's court for assault and using indecent language. A match in Barbados was abandoned because of crowd behaviour on the last day.

By April 1979 a crack was showing in the unity of the Test-playing countries. The West Indies Board, never affluent, were no help to the others because with all their best players contracted to W.S.C. – excluding Kallicharran who had a previous contract elsewhere – they were ineffectual. All the more surprising that in another 10 years they were telling England what opponents they could play and with which players! And England, under threat, were caving in and even trying to stop their players from coaching in South Africa.

During April 1979, however, talks were taking place in Australia, the Board having accepted that W.S.C. was not going to go away. At the end of the month the Board announced that an agreement had been signed. The Board granted Packer the exclusive television rights which they had always been expected to grant him when the A.B.C. contract expired in 1981. They granted the relevant company, PBL Sports Pty Ltd, the exclusive right to promote the Board's cricket for 10 years. For their part, W.S.C. would cease to promote cricket in Australia and elsewhere.

"It was envisaged," read the statement, "that the programme each season will comprise five or six Test matches and an international one-day series to be known as the Benson and Hedges World Series Cup." It was announced that, though England had only just returned from a tour of Australia, they and West Indies would be the visitors in the next season of 1979–80.

Peace was not made in time for Australia to send a full-strength team to England for the second Prudential World Cup and the side captained by Kim Hughes was beaten by both England and Pakistan in their group and did not reach the semi-finals. In the final between West Indies and England, Vivian Richards played an innings of 138 not out which contained strokes beyond the capacity of most mortals. Facing a score of 286 for nine, Boycott and Brearley began with an opening stand of 129 but 38 of the 60 overs were used up and their successors came and went swiftly as they tried to hurry against the fast bowling of Holding, Croft and Garner.

Sri Lanka and Canada, the finalists in the new I.C.C. Trophy for associate member-countries of the I.C.C., made up the eight teams in the World Cup and India stayed on to play four Tests against England. They lost the first by an innings but nearly won the last at The Oval when needing 438 to win. Gavaskar (221) and Chauhan (80) began the last innings with a stand of 213 and in the last 20 overs only 110 were needed with nine wickets standing. However, from the departure of Vengsarkar, second out at 366, the innings went into decline, finishing only nine runs short at 429 for eight. Though no side had ever made that number of runs to win a Test match, it had seemed perfectly possible on this benign pitch, especially as it was Gavaskar and Indian batsmen who had made the most – 406 for four to beat West Indies in Trinidad only three years before.

With their reluctant agreement to send a team to Australia for the second successive winter, the T.C.C.B. strove to keep the one-day matches to a minimum, to avoid such gimmicks as coloured clothing for their players and to get an assurance that the next England tour of Australia in 1982–3 should be for a full tour of five or six Test matches as in the past.

They also said that the Ashes would not be at stake in a shortened series of three Tests while Australia were also playing three Tests against West Indies and all three were playing each other in a plethora of one-day matches. It was a nasty blow for English administrators to hear that the Australian Board was referring to the refusal to put the Ashes on the table as "chicken". In view of the inconvenience to English cricket caused by a domestic squabble in Australia and the support given to the Australian Board, this seemed somewhat ungrateful.

However, this appeared to be part of the build-up of tasteless publicity designed to capture and keep a new public for cricket. Another part was the depicting of the England captain as a villain out of an old melodrama. Mike Brearley was well capable of looking after himself but the booing and other noises which greeted his walk to the wicket did no credit to Australian cricket and was in sharp contrast to the respect shown in England to Allan Border and other Australian captains.

Border had played in his first Test matches against England in the previous season and, unlike another young left-hander, David Gower, who had been England's most successful batsman then, did even better at the second meeting. England had one Packer player back, Derek Underwood, but were less well equipped to cope with the full Australian batting. They lost all three Tests, though they were unlucky to have to bat on a wet pitch in Sydney. Four days before, the ground staff had been given the night off to celebrate the New Year and the pitch had been left open to a violent thunderstorm. On subsequent days the weather gave it no chance to dry out. When play started nearly four hours late, it was clear that the toss was all-important. Greg Chappell won it, put England in and they never recovered from being bowled out by Lillee and Len Pascoe for 123.

One legacy of the Packer intervention seemed to be a deterioration in conduct on the field. In Perth Lillee came in with an aluminium bat. When asked by the umpires and both captains to change it on the reasonable grounds that in its latest form Law 6 said that the bat should be made of wood, he held up play for

10 minutes before flinging the bat away. No disciplinary action was taken for what in some quarters was no doubt considered "good television". When the West Indians, having beaten Australia 2–0, went on to New Zealand – and lost 1–0 – Holding, on being refused an appeal, advanced on the batsman's wicket and, with a kick which spoke eloquently for his suppleness but not for his sportsmanship, sent the stumps flying.

While West Indies went on to New Zealand, England returned via Bombay where they played a Test match against India to mark the golden jubilee of the Indian Board of Control. This was a remarkable match for several reasons. The pitch was grassier than any that most visitors had seen on the sub-continent. The ground, usually packed, was only half filled, which could be attributed to the fact that India had already played 12 Tests against Australia and Pakistan that season and, including those in England, 16 in seven months. The surfeit of cricket was doubtless the reason for the approach of the Indian players which was amiable and uncompetitive. This is probably also the only Test match to have had its rest day decided by an eclipse of the sun.

The match, which England won by 10 wickets, was a great triumph for Ian Botham and indeed for Bob Taylor. Botham took 13 wickets for 106 runs and made 114, sharing in a sixth-wicket stand of 171 with Taylor who also took 10 catches, seven in the first innings. Taylor had been given out early on to an appeal for a catch at the wicket. His surprise was shared by the Indian captain, Viswanath, who was well placed to see at first slip and walked slowly up to the other end and withdrew the appeal.

The idealist might think that this quixotic piece of camaraderie augured well for the 1980s. Unfortunately, less attractive events in Australia proved more accurate omens.

18

Botham and the Australians

MIKE BREARLEY was now 38 and, despite the recent defeat by Australia, was retiring from the England captaincy with the reputation of being an intellectual wizard at man-management. He was staying on as captain of Middlesex in which role he had to sort out some frailties which had developed since Emburey and Edmonds had bowled them to the Championship at the end of the dry summer of 1976, indeed since the shared title of 1977.

In this task he had a quite remarkable success in 1980, for which members of his county's committee, acting while he was in Australia, could take credit. They signed up for one season probably the best fast-medium bowler in the world at that time, Vintcent Van der Bijl.

Vintcent's father, Peter, a Rhodes Scholar, had played for Oxford in 1932 and, opening the innings for South Africa, had made 125 and 97 in the historic Durban Test of 1939 which had to be left as a draw after 10 days so that the M.C.C. team could catch their ship home. The young Vintcent had not been an outstanding schoolboy cricketer at Bishops in the Cape. He was six feet seven and a half inches tall and his elevated skill in the line-out and immense range as a place-kicker had suggested that he might make a bigger impact as a rugby footballer.

However, during his years at Natal University and as a schoolmaster in Pietermaritzburg, he became the biggest wicket-taker in Currie Cup history and captained Natal when they won the Cup in 1976–77.

Though the Natal Cricket Association took the unusual step of awarding him a benefit in 1979–80, he had not been a professional cricketer. By early 1980 he had given up teaching and had gone into business. When he was approached by Middlesex, his employers, Wiggins Teape, agreed to let him go to London for six months to fulfil, as he said, his personal ambition. He was immensely successful for Middlesex, taking 85 wickets at 14.72, playing some invaluable innings of controlled hitting at number nine and cheering everyone up with his infectious enjoyment of cricket. Middlesex won the County Championship, then sponsored by Schweppes, and the Gillette Cup.

Brearley's departure from the Test scene had caused problems. In theory he made room for another of the unusually promising generation of young batsmen including Graham Gooch, David Gower, Mike Gatting and Ian Botham, but his successor as captain was facing a tough first year with two five-match series against West Indies who had just won two out of three Tests in Australia by huge margins.

Easily the most dominant character of recent years had been Botham and he was appointed captain in 1980 at the age of 24. Many thought that to saddle a match-winning all-rounder with the captaincy was putting an undesirable burden on him, but Botham was not a normal young cricketer. He was tremendously strong and could perform feats beyond the physique of almost anyone else.

What would have happened if the opposition in 1980 had not been one of the best West Indies sides – with five fast bowlers of the highest class in Garner, Roberts, Holding, Croft and the youthful Malcolm Marshall – is anyone's guess. In fact, after losing at Trent Bridge by only two wickets, England drew the remaining four Tests with help from the weather.

In the West Indies after Christmas the England team met some dreadful weather, none worse than that in Georgetown, Guyana, where they spent a week before the Guyanan Government revoked the visitors' permit of Robin Jackman because of his associations with South Africa. He had been flown in to replace the injured Bob Willis.

The team moved on to Barbados where an infinitely worse fate hit them in the sudden death, after play on the second day of the Test match, of the well-loved assistant-manager, Ken Barrington. He had given up first-class cricket in 1968 aged 38 after a heart attack in Melbourne but in the 12 years since then had worked unstintingly as a conscientious manager and assistant-manager of England teams abroad.

The tour was not a complete failure, for it included several brave and highly skilled innings – Graham Gooch's 116 on a

rough pitch in Barbados, an undefeated hundred by Peter Willey
in Antigua, another remarkable innings of 153 (out of a total of
285) by Gooch in Jamaica, followed in the second innings by
David Gower's 154 and his courageous unbroken stand with Paul
Downton which saved the match. But these were also the great
days of Viv Richards, who averaged 85, and of Clive Lloyd who
was not far behind him.

Unfortunately, the form of the young England captain declined
sharply. Botham was the main English wicket-taker, taking 15
Test wickets, but he mustered only 71 runs in the four Tests. It
was not difficult to blame this on the cares of captaincy. It was
realised, of course, that the damaging effect of the West Indies
players also had plenty to do with it, but the fear remained that
he was being over-taxed, strong as he was. In June the selectors,
in Alec Bedser's 13th and last season as chairman, prepared to
take action.

The Australian touring team of 1981 was clearly beatable and
when England, still under Botham, lost the Prudential one-day
series and more importantly the First Test at Trent Bridge, a crisis
of captaincy was looming. After a draw at Lord's in poor weather
Botham forestalled the selectors by resigning. He had not scored
in either innings but that was irrelevant as he had been out twice
in trying to press on after earlier batsmen had been bogged down.

The selectors then recalled Mike Brearley who had conveniently made 132 not out for Middlesex against the Australians
three weeks before and 131 against Nottinghamshire who were a
strong side that year and won the Schweppes Championship.

How much of what followed was coincidence and how much
the result of relieving Botham of the captaincy is one of those
questions without an answer. At first the Third Test at
Headingley went Australia's way as they batted solidly until,
towards the end of the second day, Kim Hughes declared at 401
for nine. Botham had taken six wickets which was not a good
omen, for he had bowled 40 overs in the process. It seemed likely
that, as in Perth 18 months previously, he had to bowl that much
because the other bowlers were so ineffective.

On the third day, Lillee, Alderman and Lawson bowled
England out for 174. They followed on 227 behind, soon losing
Gooch for nought.

Nothing happened on the Monday morning to halt Australia's
progress towards an easy victory and at 135 for 7 England still
needed 92 to avoid an innings defeat and to go 2–0 down in the

series. With a day and a half to go, this was a losing position if ever there was one, and Messrs Ladbroke availed themselves of Headingley's new electronic scoreboard to offer 500–1 against England.

At this point a stand began between Botham, top scorer in the first innings with 50, and the left-handed Graham Dilley. The importance of Dilley's 56, made when batting two places higher than for much of his career, was incalculable, for he gave Botham time to settle in. It was Dilley, too, who was the first to turn to the attack, putting his right leg down the pitch and swinging the bat heartily in the general direction of mid-off.

Botham was not slow to follow suit and in 80 minutes they added 117, which meant that those who had checked out of their hotels anticipating an Australian win in four days had been premature. Another tall left-hander, Chris Old, replaced Dilley and made an active partner for Botham who by now was showing up the limitations of the Australian bowling and hitting with immense gusto the unfortunate Lillee, Alderman and Lawson. These three bowled all but four of the 84 overs which the innings lasted. Another 67 runs were added for the ninth wicket and Botham was still there, 145 not out, at the end of the fourth day.

England were now 124 ahead, which seemed not enough on one of the better Headingley pitches of that era. After Willis was out early on the last day, leaving Botham undefeated on 149 and Australia needing 130, Dyson, Wood and the youngest of the three Chappell brothers, Trevor, reached 56 for one. It looked as if the great recovery of Botham and partners had been unavailing.

Then came an unexpected development. Bob Willis had not so far taken a wicket in the match and had tended to overstep. In this short vital innings 14 runs were conceded in no-balls and Brearley had not so far risked bowling Willis down the slope. Now he did.

In his second over, downhill and downwind, Willis removed Chappell with a ball which lifted awkwardly. Suddenly he looked a totally different bowler – fast, accurate and turning what had been a pitch of only occasional eccentricity into one of many dangers. Taylor, Gatting and Dilley held missable catches. Chris Old bowled steadily up the hill and produced an unkind ball which came back sharply to bowl Allan Border. There was a frantic ninth-wicket stand of 35 in four overs between two experienced cricketers in Bright and Lillee. Willis removed them both and marched off, having taken eight for 43. England had won by 18 runs.

Only once before in more than 100 years of Test matches had a
side following on been victorious – when England won by 10
runs in Sydney in 1894–95. For a match with a similar transformation to that at Headingley the historians had to go back to
"Fowler's Match" at Lord's between Eton and Harrow in 1910.
R. St L. Fowler, the Eton captain, made 64 to save his side from
an innings defeat and then, when Harrow needed only 55 to win,
took eight of the first nine wickets, reducing Harrow to 32 for
nine. After a rally by Harrow's last pair, the future Field Marshal
Earl Alexander of Tunis was caught at slip and Eton had won by
nine runs.

Botham had not finished with the 1981 Australians. Australia,
having led by 69 on first innings in a low-scoring match at
Edgbaston, needed only 151 to win in the last innings and at 114
for five seemed to be grinding their way towards victory. Brearley
then brought a reluctant Botham back at the City End. Botham
thought others had been bowling better than he had but in 28
balls he took five wickets for one run and England were home by
29 runs.

The Fifth Cornhill Test of that extraordinary series was played
at Old Trafford on what became an excellent batting pitch. In the
first innings Botham was out first ball but in the second he gave a
brilliant exhibition of hitting, making 118 in 123 minutes, including six sixes. After a brief reconnaissance, he played two strokes
against the left-arm spin of Ray Bright which prompted the taking of the new ball as soon as available.

At this, Botham was away at full blast. Lillee's first over cost
22 runs, including two hooks for six, one of which the capless
batsman achieved with eye well off the ball. While Chris Tavaré
was doing a valuable if unexciting job at the other end, Botham
made 47 out of 52 runs scored in 4.2 overs and 65 out of 76 in
eight overs before tea. He went from 28 to 100 in eight overs and
made his last 90 runs out of 103 in 13½ overs and 55 minutes.
He gave only two slim chances to fielders running hard in the
deep.

This onslaught allowed England ample time to bowl Australia
out, which on this pitch was not easy, and there were even
moments when it was conceivable that Australia might make the
record 506 required. The left-handers, Yallop and, with a broken
finger, Border, each made a hundred but Australia went down
honourably by 103 runs. The sixth and last Test at The Oval was
drawn.

This tremendous series was not exactly the shape of things to
come. In just over four years in Test cricket Botham had taken
202 wickets in Test matches and had made eight Test hundreds.
Even allowing for the modern proliferation of Test series this was
an astonishing record. But there were already fears about his fitness. His strength was such that he was able to set these fears at
rest but his action sometimes seemed less fluent and he bowled
more overs for his wickets.

For three years from the spring of 1982 England had to do
without the players who had made up a touring team in South
Africa in March 1982. Their suspension was harsh, as they had
broken no laws and were touring in a month when they were not
required elsewhere. But the Board, fearful of losing the income
provided by home Tests against touring teams, had circularised
players in the previous year warning them of severe penalties for
undertaking such a tour.

Thus in 1982, against India and Pakistan, the selectors could
not pick Gooch, who had captained the touring team, Boycott,
Emburey, Woolmer, Old, Knott, Larkins, Willey and Hendrick of
those who had played against Australia in the previous year. Also
banned was Derek Underwood, who had just played in every Test
match in India and had 297 Test wickets to his name.

At this time things were looking up on the sub-continent. In
1978–9 India and Pakistan had resumed playing each other after
an 18-year interval for wars and other differences. Each side won
a home series 2–0 but the greater talent was beginning to appear
in Pakistan sides and though both lost in England in 1982,
Pakistan were the unluckier.

Captained by Javed Miandad, they had just won a Test match
in Australia by an innings and in England, under Imran Khan,
they looked capable of improving on this. England won the First
Test at Edgbaston but it needed a splendidly improvised 105 by
Derek Randall and a last-wicket stand of 79 between Taylor (54
not out) and Willis (28) to put them out of range. In the Second
Test, at Lord's, Pakistan won by 10 wickets after making England
follow on. When England had to make 219 to win the deciding
match at Headingley, not many would have backed them with
much confidence. The pitches and the bowling now were less
accommodating than they had been earlier in the season when
Botham's three innings against India had been 67, 128 and 208.

In the event, England's first three batsmen, the painstaking
Chris Tavaré, the normally lively left-hander Graham Fowler and

Mike Gatting put their heads down and with the help of the byes
and leg-byes which accounted for most of the 42 extras, they
reached 168 for one. From there England scrambled home by
three wickets.

In this match Imran had made 67 not out and 46 and had
taken eight wickets in 56 overs. He was now not only one of the
world's best all-rounders but a captain who could bring stability
to the talent under his command. He was vastly experienced.
Since he first came to England with the 1971 Pakistanis at the age
of 18 he had spent a year at the Royal Grammar School,
Worcester (averaging 58 with the bat and taking 30 wickets at
7.50 each), had captained Oxford and played for Worcestershire
and then Sussex. He was, when fully fit, a genuine fast bowler
and he was a consistent batsman full of strokes in the middle of
the order.

Ahead of him in Pakistan's batting order would come batsmen
of the consistency of Mudassar Nazar and the brilliance of
Zaheer Abbas and Javed Miandad. He had the world's best leg-
spinner in Abdul Qadir, a potential match-winner, and an underestimated medium-pace bowler in Mudassar.

Within a fortnight of their disappointment at Headingley the
Pakistanis were home and preparing to demolish Australia under
Kim Hughes, who seemed to be given all the below strength
Australian sides to captain. Pakistan won all three Test matches
by big margins and would doubtless have won the three one-day
matches too, if the third had not been cut short by a Karachi riot
after 12 overs, which was rather earlier than usual.

By late November the Indians had arrived in Pakistan for a six-
Test series in which Pakistan won three matches, two by an
innings. Hearts of bowlers the world over must have bled for the
Indian bowlers, as Zaheer averaged 130, Mudassar 126 and
Miandad 118. Imran himself made one hundred and, most
remarkable of all, took 40 wickets at under 14 each.

While the triumphant Pakistanis were able to relax and look
forward with some optimism to the Prudential World Cup in
England in June, the hectic programme of modern Test cricket
required that within 10 days that February the Indians were arriving in Jamaica to start a series of five Tests against the West
Indies. Somewhere on the way Gavaskar had been replaced as
captain by the burly Kapil Dev, under whom only two Test
matches were lost.

Judged on these events, Pakistan could go into the Prudential

World Cup of 1983 with hopes high, India with only limited
ambitions. Yet, though West Indies, true to form, had won the
two previous runnings of the World Cup, it was already recognised that success in five-day Test cricket was no guarantee of victory in one-day cricket, as England's opponents were to find out
in the later 1980s. In England in 1983 India took the opportunities which opened before them in a way which did the captain –
and especially his bowlers – much credit.

It was India's good fortune that in three vital matches they
found pitches and to some extent atmospheric conditions ideally
suited to medium-paced bowlers. Bowlers such as Mohinder
Amarnath and Roger Binny, who might not have bowled much in
a Test match, if at all, were just the right pace. At Old Trafford
and in the final at Lord's the ball did not come readily on to the
bat and batsmen who could cope with the faster bowlers and the
flightier spinners were in trouble as soon as they had to take risks
against tidy medium-pace and a measure of swing.

In their first match India beat West Indies at Old Trafford by
34 runs but this was considered a bit of a fluke, especially as West
Indies won their way to the final without losing another match.
Moreover, at Tunbridge Wells, after choosing to bat, India were
17 for five against Zimbabwe and it required a spectacular
innings of 175 not out by Kapil Dev to take them to 266 for eight
and eventually victory by 31 runs.

Their semi-final by a happy chance was at Old Trafford, for
which they were far better equipped than England. They won by
six wickets while West Indies were beating Pakistan at The Oval
by eight wickets. It still did not occur to many neutrals that West
Indies, who had beaten Australia on a good pitch at Lord's a
week before, making 276 for three, were in much danger of losing the final there.

Yet though Clive Lloyd chose to field and India mustered only
183, including a priceless last-wicket stand of 22, West Indies
struggled even more uncomfortably against Kapil Dev and his
medium-paced colleagues. Briefly Viv Richards rushed the score
up to 50 for one but when he mishooked Madan Lal and Kapil
Dev took an awkward running catch, the innings went into
decline. Dujon and Marshall added 43 for the seventh wicket but
both perished during the seven overs which Mohinder Amarnath
bowled for 12 runs and three wickets. India won by 43 runs. The
massed ranks of fast bowlers, as represented by Roberts, Garner,
Marshall and Holding, had suffered a rare reverse.

When the two sides met in India a few months later, things were back to normal.

The oldest Test-playing countries had varying fortunes in the 1980s. Australia, like England before them, suspended players who went to South Africa but, unlike West Indies, who were also affected, did not find them easy to replace. What they did have, after the resignation late in 1984 of Kim Hughes when the "constant criticism" became too much for him, was a regular captain in Allan Border, who was to see them through the rest of the 1980s.

Early on, Border had some difficult times. In 1985 the Ashes, which had been comfortably won back by Greg Chappell's side in 1982–3, were lost again in England. In 1985–6 Australia played two three-match Test series, home and away, against New Zealand and lost both of them, a reverse not likely to be taken lightly in Australia. It was four years since, in a tight finish to the deciding match in Melbourne of the Benson and Hedges World Series Cup, Greg Chappell had scandalised the cricket world by telling his brother Trevor to bowl the final ball underarm along the ground to ensure that the New Zealand batsman did not hit it for the six runs required. The condemnatory voices heard, including that of the New Zealand Prime Minister, may not all have claimed profound cricket knowledge but their owners all knew what a "sneak" was.

Border proved to be a great survivor and during several seasons playing for Essex became a popular figure in English cricket.

England had many more captaincy problems, some self-inflicted but most after a series with West Indies. In 1981–2 Keith Fletcher, aged 37, took the side to India. The tour, like others in this era, was preceded by political discussions in high places. In July the I.C.C. had agreed unanimously that team selection must be a matter solely for the governing body concerned but in October the Indian Government was saying that Geoff Boycott and Geoff Cook were "unacceptable". A declaration of repugnance to apartheid seemed to placate Mrs Gandhi and the tour went ahead, India winning the first of six Test matches and drawing the rest.

For the 1982 season the captaincy passed to Bob Willis, a rare distinction for a fast bowler. The decision for the selectors, the chairman of whom was now Peter May after the 13-year-stint of Alec Bedser, seemed to be influenced by the need to find places for young batsmen of quality, who now included Allan Lamb from South Africa. By contrast there was no one likely to challenge

Willis who was fitter than for some time and did, in fact, remain the most regular wicket-taker in his two years as captain.

Willis was in command in 1983 when after the World Cup New Zealand stayed on to play four Test matches. England won 3–1 but New Zealand's win at Headingley was their first in England and yet another sign of the increasingly stiff opposition England could expect at home. By now New Zealand had in Richard Hadlee an all-rounder who was one of the most accomplished fast-medium bowlers in the world, relying little on the bouncer. They had usually been concerned about the lack of depth in their cricket at the highest level and had suffered a grievous blow by the death in 1976 of a fine wicket-keeper-batsman, Ken Wadsworth, aged 29. But now they had in Martin Crowe one of the most promising young batsmen in the world and a number of other players whose ability was advertised by the Headingley victory. By some weird distribution of justice by the gods that first win was achieved without Hadlee taking a wicket – he took 21 in the other three Tests – and with only 38 runs in two innings from Martin Crowe.

New Zealand had to wait only another five months before they won a series against England for the first time. Two of the three Tests were drawn but the middle one, in difficult conditions in Christchurch, was won in three days by a huge margin by New Zealand whose bowling was vastly superior to England's. This time Hadlee's contribution left nothing to the imagination. After making 99 in 110 minutes off 86 balls, he bowled 35 overs in England's two innings and took eight for 44. England were bowled out for 82 and 93 and lost by an innings and 132 runs.

The England team went on to Pakistan, leaving behind reports of police investigation into drug-taking, not exactly the best public relations with which to start any tour. Within 10 days they were losing the First Test in Karachi, having had little time in the nets to prepare them for a much hotter climate than New Zealand's and for very different conditions. Willis's fitness did not survive the Second Test and Gower took over for the last two matches, both drawn.

Gower became captain in his own right for the home series against West Indies in 1984. He could not do much about that and though Allan Lamb made three hundreds in the series, the West Indies fast bowlers and the giant off-spinner Harper were far too good. For the first time in over 100 years England were beaten 5–0 in a home series.

This was followed in 1984–5 by a tour of India which had one of the grimmest possible starts. Within two or three hours of their arrival in Delhi by air from London on 31 October 1984, Mrs Gandhi was assassinated there. After many conferences the team management accepted an invitation from the President of Sri Lanka to move to Colombo for their practice and it was nearly a fortnight before they played their first match in India. But more tragedy was on hand in Bombay.

On the eve of the First Test the British Deputy High Commissioner, Percy Norris, a keen cricketer who had entertained the players on the previous evening, was shot dead in his car on the way to his office.

From this shattering event the players had to pick themselves up and start a Test series for which at the time they can have had little enthusiasm. They lost the First Test by a large margin but were given some encouragement by Mike Gatting's 136 in the second innings and by his playing of spin. David Gower had put an end to the ridiculous failure to make the most of Gatting's many talents. He made sure that Gatting, who had not been picked for the tour of Australia two years before, was included this time – and as vice-captain. He also installed Gatting at number three instead of in the bottom half of the order where on a good pitch he was coming in just before the declaration. Four years before, in Barbados, he had been put in number three when short of practice and on a pitch producing an abnormal number of shooters. It was the only Test in which he played there.

Gower was now determined that the most consistently successful batsman at home should be given a proper chance – and he was handsomely rewarded. Gatting averaged 95 against India and 87 in the next series against Australia at home.

It was soon recognised that Sivaramakrishnan, a 19-year-old leg-spinner, could play a major part in the series. In the First Test he took 12 wickets, but only 11 in the remaining four Tests as Gatting's example was followed. At New Delhi just before Christmas Tim Robinson, playing in his second Test, made 160 and the Indian batting subsided unexpectedly on the last day to the spin of Phil Edmonds and Pat Pocock on a slow turning pitch. England were left needing 125 in two hours – with at least 20 overs in the second hour. The institution of this compulsory minimum for the last hour, almost eliminating the opportunities for time-wasting, had been one of the most successful pieces of recent legislation.

With the series level at 1–1 a certain unrest became evident in the Indian camp. Kapil Dev, the hero of the World Cup 18 months before, had been replaced as captain by Gavaskar and was left out altogether now, taking the blame for the irresponsible stroke which had helped India to lose in Delhi. But in some gloomy New Year weather Gavaskar infuriated the huge crowd by allowing the Indian first innings to run on into the fourth afternoon. England did not start to bat until only eight hours of the match remained and the pressure was off them.

This piece of oriental mystique was followed by another in Madras when, with Kapil Dev restored, India batted so energetically that they were all out for 272 in 68 overs on the first day. This gave England plenty of time to avail themselves of what was now an excellent pitch and the left-handed Graeme Fowler made 201, Gatting 207, Robinson 74 and Lamb 62 in an innings of 652 for seven at which Gower declared. India still had to be bowled out again on a benign pitch but Neil Foster, in his first match of the series, had swung the ball with considerable effect in the first innings and he brought his tally of wickets in the match up to 11. India only saved the innings defeat with their last pair at the wicket.

England negotiated the last Test in Kanpur safely and became the first touring team from any country to come from behind to win a series in India. Some consolation for India came from the performance of a slim young batsman Azharuddin who was brought in for the last three Tests and made a hundred in each of them.

One of the successes in India had been Tim Robinson and though Australia made over 300 in each innings at Headingley in 1985, his 175 set England on the way to a victory by five wickets. As usual, Australia did better at Lord's and a fairly mature leg-spinner, Bob Holland, bowled effectively into the rough in the second innings. Australia, who had been given a big first-innings lead by Border's 196, won by four wickets.

The series remained level at 1–1 until the Fifth Test when the England selectors produced a match-winner. Richard Ellison had played in three Tests in India without much success but at Edgbaston and The Oval he swung the ball with great accuracy and took 17 wickets. England won both matches by an innings.

In the public mind England teams are only as good as their last match. Those who thought that the run of success might continue in West Indies were harbouring ideas above their station.

Mike Gatting, with two very successful series behind him, now carried high hopes but in the first one-day international he was hit in the face when aiming to hook Malcolm Marshall and had to return home to have his nose rebuilt. Though he was back in time for the last Test, it was clear by then that England were heading for another 5–0 defeat. Once again a series with West Indies was going to lead to changes at the top.

David Gower was immensely popular with his contemporaries and his casual manner could help to relieve tension when things were going well. But in a 5–0 defeat it inevitably grated. He was reappointed for the Lord's Test against India but when that was lost by five wickets the axe fell.

With some reluctance Mike Gatting accepted the job. The Second Test was lost even more conclusively at Headingley and though Gatting himself made 183 not out in the Third at Edgbaston, an even match in which each side made 390 in the first innings ended in a draw.

India's 2–0 win was only their second in a series in England; New Zealand's 1–0 victory in the second half of the 1986 summer was their first. Jeremy Coney's side won the Second Test at Trent Bridge convincingly by eight wickets. Richard Hadlee added 10 wickets to the hundreds which he had taken on the ground for Nottinghamshire and made 68 runs. The only hundred in the match was the 110 of John Bracewell, the tall off-spinner batting at number eight.

Though in the final Test Gower, Gatting and Botham hammered the New Zealand bowlers, even Hadlee, to all parts of The Oval in a desperate attempt to make up for time lost to the weather, the weather won.

Modern English cricket at international level had not yet reached its nadir, for the much criticised side which Gatting took to Australia in 1986–7 won almost everything in sight. In the week after Christmas they won back the Ashes, beating Australia in Melbourne by an innings in three days. Between the last two Tests they went to Perth and won the Benson and Hedges Challenge which coincided with the America's Cup yachting jamboree off Fremantle. In the final they beat Pakistan. The also-rans were West Indies and Australia. England won the annual Benson and Hedges Cup from Australia and West Indies. In one of the qualifying matches in Sydney of this last tournament, they were in some trouble needing 18 runs off the last over. Allan Lamb, whose mistimings had stopped him from reaching the boundary once in a fairly long stay, made the runs off five balls.

In 1987 it was Pakistan who won a series in England for the first time and succeeded where they had narrowly failed four years before. Imran took 10 wickets for 77 at Headingley and formed a redoubtable pair with Wasim Akram, as England found at Edgbaston when they had to make 124 to win in 18 overs. In the synthetic playing conditions of limited-over cricket, an experienced batting side would have reckoned this to be well within their powers; but in the conventional game when the bowler is allowed to stray far off the line of the stumps England could muster only 109 for seven against Imran and Wasim. Pakistan's Headingley win by an innings gave them the five match series, 1–0.

In the final Test at The Oval Pakistan made 708 – Miandad 260, Salim Malik 102, Imran 118 – and though Gatting batted through the last day to save the match with his 150 not out and with Botham in suitably restrained support, Pakistan could be said to have made their point. So, too, had Gatting, who was making his ninth Test hundred in less than three years.

Still to come in the 1980s were heavy home defeats by West Indies and Australia but England remained remarkably successful in the one-day matches which were now financing but undermining the world's cricket. In October and November 1987 the Reliance World Cup, staged for the first time outside England by India and Pakistan jointly, should probably have been won by England who lost the final in Calcutta to Australia. The huge crowds of the sub-continent had been conditioned to expect a final between India and Pakistan but both lost in the semi-finals. On the whole the public stood the disappointment of seeing a final between Australia and England stoically.

The fall of Gatting, who in many ways had proved an excellent and unselfish captain always prepared to set an example when positive action was required, was just appearing above the horizon. His side went on from Calcutta to Pakistan for a tour which they began seemingly convinced that they would be cheated, an undesirable approach to any series. They lost the First Test in Lahore by an innings but were doing better in the Second in Faisalabad when Gatting, on being accused himself of unfair play by Umpire Shakoor Rana, boiled over.

No doubt other captains in the past have wagged their fingers at umpires and used unsavoury language to them – but not in front of television cameras and with a microphone close to the pitch. A day's play was lost in waiting for apologies, which are not freely given on the sub-continent but are expected from visitors, and the last two Tests, enjoyed by very few, were drawn. The situation became even more confused when the T.C.C.B. chairman, Raman Subba Row, flew to Pakistan and awarded the players an extra £1000 a man.

After Christmas at home the England team, slightly changed, set off for New Zealand whence they soon had to fly to Sydney for a Bicentenary Test. In this they made Australia follow on but came no nearer to winning than that. In New Zealand, they were accompanied by a posse of journalists waiting for indiscretions on and off the field. This they weathered well enough for the Chairman of the New Zealand Board to write an appreciative letter to Lord's, though the cricket in four draws, on lifeless pitches and in poor weather, had little to commend it.

In the summer of 1988 England won all three one-day Texaco Trophy matches against West Indies. Gatting, in good form, made 140 runs for once out. But after the First Test at Trent Bridge, his time was up.

A popular newspaper published a story alleging that on his birthday, the fourth day of the match, Gatting had invited a barmaid to his room. The Board accepted that nothing improper had taken place but removed him from the captaincy, presumably on the grounds that he should not have been so silly as to give the Press a chance.

His record of offences had been building up. The ill-chosen reverse sweep which had let England down when they were well placed to win the World Cup final in Calcutta, the pessimistic approach to the tour of Pakistan, the exchange with Shakoor Rana, frequently replayed on television, Gatting's dispute with the T.C.C.B. over a book which he had written on the tour of Pakistan allegedly in breach of his contract – and now this.

Captained twice by John Emburey, once by Christopher Cowdrey and lastly by Graham Gooch, England lost the last four Tests to West Indies. The selectors then named Graham Gooch as captain for a tour of India which, because of his associations with South Africa, including the brief tour in 1982 for which he had served a suspension, was considered in India to be provocative.

Though the T.C.C.B. tried harder than many would have done to heal the breach, the tour did not take place. During the winter Peter May had resigned as chairman of selectors in order to devote himself full-time to his last year in the City. An England Committee was formed under Ted Dexter.

One of Dexter's first moves was to try to restore Gatting to the captaincy. The Board would not allow it and the charming but luckless David Gower was recalled to captain England against Australia. Nearly all the good cricket came from Australia and they won 4–0. Terry Alderman, who had taken 42 wickets in the 1981 season, took 41 this time at the age of 33.

Early in 1989 the Board had given in to pressure within the I.C.C. and, after many years of helping their players to find winter jobs in South Africa, now told them that they were liable to suspension if they went there. The Cricketers' Association asked the Board to seek agreement that coaching in South Africa, which in many cases was of non-Whites, might still be allowed. When the players learnt that the T.C.C.B. had not even put this to the I.C.C., a growing disenchantment with the Board manifested itself.

When the South African Cricket Union, given no hope, even of a hearing, by the I.C.C., committed themselves to inviting players to form another unofficial tour, there were plenty of willing volunteers and Gatting, who had never previously been to South Africa, accepted the captaincy.

In their attempt to maintain the income which they now received from international cricket and to avoid a split in the I.C.C., the Board had achieved a split in their own ranks. Players who once would not have considered such a tour on patriotic grounds presumably considered that if the Board would put commercial gain above backing their players in a perfectly honourable job, they were entitled to put financial gain first too.

So the 1990s began with Australian cricket on the way up, though soon to be in need of good young bowlers; with West Indies still supreme in Test cricket; with Pakistan full of talent and highly successful when not racked by internal strife; with New Zealand in good shape but shortly to be facing a future without Hadlee; with India below their best and losing their great Test crowds through occasional one-day successes; with Sri Lanka, after a promising start to Test cricket in the early 1980s unable to sustain it and suffering from the political blood-shedding which prevented their playing Test cricket at home; and with England in a mess.

19

Then and Now

FORTY-FIVE years on, cricket has changed from the game which in 1945 began its hurried revival amid bubbling enthusiasm. So much was inevitable, and anticipated, in a society which itself was bound to change. In England the amateur survived in the first-class game for 17 years before being voted out by the Advisory County Cricket Committee, forerunner of the T.C.C.B. He became just a "cricketer", though for many years it was a transformation lamented by those senior professionals who knew what many amateurs had contributed. Other countries had not had the same distinction between paid and unpaid which was largely brought about not only by tradition but by the shortness and concentrated nature of the English season. One consequence of the amateur's disappearance has been the extra burden put on the umpires who are now called upon to arbitrate on fair play and the conduct of the game, which once would have been a matter for the captains.

First-class cricket is only the thin professional top level of the game. At lower levels many more changes were to come but it was first-class, and especially international, cricket which was affected by the most important single post-war influence – television.

Cricket was soon found to be very suitable for television, though at first this was only in the United Kingdom – and not all of that. Television was still in its infancy in Australia in the mid-1950s. It was not introduced in South Africa until the 1970s. Despite the great rumpus in Australia in the 1970s and the cheapening gimmicks which accompanied it, television in Britain was to serve the game well.

As in other games and sports this meant a greater emphasis on the game at top level to the exclusion of the minor matches. Yet without the lower levels of a game, where the best players of the future are found and developed, there would be no international sport. Thus in English cricket the counties have to suffer a loss on their County Championship matches but do so in the knowledge that they will be compensated from the riches now earned at international level. By the late 1980s the receipts for a five-match Test series against West Indies had exceeded £2³/₄ million, which may explain why the T.C.C.B. was prepared to be told by other Test-playing countries how English cricketers should spend their winters.

With television and radio has come sponsorship. In the game's Middle Ages sponsorship had come from the wealthy and often titled gentry. Now big companies came and prospered. Cornhill Insurance was said to have been particularly successful through its sponsorship of Test matches in England, begun in the difficult days of the Packer intervention.

The first limited-over competition in England, and in South Africa, bore the name of Gillette, who only dropped out in England after 18 years because the name had become so much a part of the programme that its connection with razor blades scarcely registered with the public any more.

Air travel had almost completely replaced sea voyages by the early 1960s and was a mixed blessing. Test tours until then were still rare events and all the more exciting for that. Now Test teams rush about the world, playing short series which make less impact and allow little time for the break from the game which used to be considered essential.

In Australia, however, air travel was highly beneficial, for it brought Western Australia into the Sheffield Shield. Before the War when the great players of the Eastern states were invited to Perth to play for a Combined XI against the tourists in a four-day match, they would have to take a fortnight off. Immediately after the War, Western Australia made their first appearance in the Shield and won it but then, and for nine seasons, they played only four matches against the other states' seven. It was not until 1956–7 that they won the Shield for the second time. But then they won it 11 times in the next 22 years. By then they were the richest source of cricketing talent in Australia, producing players of the calibre of Graham McKenzie, Dennis Lillee, John Inverarity, Rodney Marsh, Terry Alderman, Kim Hughes and Graeme Wood. When they won in 1967–8, their captain was

Tony Lock, formerly of Surrey and Leicestershire and now aged
38. Like Peter Loader, also of Surrey, he had emigrated to Perth.

As Test series and one-day internationals proliferated, an
uneasy feeling grew that the goose which laid the golden egg was
being exposed to the dangers of familiarity. Even in India, where
every day's play in a Test match used to be watched on a packed
ground built or rebuilt to accommodate 40,000, and double that
in Calcutta, one-day matches began to take crowds away from
Test cricket. In India, as in Australia, the one-day game had been
slower to become popular than in England. But English administrators soon recognised the dangers and though they had saddled
themselves with three limited-over competitions, they kept international one-day matches to a minimum and retained the Test
series as the major money-maker.

On the whole, England, where cricket began, retained a sense
of responsibility for doing what the game needed, even though it
was not likely to improve their own chances. Nationalism is not
the force in England with its huge polyglot population that it is
elsewhere. It was when the T.C.C.B. allowed themselves to be
badgered by other countries into cutting links still further with
what was now non-racial cricket in South Africa that they lost
some old friends at home.

On the playing side, England have not been helped by the massive population of the United Kingdom. It is easier for coaches
and administrators to sort out the best players in a more compact
society and in a better climate. A coach, say, in South Australia
will find the bulk of his players in Adelaide and will be able to
watch and develop the most gifted of them from an early age. In
Britain a talent for cricket may turn up almost anywhere.

There is a parallel in rugby football where the selectors of
Wales, Ireland, Scotland, Australia and especially New Zealand
are wont to have a clearer choice than England's.

In English cricket, too, there have been 17 first-class counties
since 1921, which means that in theory a county is one-seven-
teenth of the whole. In Australia a state is one-sixth and for many
years was a quarter of the country's strength at the top. Thus the
step up from county to Test cricket is always likely to be much
steeper than the one from Sheffield Shield cricket to the
Australian Test team.

To some extent the distribution around the English counties of
some of the best overseas players of the day must raise the standard of county cricket. Yet the strength of the West Indian fast

bowlers, for example, lies in the relentless hammering which four of them achieve in one side. As individuals they are relatively less formidable.

The county is a splendid unit, carrying lifetime loyalties. Heaven forbid that it should be lost. The difficulty of adding Durham as an 18th first-class county is that it would mean more travelling and more cricket in an already congested programme. It could also lead to a split into two divisions of nine. Whether or not this raised the standard of the upper nine, it would almost certainly bring lower standards in the second nine and potential England players in the lower league would find the step up to Test cricket even steeper than it is already.

The 1980s ended with England having lost Test series at home successively to India, New Zealand, Pakistan, West Indies and Australia, something inconceivable in 1946 when, indeed, Pakistan had not yet been born. It was probably not a bad thing in the context of world cricket and it may not last long. It is amazing what two or three fit and penetrative bowlers can do.

What became uncomfortably evident as the years passed, however, was the flawed technique of a generation of stroke-playing batsmen who seemed to play across the line much more than their opponents. This can often be magnified when batsmen have been pinned down by fast bowling. So much is out of reach that they are never really "in" and in desperation abandon normal concepts. It was particularly disappointing because if there was one area in which English cricket had made great advances since 1945, it was in the work of the National Cricket Association.

The N.C.A. covers non-first-class cricket and has, as a priority, not only the provision of coaching but of the opportunity for the young to play the game in the first place. By contrast with the thinking before the War individual pastimes were being encouraged. Team games were out. Competitiveness was frowned upon. Football of various codes survived but cricket is a game which requires expert coaching and the syllabuses of teacher training colleges made scant reference to it. An added obstacle was the high cost of equipment.

The N.C.A. was not founded until 1968 but it owed a great deal to the vision, enterprise and devotion to cricket of Harry Altham, who died suddenly in 1965 aged 74. Before the First World War he won a Blue at Oxford and played a few matches in 1912 for Surrey. After the War, from which he emerged with a D.S.O. and M.C., he began 30 years as a master at Winchester and played several years for Hampshire. Thereafter he filled many roles in cricket in Hampshire and throughout Britain.

In 1949 he was appointed chairman of an M.C.C. committee set up to look into the future welfare of English cricket. He was chairman of Test selectors in 1954, President of M.C.C. in 1959, co-author of the *M.C.C. Cricket Coaching Book* with G. O. Allen and the leading coach of the day Harry Crabtree, and President of Hampshire for his last 19 years. He was historian, legislator, coach. He had a fund of knowledge and good sense and he was a compelling speaker.

He was also chairman of the M.C.C. Youth Cricket Association and President of the English Schools Cricket Association. These two bodies were among those gathered in under the umbrella of the N.C.A. in 1968.

By now it was clear that an ever-growing number of boys would have little, if any, cricket at school. The onus was on local clubs to provide them with it and these responded willingly. The number of clubs with junior sections multiplied many times and before long there were Test cricketers who had not played the game at school. The independent, and especially boarding, schools now supplied an even higher percentage of first-class cricketers than in the days of the amateur. Partly this was because in their twenties players could earn enough to keep themselves and see something of the world through taking winter coaching jobs. Mostly it was because they had learnt on good pitches, helped not only by a professional coach and a master in charge of cricket but by other masters, cricketers themselves, who were expected to turn out and bowl at the nets on summer evenings – and were happy to do so.

In the Southern Hemisphere good cricketers are more easily produced because young men are used to spending leisure hours outdoors for much of the year. In Britain, the season was extended by an increase in the number of indoor schools which do brisk business even in the depth of winter.

In the North of England and in Scotland leagues have been long established. In London and the South leagues were not generally welcomed because many players feared that they would lose fixtures with old and popular opponents and would find themselves playing more competitive and less enjoyable cricket.

This may often have happened but young players were more easily attracted to club cricket if there was a competitive element in it. The league match on Saturday and the social match on

Sunday seem to blend satisfactorily. Over this changing scene the
N.C.A. presided with help from the successful fund-raising body,
the Lord's Taverners, from *The Cricketer International* magazine
and other benefactors attracted by a good cause. Soon there were
national club and village competitions each with an entry of nearly
1000 teams and a final at Lord's. *The Cricketer* also ran a successful competition for the old boys of independent schools on
the lines of the Arthur Dunn Cup, long established in soccer.

Sponsors have been found for Youth Festivals, some with sides
from overseas taking part. The benefactors must have been amply
rewarded by the success of these events. Anyone who sees at close
quarters the good done by the meeting of young cricketers from
different countries and different backgrounds must wonder at the
thinking behind boycotts and ostracism.

M.C.C., though shorn of its direct responsibility for the first-
class game, has played an active part, not least by building the
spacious and well-equipped Indoor School beside the Nursery
ground. Opened in 1977 by G. O. Allen and largely financed by
the generous gift of Sir Jack Hayward, the Indoor School is also a
reflection of the enthusiasm and energy of E. W. Swanton and his
committee. Ten years later, in the Bicentenary year of M.C.C.,
Prince Philip opened the new Mound Stand, a handsome building
with which, at a time when modern architecture was coming
under severe criticism, few could find fault. The funding of this
was launched with a gift from another cricket-lover, John Paul
Getty, who met half the cost. Thus was tackled one of the biggest
problems facing M.C.C. and the counties – the cost of modernisation.

At the heart of English cricket until his death aged 87 in
November 1989 was Sir George – Gubby – Allen, fast bowler,
captain of England, chairman of selectors, administrator, former
President, Treasurer and Trustee of M.C.C. He had first played at
Lord's for Eton in 1919. His influence and guidance in the 70
years before he died in his home behind the Lord's pavilion had
been far-reaching. Without his and Harry Altham's enthusiasm
and concern for youth and for the future of the game, English
cricket could have been in a sorry state.

It is easy to trace a downward path in English cricket since the
War through home defeats by opponents whose standards have
risen. The word "professional" is now bestowed in a laudatory
sense when all goes well, but professionalism is not all-conquering.
The most publicised part of the game concerns barely 300 players

in England and fewer than that in other countries. The rest play just for fun.

First-class players are now younger, which is probably not a good thing in itself, but it does mean that they can reach levels of athleticism in the field unknown in 1946 and before. Few first-class cricketers then were physically equipped for headlong dives at the ball in order to turn a four into a three.

Another big difference strikes the spectator of today from the moment that two batsmen walk out to start the match, wearing helmets. This custom originated in the 1970s and greatly complicates the identification of batsmen and close fielders. Somehow a helmeted figure behind bars loses his individuality.

Yet the helmet is here to stay, anyhow for batsmen. The mind boggles at the meal which the injured plaintiff's lawyer would make in court of a county committee's instruction to their batsmen not to wear a helmet. For better or for worse, the helmet will not go away – for worse because the mere fact that the batsman is protected will encourage the thinking among fast bowlers that he is fair game. It is likely to lead to more bouncers being bowled, even at tail-enders. There now are, unfortunately for the spectator, more late-order batsmen with respectable defences than in the days when numbers nine, ten and eleven came and went in a few minutes of crude but entertaining violence. Moreover, it is still possible for the ball to strike an important part of the batsman's anatomy which he has not protected.

In theory there is a stronger case for banning the wearing of a helmet by a close fielder. If it meant that fielders did not stand so close in the hope of catching a nick off bat and pad, that should reduce the number of hits registered on the close fielder's person. But sooner or later someone would be injured and counsel would wax eloquent on the employer's failure to equip the fielders adequately.

The frequency of bouncers, especially on unreliable pitches, has been one of the game's most unattractive developments since 1945. When the Australians of 1953 arrived at Southampton, a news reporter asked their captain, Lindsay Hassett: "What about bumpers?" There was an embarrassed silence among the welcoming Press at this intrusion of a distasteful subject from the past. Though, five years before, Lindwall and Miller had bowled with great success and were here again, the bumper was not an issue at the time. Those who fielded at slip to Frank Tyson in 1954–5 say that they can scarcely remember a batsman having to duck. Later

in the 1950s short-pitched bowling did become more relevant but
mainly because of throwing and dragging. Since then, intimidatory bowling has seldom been far out of mind but without a solution being found. In one-day matches in Australia the no-balling
of bouncers above shoulder-high has been tried with harmonious
results but it was hard to imagine a change in the Laws of this
nature receiving West Indian blessing.

When a proposal came before the I.C.C. (the second C. now
standing for Council) that bouncers should be limited to one per
over in a forthcoming series between England and Australia, it
was outvoted by West Indies and associate member-countries. It
had been tried in English domestic cricket and, though not ideal,
seemed worth a trial in Test matches. English and Australian
batsmen were left somewhat perplexed by this contribution from
the likes of Gibraltar and Israel. "It's all right for them," was one
comment, "they're not having their blocks knocked off."

Perhaps the greatest difference between cricket in 1945 and in
1990 lay in relations with South Africa. The anti-apartheid move-
ments overseas kept the extreme Right in South Africa increasing
in support as the Government which it opposed was snubbed
once again. The leading part played by South African cricketers in
breaking down barriers of race was sneered at as 'cosmetic', as
English cricket became more and more under pressure from countries who knew little about South Africa, did not wish to know
and did not want to lose an ever-useful scapegoat.

To play in South Africa, even to coach there, was considered to
be condoning apartheid. Yet British soccer and rugby teams were
playing Romania where the ruling party was known to be particularly evil. Nobody minded condoning that.

It was a cock-eyed world, not helped by the Declaration which
tarnished the fair name of Gleneagles in 1978 and which seemed
to be interpreted according to taste. While the cricket authorities
of other countries were stopped by their Governments from having anything to do with South Africa, English cricket authorities
employed sanctions which their Government opposed.

It was all much simpler in 1945 when the "baddies" were
unarguably Germany and Japan, who had the merit of not playing cricket and could be safely left to the administrators of other
games to readmit in due course.

A perennial concern in the post-war years has been the leisurely
over rate of modern first-class cricket. It first caused official concern in the 1950s, partly because it was occasionally being used

as a defensive measure and partly because spin bowlers with their short run-ups were being replaced by bowlers of medium pace and above. Few of the latter approached the short economical run-up of Alec Bedser. By the late 1980s all visitors to England were agreeing to a minimum requirement but at 90 overs a day, 15 six-ball overs an hour, sights were still being set disappointingly low. The eight-ball over, which, by reducing the number of gaps between overs, should in theory have improved the over rate, had been tried in England for a two-year period in 1939. War ended the experiment after one season and it is significant that though many ways of quickening the over rate have been tried in England since, the eight-ball over has not been one of them. It had been found that the faster bowlers would be going so slowly when they came to the seventh and eighth balls that any time gained by fewer intervals between overs would be lost.

In Australia the eight-ball over, introduced in December 1918, lingered on until 1977 when it fell a victim to Packerism, presumably because the six-ball over in televised matches provided more intervals for commercial advertising.

Pitches, which in parts of India and Pakistan were still of matting in the 1950s, would take spin on the sub-continent but seldom quickly enough to be lethal. The norm was a slab of rolled mud with wisps of grass. Visiting sides discovered that although Indian batsmen had been found wanting on faster, bouncier pitches in England, they were brilliant players of fast bowling on dead pitches at home.

In England in the 1970s the T.C.C.B. instructed the counties to start matches on dry pitches in the hope that they would deteriorate by the third day and provide opportunities for spin bowling. Like other reasonable and well-intentioned decisions by the Board, this proved to be hard to put into effect. The groundsman might have been forced by bad weather to keep the pitch covered, thus preventing the pitch from drying out. He may have been afraid that if he left the pitch too dry, it would be dangerous.

The helmet was not alone in destroying some of the game's charm for spectators. The bat, around three pounds three ounces, was now often nearly a pound heavier than that wielded by great players of the past. The new fashion of holding it aloft while awaiting the ball did not seem to be the direct result of using a heavy bat but it spread with a speed which suggested that it was needed. Coaches might query the new stance but, if told by the batsman that it had given him a new confidence, hesitated to take stronger action.

If there was a fashion-setter, it was Tony Greig who had considerable influence during his brief tenure of the England captaincy. Standing nearly six and a half feet, he had presumably found that if he picked the bat up from the block hole, he had to hurry with it. Whereas if the bat had already been taken back, he had ample time to play the turning ball off the pitch. To the regular watcher of that era Greig seemed to adopt the uplifted bat not as an answer to fast bowling but as a counter to the Indian spinners in India.

With the increase in overseas tours, not least those to and from the sub-continent, umpiring became so variable that it led to the inexcusable sin of dissent by the batsman. Efforts were made to achieve a uniform interpretation on lbw and other matters in which the umpire's opinion was required. In February 1971 the senior English umpire Charles Elliott, on a visit to New Zealand made possible by a Churchill fellowship, stood in a Test match between New Zealand and England in Christchurch. For some years the T.C.C.B. invited other countries to send umpires to stand in county matches in England but the best overseas umpires could not always spare the time from their main jobs and the enterprise had less success than it deserved.

There was general agreement that English umpires were the best because they were mostly recruited from former first-class players and because, through the heavy programme of English first-class cricket, they had more experience. It was also agreed that what was needed was not neutral umpires but a panel of the best umpires.

Over the years the policy of allowing a touring side to turn down an umpire nominated by the home authority had worked reasonably well, helped by the fact that objections to individual umpires were not usually made public. In 1988 the Pakistan touring team asked for David Constant, a senior English umpire, to be replaced. The T.C.C.B., presumably thinking that an objection to a long-respected umpire was the latest ploy by a Pakistani manager who had been making lurid comments to the Press, refused to replace Constant. In the following winter, therefore, England were less well placed to ask for an unsatisfactory umpire in Pakistan to be withdrawn. Pakistan took a step forward in the following season by inviting two English umpires, John Hampshire and John Holder, to stand in a series with India, which they did with success.

Another long-running serial, trouble in Yorkshire, was given another instalment brought about by a continued lack of success on the field. The committee's first step of the 1990s was to invite Sir Leonard Hutton to be President, providing another reason for wishing Yorkshire well in their continued determination to employ only Yorkshire-born players.

Since one of their golden eras ended with three successive Championships won between 1966 and 1968, Yorkshire had only seven times finished better than 10th in the table. They had not reached the final of the Gillette/NatWest Bank competition since the 1960s, had won the Sunday League only once in 1983 and the Benson and Hedges Cup only in 1987.

The strong counties now were Essex who, since winning the Championship for the first time in 1979 under Keith Fletcher, had won it three times in the 1980s; Middlesex, who had won it four times in the last 13 years, twice under Mike Brearley, twice under Mike Gatting; and Nottinghamshire, who won twice with two outstanding overseas players, the South African captain Clive Rice and the great New Zealand bowler Richard Hadlee. The knighthood with which Hadlee was honoured in 1990 was wholeheartedly acclaimed throughout the cricket world. As well as being the first bowler to take more than 400 Test wickets, he had given so much that was good to the game, as indeed had his father, Walter.

In 1989 Essex were widely considered unlucky to have been docked 25 points under a new rule for a sub-standard pitch at Southend. At the time they were leading the field by 50 points but in the end finished six points behind the 1988 Champions Worcestershire. Nottinghamshire also had 25 points deducted but Worcestershire, to the surprise of many who played there, suffered no penalty for the pitches on their county ground. If they were lucky in this respect, they had more than their share of injuries.

Despite the difficulties for batsmen at Worcester, the young Zimbabwean Graeme Hick, who had first played for Worcestershire in 1984 aged 18, averaged 57 in the Britannic Assurance Championship, as it had been known since 1984.

Tall and more strongly built than others of his age, Hick had borne a rare look of quality long before, in one of the first four-day matches in 1988, he made 405 not out at Taunton, a score only exceeded in English first-class cricket by A.C. MacLaren's 424, also against Somerset on the same ground in 1895. He had a wide range of strokes, immaculate timing and he played very straight. He seemed likely to be the latest addition to the select list of cricketers with a genius for the game.

Hick's huge score at Taunton was made two years before the experiment with a ball with less pronounced seam. When this was introduced in 1990 the combination of four-day matches, a ball which seldom swung or deviated off the wicket and the flat pitches and fast outfield of the sunniest spring for years, brought an early season flood of individual scores of over 200, even 300, and innings totals of 700 and 800. The difficulty of achieving an ideal balance between batsmen and bowlers was seldom more vividly demonstrated.

Hick opted to qualify for England and was required to wait eight years. During this period Dipak Patel, born in Kenya, who had not been far out of the England selectors' minds while playing for Worcestershire, decided that his future lay in New Zealand and was soon playing in Test cricket. Also in the 1980s Kepler Wessels, a South African batsman who played several seasons for Sussex but acquired Australian citizenship, played 24 times for Australia before returning home to South Africa.

Those bemused by such contrasting rules of qualification who think that it would be for the good of cricket to have a player of Hick's talent at Test level already, have to weigh against that view the need to protect young English cricketers from overseas competition.

Anyhow it leaves a rich pleasure in store for 1992.

Index

232

238

After the Interval

Surridge, Stuart 73, 116–8
Swanton, E.W. 225

Tallon, Don 25, 65
Tattersall, Roy 63, 66–9, 73, 95
Tavaré, Chris 208, 209
Tayfield, Hugh 67, 81, 82, 100,
103, 109
Taylor, Bob 200, 203, 207, 209
Thomas, Bernard 183, 188, 189
Thompson, Alec 38
Thomson, Jeff 99, 177, 180, 181,
183–5, 194, 197
Titmus, Fred 135, 142, 143, 151,
152, 182
Tolchard, Roger 188
Toshack, Ernie 29, 30, 34
Traicos, Athanasios 149
Trueman, Fred 62, 77–80, 86, 87,
92, 94, 98, 101, 110, 112, 113,
118, 120, 136, 151, 157, 158,
192
Trumper, Victor 26
Turnbull, Maurice 71
Turner, Cyril 21
Turner, Glenn 174, 175
Tyson, Frank 45, 46, 92, 94, 96,
100, 227

Umrigar, "Polly" 160
Underwood, Derek 147, 153–6,
164, 180, 182, 183, 187, 190,
194, 200, 202

Valentine, Alfred 57, 58, 60, 62,
70, 88, 127
van der Bijl, Vintcent 171, 205
van der Merwe, Peter 140, 143,
145
van Ryneveld, Clive 54, 67, 109
Varachia, Rashid 150
Veivers, Tom 142
Venkataraghavan, S. 161, 163,
184
Verity, Hedley 11
Viswanath, G.R. 203
Voce, Bill 27, 29
Vorster, John 148

Wadekar, Ajit 164
Wadsworth, Ken 213
Waite, John 67, 82, 102, 104

Walcott, Clyde 15, 59, 70, 89,
110, 125
Walker, Max 179, 181, 183, 185
Walker, Peter 136
Wallace, Boon 191
Wallace, Mervyn 52
Walsh, Jack 38
Walters, C.F. 175
Walters, Doug, 184
Ward, Alan 156
Wardle, John 39, 72, 85, 89–94,
98, 101, 109, 118, 119, 147
Warner, Sir Pelham 9, 43
Warr, J.J. 46, 49, 62–4, 118, 122
Washbrook, Cyril 15, 28, 31, 53,
62, 99, 105, 106
Wasim Akram 217
Wasim Bari 196
Watkins, Allan 71, 79
Watson, Willie 67, 69, 72, 84, 86,
103, 112
Wazir Mohammad 93
Weekes, Everton 10, 57, 59, 70,
88, 89, 110, 111, 125
Wessels, Kepler 231
Whitcombe, Philip 54
Wilkinson, C.T.A. 73
Willey, Peter 206, 209
Willis, Bob 156, 181, 183, 187,
194, 207, 209, 212, 213
Winn, Christopher 54
Winslow, Paul 102
Wood, Graeme 207, 221
Wooller, Wilfred 71
Woolley, Frank 18, 142
Woolmer, Bob 194, 200, 209
Worrell, Sir Frank 10, 57, 59, 70,
88, 89, 110, 125, 126, 129,
157, 158
Wright, Doug 26, 27, 31, 41, 44,
62
Wright, John 173
Wrigley, Michael 54
Wyatt, Bob 62, 76, 84

Yallop, Graham 208
Yardley, Norman 27–9, 31, 34,
54, 55, 62, 72, 76, 84, 93, 98
Young, Jack 22, 39, 41

Zahir Abbas 164, 196, 197, 210
Zia, President of Pakistan 197
Zulfiqar Ahmed 93